What Next after School?

SORT IT OUT!

FINISHING SCHOOL AND NOT SURE WHAT YOU'D LIKE TO DO?

Check out our new edition of the City & Guilds Guide for 14-19 year olds – and get the low down on what qualifications you'll need to get you where you want to go.

For your free copy, text GUIDE with your name, house number and postcode to 62299.

HOW DO I KNOW WHICH JOBS ARE RIGHT FOR ME?

No problem, you can also log on to www.cityandguilds.com/myperfectjob and be amazed by the careers you can choose from! It only takes 20 minutes to discover some great job options, get all the information on how to get started and where you can go to study.

Advice and information is also available from your Careers Advisor and local Careers Wales office, check local listings for details.

THE TIMES

What Next after School?

All you need to know about work, travel and study

6th Edition

Elizabeth Holmes

KOGAN
PAGE

This book is dedicated to Callum Stannard

Publisher's note
Every possible effort has been made to ensure that the information contained in this book is accurate at the time of going to press, and the publisher and author cannot accept responsibility for any errors or omissions, however caused. No responsibility for loss or damage occasioned to any person acting, or refraining from action, as a result of the material in this publication can be accepted by the editor, the publisher or the author.

The views expressed in this book are those of the author, and are not necessarily the same as those of Times Newspapers Ltd.

First published in Great Britain in 1996 as *The School-leaver's Handbook*
Second edition 1999

First published as *What Next?* in 2001
Second edition 2003
Third edition entitled *What Next After School?* 2004
Fourth edition 2006
Fifth edition 2007
Sixth edition 2008

Kogan Page Limited
120 Pentonville Road
London N1 9JN
United Kingdom
www.kogan-page.co.uk

© Joanna Grigg, 1996, 1999, 2001, 2003
© Elizabeth Holmes, 2004, 2006, 2007, 2008

British Library Cataloguing in Publication Data

A CIP record for this book is available from the British Library.

ISBN 978 0 7494 5102 8

Typeset by Jean Cussons Typesetting, Diss, Norfolk
Printed and bound in Great Britain by Bell & Bain Ltd, Glasgow

gap year ✈
working holidays

Make the most of your time out from studies with BUNAC's wide range of exciting work and volunteer programmes.

With the benefit of BUNAC's support, you'll be able to gain work experience while exploring another country. Taking part in a BUNAC programme also looks great on your CV!

■ Work and travel for up to twelve months in Canada, Australia or South Africa or, up to two years in New Zealand

■ Volunteer or teach in Ghana, South Africa, Costa Rica, Peru, Cambodia, China or the USA

■ Summer camp jobs in the US on *Summer Camp USA*

For further information or to download an application form, please visit the BUNAC website.

YEAR OUT
GROUP
FOUNDER MEMBER

Thinking of taking a break before going to university? Need some time off before another three years of studying? Still not sure what you want to do with the next few years of your life? Whether you're looking to fill a few months or a year with an exciting adventure before going to university then BUNAC could be your answer.

BUNAC offers young people the chance to explore some of the most exciting destinations in the world. As a non-profit, non-political national student club BUNAC's work and travel programmes are both fun and affordable. By travelling with BUNAC you will have the opportunity to see different countries and cultures as a member of their community rather than just as a tourist. You will also gain independence and transferable job skills, internationalise your CV, make new friends and earn money to travel after working. BUNAC takes care of the visa paperwork and travel arrangements so that you can concentrate on having fun. They are also there to offer help and advice when it's needed while you're travelling.

BUNAC has been organising work and travel programmes for young people since 1962 and the last four decades have seen BUNAC develop from pioneer to market leader in the field of work abroad programmes. Today, having grown significantly from its North American roots, BUNAC is recognised as a truly global organisation offering students and other eligible young people affordable work/travel opportunities in countries to and from as far afield as New Zealand, Africa, Cambodia and Costa Rica. With BUNAC your dreams can become reality.

Work America is BUNAC's longest running programme, giving you the opportunity to combine work and travel. The programme lets you take almost any job, anywhere in the USA during your trip and allows for time to travel throughout North America afterwards.

Or if you want to spend a fun and energetic summer in the US then *Summer Camp USA* could be for you. As a camp counsellor you'll have the opportunity to enjoy a real cultural exchange and the chance to experience the most amazing, fulfilling and exciting summer you can possibly imagine. But if you don't like the idea of working with kids all summer then why not consider *KAMP*? *The Kitchen and Maintenance Programme* lets you enjoy the camp benefits and facilities while doing a job that is more suited to you.

Alternatively you can spend an exciting 6-12 months working on the other side of the world. *Work Australia* and *Work New Zealand* are especially suited to Gap Year students and offer you the chance to spend extended time in another culture, again allowing you to take almost any job, anywhere. The *Work Australia* programme also offers you the chance to gain CV-enhancing skills combining practical training and some great sightseeing tours in and around Sydney.

BUNAC's Canadian programmes give you the chance to spend anything from eight weeks to 12 months working and living in the second largest country in the world. If you want to relax on the beach, spend a ski season on the slopes or enjoy the city life, Canada has something for you. Employment opportunities are equally diverse and with an open work authorisation obtained with BUNAC's help, you can again take virtually any job, anywhere in Canada.

If you're looking for a more exotic travel destination such as Costa Rica, Peru, South Africa, Ghana or Cambodia, you could combine volunteering with your travels. Working as a volunteer is a truly rewarding experience, whether you help to raise awareness of HIV/AIDS in Africa, teach street children in South America or work in a community project in South-East Asia.

For many young people, participating in a BUNAC working holiday is one of the most rewarding and memorable experiences of their lives. It gives you a chance to develop confidence and self-motivation, a broader outlook on life and a wider view of the world as a whole. Taking part in a BUNAC programme also provides a talking point for potential employers once back in the UK.

ROYAL FLEET AUXILIARY
CAREERS AT SEA

HOW FAR COULD A CAREER WITH THE RFA TAKE YOU?
ANYWHERE AROUND THE WORLD, AT ANY TIME.

"When I discovered the RFA offered greater opportunities for training and experience across a broader spectrum I decided that it was the best route for me." N Stubbs

MERCHANT NAVY
MILITARY ACTION
0845 04 05 20
RFA.MOD.UK

THE RFA
Unlike a commercial shipping company, you never know where your next destination will be. No foreign land or port is out of the question because the RFA is responsible for supporting the Royal Navy, keeping them supplied with everything they need - fuel, food, spares and ammunition. Or you could be delivering vital humanitarian aid whenever it is needed.

YOUR ROLE IN THE RFA
Imagine being in charge on the bridge of a ship, taking responsibility for the engine room, overseeing the efficiency of all the electrical systems on board or catering for a hungry ship. If you can picture yourself in any of these roles, you may have what it takes to become a Rating or trainee RFA Officer.

WHAT'S IN IT FOR YOU
The RFA offers "a life less ordinary" for practical individuals with initiative, who enjoy a challenge and would relish the opportunity to travel around the world. The salary, training and leave entitlement is highly competitive combining all the benefits of a merchant shipping organisation with a true vocation and the excitement of supporting military operations or providing disaster relief.

FIND OUT MORE
You can find out more by visiting RFA.MOD.UK or by calling 0845 04 05 20.

ROYAL FLEET AUXILIARY

Engineering your Career

Engineering is a tremendous career option. It offers variety and excitement and is rewarding both intellectually and financially. The career opportunities associated with engineering are vast because, as society progresses, so do its requirements for housing, heating, medicines, communications, food and entertainment.

To enable students to get a taster of it even before leaving school, the Royal Academy of Engineering has a Programme of extra-curricular activities called the Best Programme.

Young Engineers clubs around the country are often the first port of call for many aspiring engineers, and many take part right up until university.

Go4SET offers Year 9 pupils an 8 week Science, Engineering and Technology experience and the Engineering Education Scheme introduces sixth formers to the world of engineering via a programme of joint projects between participating schools and sponsoring industrial companies.

There are loads of Smallpeice Trust schemes to choose from, Headstart courses provide opportunities for students at the end of Year 12 to spend up to a week during the summer holiday at a university engineering facility and The Year in Industry scheme provides top quality work placements in industry for pre-university students.

The support continues throughout university and even qualified engineers can continue to benefit from the Best Programme.

advertisement feature

This exciting company has just returned from a successful stint at the Edinburgh Fringe Festival. The twenty-five strong ensemble performed *Story Shakespeare: The Two Noble Kinsmen* and received excellent reviews.

"Combining exhilarating ensemble work, song and a keen ear for comedy, this troupe are well worth a watch. Pacy, slick, and professional this company excel en masse...Forget building a wall in Ghana, this should be every aspiring actor's gap year."

Three Weeks Daily Edition August 2007 rating 4/5

Each September a new Year Out Drama Company is formed, and this year celebrates twenty-one highly successful years. Students apply from all around the UK, and often from Europe and America. Suitable candidates are selected not by audition, but after an extensive interview. Personality, strength of character, enthusiasm and the potential to work well in an ensemble has proved to be the most important elements in building on the success of this unique group.

This full-time course is based in Stratford-upon-Avon College and has the full use of its high quality performance facilities. Students stay in the new Halls of Residence block on the college campus. Each room is en-suite and the company lives together in specific Year-Out-Drama flats.

Stratford is world renowned for the Royal Shakespeare Company which is closely linked to Year-Out-Drama, inviting students to attend workshops, seminars and see performances on a regular basis, and to explore the work of different back stage departments.

Each intensive year is packed with a diverse range of performance projects, all exploring different theatre skills and disciplines.

Deborah Moody, the course director, invites working professionals from various fields to work with and inspire the students, and give them a real insight into the world of theatre.

Through classes and practical workshops the Company are taught acting techniques, movement, dance, singing, voice work and combat. They also have the opportunity to pursue stage management, lighting, sound, costume, script writing and directing. The organic nature of the course allows each year to have different experiences uniquely tailored for its students.

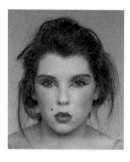

Deborah Moody believes that seeing live theatre is important for an actor's development, so the students regularly travel around the country to watch productions. Recent trips have included *The Bacchae* at the Lyric Theatre Hammersmith, *Henry V* at the Manchester Royal Exchange and *Brief Encounter* by Kneehigh Theatre Company at Birmingham Rep. Each year they see at least 20 productions.

The course offers individual help for all those wishing to gain entry to the top Drama Schools and University places. There is one to one audition practice and interview support giving students the techniques and confidence realise their potential and win the places they deserve. The success of these processes can be seen by the alumni of the course:

Tobias Menzies who went on to RADA has been very busy filming *Casino Royale* and *Rome*, as well as working at the National Theatre in *The History Boys*, and a highly acclaimed *Hamlet* with director Rupert Gould.

Michael Johnson developed his writing skills while in Stratford, went on to the London International Film School, and is now writing a Sherlock Holmes script for Warner Brothers.

Justin Edwards went on to at Manchester University and Mountview, won the Perrier Best Newcomer Award in Edinburgh with his comedy team *The Consultants* in 2002, and has since appeared in numerous TV comedies. He is now filming his own sitcom, based on his stand up character Jeremy Lion.

Currently, the Company has ex-students studying at top universities and drama schools including Bristol Old Vic Theatre School and Bristol University, Oxford and Cambridge Universities, Drama Centre London, Rose Bruford, Warwick University, and Royal Welsh College of Music and Drama.

Contents

Amazing Career Awaits

Tipped for the top
When the biggest names in business want to create and shape strategy, they turn to chartered accountants. Around 80% of FTSE 100 companies have at least one chartered accountant on the board either as Chief Executive Officer or Financial Director. Employers are keen to secure exceptional business advisers. Newly-qualified chartered accountants are amongst the highest earners when compared to other newly qualified individuals in areas such as Banking and Law!

To become successful in business, your first major decision is which professional or business qualification to take. If you want a valuable and versatile career offering unparalleled career opportunities, excitement, challenges and the chance to work in any sector anywhere in the world, there's really only one option. The ACA qualification.

The ACA
Offered by The Institute of Chartered Accountants in England and Wales (ICAEW), the ACA is viewed the world over as the one of the most prestigious financially based business qualifications. By choosing to join the profession you'll work alongside people your own age and experience a whole range of challenging projects.

There are several routes to enter the business world with the ACA. You may be surprised to know you can study for the ACA straight after your A-levels. This is a great opportunity for those who decide university is not for them.

Another route to the ACA is via the Association of Accounting Technicians qualification (AAT). The AAT-ACA Fast Track allows you to qualify in as little as four years. Two years to qualify as an AAT and further two years to qualify as an ACA.

'Even though I applied to go to university and was accepted, I decided that I wanted to get a professional qualification and practical work experience as soon as I could, so I saw the AAT-ACA Fast Track as a great alternative'
James Houston – School leaver

The majority of ACAs start their training after university. All students combine exam study with a paid full-time job in one of our 2,200 authorised training offices. Training last between three and five years dependant on your entry route.

'We get great exposure to some very influential figures in the business world'
Bonnie Tham – Graduate

Making the grade
You don't need A-level Maths or an accountancy related degree to be eligible to train for the ACA. If you choose to go to University you should try to achieve a First or upper second class degree. Whichever route you chose to take we recommend a minimum of 220 UCAS Tariff Score (employers expect 280 to 300 UCAS Tariff Score when recruiting for trainee ACAs), two A-levels and three GCSE C grades or above (including an A or B in Maths and English) or international equivalents.

One sure fact is that the ACA qualification gives you the competitive edge needed to achieve such an amazing career.

Find out more: T +44(0)1908 248 040 E careers@icaew.com
www.icaew.com/careers

The UK's fashion and textiles industry offers a range of highly-skilled and well-paid career opportunities.

Want to know more?

Can U Cut It? In Fashion

www.CanUCutIt.co.uk

If, when you think of a career in fashion, you think of a "designer", then you are not alone. But this isn't the only fashion-related career on offer.

To find out more, visit Can U Cut It? where you can read job profiles, real life case studies and top tips from leading names from Savile Row, Lulu Guinness and TopShop.

Just The Job

www.skillfast-uk.org/JustTheJob

Today's UK clothing, footwear and textiles sector is a modern and exciting place to work – one that has opportunities for all levels of experience and ability.

So whether you want to work with your hands, with IT / technical equipment or you enjoy creative thinking and developing strategies, then there is a career for you. Simply go to Just the Job to find out more.

Future Textiles

www.FutureTextiles.co.uk

The world of textiles has changed considerably over recent years, particularly the area of "technical textiles".

This exciting sector has opportunities for those with textiles and scientific-related knowledge. Visit Future Textiles to find out about the careers on offer and how you can learn the necessary skills.

The Sector Skills Council for fashion and textiles   **skillfast-uk**

If you think of the UK's clothing, footwear and textiles industry, do the words exciting and dynamic come to mind? If not, it might be time to re-think, as the industry has undergone huge changes over recent years. It offers well paid career opportunities in areas such as:

Fashion:

Despite 3,000 students graduating from fashion-related courses each year, which is more than industry needs, employers continue to report a lack of "technical" skills amongst potential recruits.

These skills include pattern-cutting, pattern-grading, garment technology and garment construction. In fact, they are so important they are jobs in their own right.

To find out about these jobs and the role of a fashion designer, you need to go to the Can U Cut It? website, which has been created specifically for those interested in a career in fashion.

Footwear & Textiles:

There are now a broad range of careers within the footwear and textiles sector, since companies were forced to become more competitive due to increased competition from overseas.

With many now producing high quality, luxury goods, opportunities range from operative level to highly skilled technical and management roles. To find a career to suit you, visit "Just the Job".

Technical Textiles:

Believe it or not, automotive tyres and aircraft wings actually contain textile components. And because of this, they are part of the high performing area of technical textiles.

Currently contributing £1.2 billion each year to the UK's economy, there are a host of well-paid, skilled professions that require new recruits in areas such as design, research & development, sales and marketing. As a result, textiles, design and science graduates are needed. To find out more, including job profiles and real-life case studies go to the Future Textiles website.

BE PART OF SOMETHING BIG.

As a global network of innovation, we make technology that most people take for granted. Whether you are travelling by train or car, communicating with friends and colleagues by phone or email, doing the weekly shop, attending a hospital appointment, applying for a passport, taking money from a cash-machine or making a cup of tea, there is a good chance our ideas are somewhere in the background making life easier for you.

We employ over 20,000 people in the UK alone. Considering our size and scope, it's no surprise that we offer a wealth of opportunities for those in search of a successful engineering or commercial career that offers a real challenge.

There are two types of apprenticeship to choose from:

Commercial Apprenticeships

For those interested in a commercial future, our Commercial Academy will equip you with work experience across finance & commercial departments, as well as recognised qualifications. In two years you'll have an HND in business; in four a bachelor's degree. All without the student debt of university study.

Engineering Apprenticeships

Alternatively, you can work towards an NVQ level 2 or 3 on our Engineering Apprenticeships. Based all over the UK, we offer real opportunity to gain hands-on experience in Engineering in areas such as Power, Transportation, and Broadcast Technology.

We have opportunities all over the UK including: Newcastle, Manchester, Poole, Northampton, Frimley, Lincoln, Glasgow, York and many more.

Wherever you join us, you'll be laying the foundation for a permanent career here. Learning and working with other apprentices, you'll be in contact with people who are the best in their field. With this calibre of people, it's essential you've got what it takes to keep up. To make sure, we'll give you plenty of training and ongoing support.

Your first step is to visit www.siemens.co.uk/apprenticeships

Siemens Apprenticeships

www.siemens.co.uk/apprenticeships

SIEMENS

Name: Neale Burrows
Business: Siemens Traffic Controls
Year joined Siemens: 2004
Job Title: Technical Support Engineer

I've been with Siemens Traffic Controls since Summer 2004. I started of as a Field Services Trainee with the aim of becoming an Engineer after 3 years. I found the technical aspects of the role really suited me and I already had some of the qualifications required for the Programme, so I fast-tracked and completed the scheme within 2 years. I was fortunate to be on a scheme that was flexible enough to allow me to do that. Now I'm a Technical Support Engineer and I'm responsible for Southern Aberdeen to the furthest of Northern Scotland. My main customer is Aberdeen City Council and my job is to rectify faults on the urban traffic systems.

No two days are the same, but a typical day form starts off with driving my company car to the office and getting a drink of coffee when I get there. Then I check my emails; usually they are from the customer and are to do with queries that haven't been answered. Someone else will have thought they'd fixed the problem, but the customer doesn't think it's been resolved properly. As I said, no two days are the same, and no two faults are the same – every day is a new challenge! Mainly I have to resolve problems with the computer system that oversees the co-ordination of the traffic, and co-ordinating with the Police to maintain the bus lane enforcement cameras. As well as day to day faults I have larger projects to work on as well. Due to the nature of the work my job is reactive and not preventative, it's quite difficult to plan time. Someone will phone and I have to be there in the next five minutes.

There's a good social life too. Even though I do a lot of my work on my own, there are plenty of team and customer nights out planned in.

This Summer I became a Mentor for our latest Trainee. I thought it would be much easier than it is and now I appreciate just what my Mentor had to go through when I first started! I think the best thing about being on the Trainee Programme is that it acts as a cushion for your mistakes, so you get to learn the skills of the job in a "safe" environment.

Preface

Over recent years, it seems that the decisions that people must make when facing a new phase of life after school or college have taken on an extra significance. The world of study and work has been changing; there are more choices to consider and possibilities to take on board. But at the same time, the costs associated with some of these choices are significant, meaning that a solid understanding of just what you might be taking on and the potential consequences of each choice is essential.

For this reason, this latest edition of this book includes plenty of advice and ideas on how to make good decisions, and how to support yourself most effectively through this important stage of your life. There's a greater emphasis on how to become your own life coach, as well as the usual up-to-date information on all the many options facing 16- and 18-year-old school leavers.

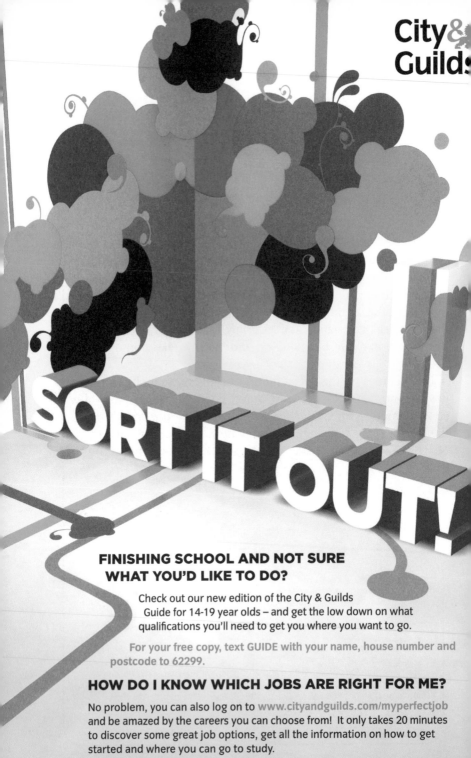

City& Guilds

SORT IT OUT!

FINISHING SCHOOL AND NOT SURE WHAT YOU'D LIKE TO DO?

Check out our new edition of the City & Guilds Guide for 14-19 year olds – and get the low down on what qualifications you'll need to get you where you want to go.

For your free copy, text GUIDE with your name, house number and postcode to 62299.

HOW DO I KNOW WHICH JOBS ARE RIGHT FOR ME?

No problem, you can also log on to www.cityandguilds.com/myperfectjob and be amazed by the careers you can choose from! It only takes 20 minutes to discover some great job options, get all the information on how to get started and where you can go to study.

Advice and information is also available from your Careers Advisor and local Careers Wales office, check local listings for details.

YOUNG BRITONS SWITCHED ON AT SIXTEEN

An astute new breed of 16 year olds is emerging in the UK, challenging the old notion that the youth of today lacks drive.

According to the second City & Guilds Youth Aspiration Index – an annual monitor of the career goals of Britain's 11-18 year olds – 16 year olds have surfaced as the most savvy of the group, more likely than any other age to choose hard work and happiness over remuneration.

Despite common misconceptions of young people being lazy and unmotivated, the Index reveals that today's school leavers are not afraid of grafting, with most 16 year olds (81 per cent) prepared to work long hours to reach their goals.

Inspired by role models such as Richard Branson, Sir Alan Sugar and Jamie Oliver – who they believe got to where they are through hard work and determination – many 16 year olds (23 per cent) also have visions of running their own business. This ambition grows stronger as they get older,  with 25 per cent of 17 year olds and 38 per cent of 18 year olds hoping to set up shop.

With GCSEs results approaching and A-levels around the corner, 16 year olds are at a 'careers crossroad', considering whether to remain in education or seek employment. The Index shows they put more thought into their careers than any other age group, with a fifth (19 per cent) thinking about getting a job more than anything else and a quarter (24 per cent) considering their future all the time.

They are also the most optimistic of all young people, with 90 per cent of 16 year olds expecting to be happy in their future career. Thirty-nine per cent put happiness, rather than money (17 per cent), at the top of their career wish list – a remarkable difference to their younger 13 year old counterparts who prioritise money (32 per cent) over happiness (27 per cent).

Keith Brooker, director of group markets and products at City & Guilds comments: 'It's enlightening to see that many 16 year olds today are extremely ambitious and possess real entrepreneurial spirit. It's vital that, as a society, we encourage them to fulfil their vision by giving them as much support, guidance and training as possible at this critical stage in their lives. Deciding on a career is a very daunting prospect and it is great to see that most young people are taking their future seriously and considering all the options open to them.

'I am also pleased that the next generation are looking for jobs that will make them happy over those that will just pay the best wages. Nowadays, true job satisfaction and happiness is about fulfilling your full potential, tapping into your own creativity and feeling that you can make a difference. As we spend so much time at work, it's important that we enjoy what we do and build on the skills that we're good at.'

DREAM JOBS AND THE GENDER DIVIDE

Britain's future workers also have clear ideas about the professions they admire and want to work in, with gender stereotypes for girls and boys set at a young age.

Twelve per cent of 11-14 year old girls want to be hairdressers or beauty therapists when they grow up, rising to 18 per cent when they are 15-18 years old.

And World Cup fever seems to have captured the imagination of the younger 11-14 year old boys more than the 15-18 year olds, with over a quarter wanting to be footballers.

While boys tend to prefer sports roles, girls look towards nurturing positions, such as working with animals. However, as they get older, perspectives change and horizons broaden, with the medical profession becoming more appealing.

Brooker adds: 'With the wide range of professions available today it can sometimes be confusing to choose your direction. This is why we launched 'The real you' campaign last year to guide young people through the career maze and to demonstrate how vocational training can be their route to success. We are continually developing this campaign and hope to include more careers advice in the future.'

INDEX REVEALS YOUNG PERSON'S IDOLS

It would seem there are a number of successful celebrities motivating young talent. David Beckham tops the league of most inspirational celebrities for 11-18 year olds with 16 per cent putting him top of their list, followed by Ant & Dec (10 per cent). Other celebrities admired include Sir Richard Branson and Sir Alan Sugar. And almost half

(46 per cent) of young people admire their favourite celebrity because they believe they worked hard to get where they are.

The altruistic pursuits of favoured celebrities like Jamie Oliver and Bob Geldof are encouraging some young people to give something back. Fifty-five per cent of 16 year olds do not want to work in a big office, and of those, over seven in ten (72 per cent) think that the most important aspect of a future job is the positive difference it will make.

Brooker continues: 'Admiring celebrities plays a big role in all young peoples' lives and it is enlightening to see that they are choosing celebrities that enjoy their jobs as well as looking towards the financial rewards. While this is encouraging to hear it's essential that young people are aware of all their career options before making any important decisions about the profession that they would like to pursue.'

NEW Careers Calculator for young people

Builder, lawyer, care worker, doctor, actor – there are hundreds of careers out there – but finding the right one isn't easy. City & Guilds has got together with icom™ to create an online tool that provides the resources and information young people need to help them find the right job.

You can complete *four online tests* that will match your personality and ambitions to a number of jobs and careers. You'll also get advice on the qualifications you need to get in and get on!

Your very own *online portfolio* will allow you to store relevant information such as notes, pictures, CVs and information on qualifications which you can share as much or as little as you like with others.

To discover your perfect job go to:

http://www.cityandguilds.com/myperfectjob

Acknowledgements

Throughout the course of writing this book I visited many schools and colleges to get ideas about the kind of information and advice that school leavers *really* need. Although too numerous to mention individually by name, I would like to thank all of the teachers, lecturers, students and careers advisers who willingly gave their time and thoughts; your help was very much appreciated.

I would also like to thank Charlotte Howard of the Fox and Howard Literary Agency, Jon Finch, Ian Hallsworth and the Kogan Page team.

The information in this book is correct at the time of going to print, but be aware that some of the detail will be subject to change on a regular basis. Where this might be an issue, relevant website addresses have been included so that you can find updated information if necessary.

Introduction

It doesn't matter how much you may be looking forward to leaving school and moving on to your next challenge, this can still be a nerve-racking time. Many people of your age find themselves thinking: How do I know what I want to do? What options are open to me? Have I made the right decision? What should I do next?

On top of any uncertainty you might be feeling, you are probably really pushed for time. If you are in the middle of your GCSEs you will be up to your eyes in coursework, studying, revising and exams and finding time even to *start* thinking about your next steps in life can be impossible.

It's tough that so much seems to happen all at once. Just as you are ploughing through the most demanding period of your school life so far, you are expected to search out new courses that you would like to take, think about where you want to work, even consider leaving home. This means gathering information, application forms, writing CVs and creating personal statements that reveal who you are and why you would be great for the course/job/voluntary position (delete as appropriate). It also means thinking just as much about the past as about the future. What have you done so far in your life that you have enjoyed? What have you learned from the experiences you have had? What have the holiday or Saturday jobs you have had taught you?

That's where this book comes in to help you out. Packed with information on the kinds of choices that you face right now, as well as information on options you may not even have thought of, this book helps you to take a good look at where you have been, where you are now, where you want to be in the future and how you can get there. It helps you to take a good look at yourself, to see yourself as clearly as possible and to think about life goals that you know will give you that kick.

This book will not tell you what will earn you the most money, or what qualifications you need to do certain jobs. There are other sources for this information that your school or local library can help you find out. Instead, when you have gone through all this book has to offer, you can expect to know where it is you want to head for in life and what you might find when you get there.

You may not always feel totally in control of your life; growing up and being at school has to be like that. But with the help of this book, you will see what opportunities lie ahead of you and can start to direct the next scenes of your life. Good luck!

Who this book is for

If you are looking ahead to when you leave school, then this book has been written for you. However, it will also be invaluable for teachers and parents who are supporting teenagers through the decision-making processes linked to leaving school at either 16 or 18 years old.

How to use this book

Now that you have picked this book up and started reading it, don't feel that you have to continue from this point and plough your way through to the very end. *What Next After School?* has been written in a way to allow you to dip in for specific chunks of information or treat it like a cover to cover read. Either way, I hope you get what you need from it.

Features of this book

Each part of *What Next After School?* has been broken down into parts to enable you to find the information you need as quickly as possible. At the start of each chapter is a list of what you will find within it and at the end of each there is a summary.

Action features

These are questions for you to consider or activities for you to do. They have been designed not as essential tasks that you *must* do, but as interesting 'thought-provokers' that will help you to clarify your thinking. Do what you think will help you and leave out what you don't feel you need to do. Your responses are for your eyes only. Don't feel that you need to share them with anyone if you don't want to.

Information points

Here you will find website addresses, e-mail addresses and telephone numbers where you can find further information about what you have just read.

'View from ...' boxes

Many young people, teachers, lecturers and parents gave their views, experiences and opinions to me when I was writing this book. You will find these throughout in 'View from ...' boxes (for example, 'Perfectionism ... View from Amy'). Although the names have been changed, and sometimes some of the ideas have been merged, the views are of real people.

Glossary

There may be words or abbreviations in this book that you have not come across before. If this is the case, take a look at the glossary in Appendix 1, page 281, where you should find an explanation. It might be a good idea to read through this section anyway, so that you know what is covered there. If you can think of anything that should be included in the glossary in future editions of this book, you can e-mail your suggestions to eh@elizabethholmes.info.

The internet

Just about everything you need to know about the options you have can be found on the internet but it can be hard tracking down just where to look. To save you the trouble of trawling through what search engines churn up for you, I have included details of useful websites that you might like to visit. These appear in the main text of the book as well as in the directory of useful information in Appendix 1.

For those in Scotland, Wales and Northern Ireland

There are some significant differences between the countries that make up the United Kingdom regarding education. Since devolution, Wales and Northern Ireland have been developing their own (but similar) education systems, and the education system in Scotland has long had significant differences when compared with the English education system. For example, Scottish readers should be aware that in order to simplify the text I refer only to NVQs in this book. In nearly every respect, these are the same as their Scottish equivalent, SVQs. You can find out more about the education systems in Wales, Scotland and Northern Ireland from the following websites:

Wales: www.wales.gov.uk
Scotland: www.scotland.gov.uk
Northern Ireland: www.niassembly.gov.uk
England: www.dius.gov.uk.

A word about change

The world of education is changing at a fast pace and in particular, the education choices of 14- to 19-year-olds are about to change dramatically, even though this change will be phased in over several years. This may mean that you need to do some additional research on the choices that you have in front of you. The best place to start looking for further information on the changes for 14- to 19-year-olds is www.dcsf.gov.uk/14-19/.

Part One

Career planning

1 *Being your own life coach*

This chapter looks at:

- where you are now;
- life coaching as a concept;
- how to become your own life coach.

So, you're about to make the move into the next phase of your life. Your compulsory school career is over and the next steps are for you to decide. How does it feel? Is it a relief to be free and in charge of your life? Or is it all a daunting responsibility?

You're probably sick of hearing people telling you that 'you're at an important stage of your life' and that 'the choices you make now will affect you for the rest of your life' and so on. As if you might have missed that fact! Most teenagers know exactly how crucial their decisions are likely to be, but what is the best way of making them?

If anyone passes on any gems of advice to you, they almost certainly mean well. But it can be incredibly confusing when you are bombarded with opinions from others who simply want to make sure that you don't make the same 'mistakes' that they think they made. It's at times like these that you need to be able to trust in your own decision-making abilities (see Chapter 2), based on sound advice from people in the know. And knowing who and where to go to for that advice is essential. Basically, to find your way round the potential pitfalls so that success is yours, not just at this stage of your life, but beyond into the future, you need to become your own life coach.

Life coaching... what does it mean?

Life coaching is just what the name implies. It has become very popular, particularly among those who are keen to make changes in their lives, or who envisage combining several careers throughout their working lives. There are many reasons for this, probably to do with the fact that people increasingly have a variety of careers rather than just one, as used to be the case. Instead of reacting to opportunities that may present themselves to you throughout the course of your life, life coaching helps you to seek out and create the kind of opportunities you need in order to get where you want to go. A life coach typically talks you through what you hope to achieve, what resources you have to help you achieve that, and what next steps you can take to set you on the right course. It should be a really positive process, although it may sometimes involve facing up to self-sabotaging habits.

Making decisions ... View from Lee

I don't think I ever thought about what I wanted to do that much. I just took whatever next step was in front of me. I didn't really ever plan anything. But then I started to think that I should have some idea of my goals and what I want to achieve. It boosted my confidence because I started to see that planning and making goals are important steps to achieving what you want to achieve. That sounds really obvious now, but I don't remember ever being told that, or being told how to do it effectively. I think it's about seeing your life as something that you can create, rather than something you are stuck with and can't do anything about.

Becoming your own life coach

You are bound to have the support of others around you, whether at school or college or at home, to help you sort out what your next moves might be, and you may even have the benefit of a mentor who works closely with you, but it is important not to forget what a great resource *you* are!

There are some key ways to help you become your own life coach. And it's always going to be worth doing that, rather than risking unintentionally standing in your own way. As you read through this book, which contains stacks of information on decision making, goal setting, studying, taking time out, travelling, moving away from home, money management and much more, keep in mind these key life-coaching ideas:

- **Stay confident** – As soon as you start to doubt your skills and abilities, or to doubt your value as a person, your confidence will nose dive. Clearly there's a balance between healthy confidence and excessive confidence, but severe self-doubt is rarely, if ever, useful or constructive. Talk to a trusted friend, teacher, tutor or family member if you think your confidence may be sliding downwards. There are many reasons for this happening, and nearly everyone experiences it from time to time, but it is important to talk to someone about how you are feeling, sooner rather than later.
- **Build up a support network** – It can be easy to feel isolated and as though you must tackle everything alone, but that isn't the case. There will always be someone you can turn to for advice, so make sure that your inner life coach remembers that. In each section of this book there are contact details for organizations and other sources that will be able to help you through any problem you may come across.
- **Follow your interests** – It can really make life easier if you pursue the things you are naturally interested in (and it's amazing how many people find themselves in jobs or on courses that they aren't really that keen on). Aim to nurture your natural talents and interests and whatever you choose to do is bound to be more achievable.
- **Aim to anticipate obstacles** – You're likely to hit potential problems along the way, whatever path you choose to follow after the age of 16, but there will be a way over them (or under, round or through them). Obstacles are always easier to deal with, though, if you have seen them coming, rather than crashing into them

blindly. Arm yourself with information and knowledge about your choices as this will help you to anticipate all the potential difficulties that may arise. And 'difficulties' aren't always what they seem. Sometimes they are 'blessings in disguise', leading us to better, unanticipated outcomes.

- **Be positive about your next steps** – The more positive you can be about the possible directions your life can take, the more likely you are to make a go of it. If you can really look forward to your new job or your move to college or university, you'll get the most out of it. It's natural to feel some nerves, but if you are dreading it, or feel a sense of doom about the whole thing, then the chances are you may need to rethink your plans. Being positive can only help, but if it's impossible to muster positive thinking, talk to someone you trust, sooner rather than later.
- **Keep an eye on your money** – The chances are you'll be budgeting through your next steps, whatever they are, and while it's important not to completely deprive yourself, it's essential not to overspend and pretend it didn't happen (something many people seem to do). Keep on top of your money and ask for help sooner rather than later if you think you may be getting into debt or you need help with budgeting. There is plenty of advice on this in Part Six.
- **Don't succumb to peer pressure** – *You* have to live your life, not your friends. It's easy to feel pressured by those around you, but don't let this affect the decisions you make. What *you* want to achieve is important.
- **Keep your eyes on the prize** – Know what you want and go for it. And if you don't know what you want, you will by the time you reach the end of this book!

Action

Take a few minutes to think about how you feel about what you have just read. Do you feel able to be your own life coach? Or do you feel in need of talking to someone about how you might best make your next moves? How confident and positive are you at the moment? If at all possible, talk through your thoughts on these questions with someone else, maybe a family member, tutor or mentor. Even if you feel completely on top of things, it can be great talking about that.

Keeping an eye on the bigger picture

When you're focusing on one aspect of your life, such as whether to study or work, where to live or what career to have, it's really important not to lose sight of the bigger picture. This means taking what's known as an holistic view of your life. You are more than what you study or where you work. You are a complete and developing human being. You probably have family relationships with parents or carers, siblings and extended family such as aunts and uncles; friendships and maybe partnerships with a girlfriend or boyfriend; work commitments and goals for the future; study commitments and plans for the future; hobbies; activities to keep you fit and healthy such as taking part in sport and maybe belonging to a team; or perhaps you follow a particular religion or faith. Of course you need to work hard at your job or your course, but there's far more to your life than that. There are many facets to who you are so remember to keep this in mind as you read through this book and decide on your next steps.

A word about change

Change is one of the few inevitable facts of life and yet it can be difficult to cope with, whatever age you are. Sometimes we can fall into the trap of thinking that change has to be big to be significant. It doesn't. Often it is the smallest changes that can bring about the biggest results. For example, making a commitment to spending just 10 minutes a day studying something we don't understand, or getting fitter, can have an amazing accumulative impact, without causing too much pain! It is always possible to bring about change through small steps, and sometimes that's all that feels comfortable. It doesn't make it less effective though.

View from Anna

I was fine when I was deciding what I wanted to study at uni. I looked at all my options but I knew I really wanted to do something textiles related. I found a great course in a town I knew I wanted to live in but I wasn't happy with my weight. I'd got heavier while I was doing my A levels and wanted to get back to how I was before. I knew it would help boost my confidence when I started my course and had to meet new people, but I had friends who had been on crash diets and I knew they didn't work in the long run. So I decided to run for 10 minutes twice a day. I was careful with what I ate too but didn't diet. Just making those small changes meant that I lost the weight that I had put on through my exams. It sounds odd, but I hadn't realised what a little effort can do if you stick at it.

Summary

The key points from this chapter include:

- Life coaching can be a useful tool to help you to make decisions at key points in your life.
- It is possible to be your own life coach if you follow a few basic steps such as aiming to anticipate obstacles and building up a support network.
- Change is inevitable, and it can be achieved through small steps as well as large steps.
- Advice, suggestions and sources of further information for anything you may come across in your decision-making processes are included throughout this book.

2 Decisions

This chapter looks at:

- how to make decisions;
- where to go for help.

The chances are, if you have picked up this book, that you are not entirely certain about what your next step should be. That's not at all unusual. Although some lucky people seem to be born knowing what they want to do, others may take years to find themselves in a job or career that feels right. For others still, choosing the right courses to do can prove to be virtually impossible, resulting in a series of false starts.

In some ways it seems that there are far more choices now than there ever have been. In years gone by career choice was often limited by what sex you were. Females would have followed 'feminine' jobs such as going into service or becoming a dressmaker and males would have done the jobs that men did such as physical labouring, office work or engineering. Sometimes young people would do what their father or mother did. For example, some may have been expected to follow in the footsteps of their father and work for the family business.

It is not like that now though, and in some ways that's harder, although it is ultimately better that many people have more career freedom. Because of this, you may need to seek career and job advice. In fact, even if you don't feel that you *need* career advice, it is a good idea to have some just in case options that you had not even considered come up. It is important to take a look at everything that is available to you so that you really can make an informed decision.

Decisions – the issues

Whether you are reading this at the age of 15 or 16 or at 17 or 18, you face choices, which means making decisions. Basically, you could stay in education, go into a work-based training programme or apprenticeship, join the armed forces, get a job or work for yourself. You could also go travelling, work as a volunteer or join the ranks of the unemployed.

What you do can be a tough decision to make. It is likely that many people will want to influence you. But as you read through this book and work through the activities that you feel are relevant to you, you will see that it is possible to know for yourself the direction that you should take. As long as you explore all the options open to you and honestly answer the questions you ask yourself, you will be giving yourself the best possible chance.

Making decisions can be one of the hardest things that humans have to do. So many things can stand in our way. Sometimes we feel that we will not be able to stick to the decisions we make and at other times we think that we are not good enough to follow them through. We may even think that we are too good for something once we start it or our lack of self-esteem may prevent us from giving it a go. The question is: how can we give ourselves the chance to make sound decisions that stick?

Making decisions ... View from Taylor

I don't think I'm good at making decisions. I don't think I've ever given it that much thought. I've always just done what seemed most obvious but that's not always what's best for you. The thing is that if you really think about each decision, about all that could happen if you did a certain thing, you'd have to make a lot of effort. I think lots of people don't want to put in that effort. Or perhaps they think they don't have to because they'll just change their minds and do something else if it doesn't work out. I can see now that's not a good idea but the thought of sitting down and actively *deciding* rather than doing one of the first things that comes to my head is quite frightening. What if I can't follow it through perfectly? What if I fail?

Perfectionism

Wanting to do things perfectly is one of the most common reasons for not having a go at something. Suppose you want to be a singer. Would you want to do this as a hobby or would it have to be your career? Would you be happy to sing to yourself and your mates or would you want to give a proper performance? Would you sing in your local pub or want to be in front of an audience of thousands? Or broadcast your music via a webcam like singer/songwriter Sandi Thom? How much, or little, would you settle for?

Wanting to do things perfectly can be paralysing. It can actually prevent us from taking action and mean that we might never know what we could have achieved. If perfectionism is something you sometimes suffer from you need to try to take a step back for now and give yourself the chance to follow your dreams.

Action

Are you a perfectionist? Take a moment to answer these questions. If you jot your answers down you can see how many times you answer 'yes' and how many times you answer 'no'.

- Does making mistakes make you feel self-conscious – over-aware of yourself?
- How do you feel when other people make a mistake? Do you tend to comment and point out their errors?
- Do you get anxious if your appearance is not perfect?
- Do you tend to write rough drafts before completing a neat version?
- Do you give yourself a hard time if you do something embarrassing?
- Are you always neat and tidy in everything you do?
- Do you tend to stick to set routines – for example, when you get ready in the mornings, when you do your homework and so on?
- Do you work extra time to ensure that your homework is just right?

- Do you know exactly how you will spend each day when you wake up in the morning?
- Do you sometimes put off making decisions out of fear that you might do the wrong thing?

How did you do? Did you answer 'yes' to all or most of them? If that is the case it looks like you just might have some perfectionist tendencies! Keep this firmly in mind as you go through your decision-making processes and don't give yourself a hard time! Perfectionism doesn't exist and if you think it does, it will be something you will always strive for and never achieve.

Perfectionism ... View from Amy

It took me years to realize that you don't have to think of the decisions that you make about your career as being permanent. Just because you decide to train as a hairdresser, for example, doesn't mean that you will have to do that for the rest of your life. People are increasingly changing their jobs completely and having several careers in their lives. That can really help the decision-making process if you say to yourself that you will pursue a job or career for as long as it fulfils you rather than looking on it as a life sentence.

How to make decisions that stick

Whenever you face having to make a decision in your life there are certain techniques that you can use to help you. These are described for you below.

Brainstorming

Whether you call them maps, thought showers, spider diagrams or mindblasts they all, essentially, amount to the same thing: brainstorming. Basically, this means taking a large sheet of paper, putting the issue that needs a decision at the centre of the page and writing the possibilities open to you all around the outside in as much detail as you like. Perhaps there are connections that you can make between what you write down. Can you find any linking themes? Make sure that you include things that might seem a bit 'way out there'. The purpose of the exercise is to bring to your awareness all the possibilities that could conceivably be facing you. You don't have to make judgements on these ideas. Brainstorming can be as orga-nized or as chaotic as you like. As long as it helps you, feel free to develop your own techniques!

Action

Think of a decision that you have to make. Don't choose a massive question such as 'How shall I spend the rest of my life?' Instead, go for something like 'What shall I do on Saturday?'

Now take a large sheet of paper and write your question right in the middle of the page. After that, scatter all the possible ideas you can think of around the outside of your question. Don't stop after just one or two, but keep going. You will probably find that all your really good ideas start to flow after you have already written down about five or so.

Now look at what you have produced. Are you surprised by the quantity of ideas that you have?

Gathering information

In order to make effective decisions you need to have all the relevant information available to you. This may not involve additional work but the chances are that you will have to do at least some research in order to make most decisions. For example, supposing you want to go out for the day with your friends. You cannot decide between two possible choices so what do you do? You find out:

● how much each option will cost you;

- how far you would have to travel for each option;
- whether you would have to take food with you or could buy something when you get there;
- what preference each of your friends has.

Only when you have this information can you make a decision about where you should go for the day.

Whether your decisions are small like the example above, or big like deciding what to study at university, the information-gathering stage will probably be a pretty important part of the whole process.

Pros and cons

Sometimes it can really help to write a list of pros and cons about a particular course of action. In case you have not come across this before, 'pros' are the good points and 'cons' are the bad points. So, for example, if you were writing a list of pros and cons about buying a new bike you might end up with something like the list below.

Pros	Cons
I need a new one as my bike is quite old now and needs some repairs.	I could get my bike repaired and save some money.
I'll be able to get a mountain bike and cycle off-road.	I'd have to ask Dad to put a bike rack on his car so that I could get out to the country.
I've got just enough money saved.	It would leave me with no savings at all.
The local bike store has got a discount on the bike I've chosen.	The bike shop has always got something on offer, so there's no hurry.

Faced with the list of pros and cons in the table above, what would you choose?

Visualizing

Visualization means imagining, or picturing, something in your mind. If you were to visualize yourself working in a bakery shop you would see yourself, in your mind's eye, standing behind the counter. What have you got on? You're probably wearing a uniform and there may be something on your head to keep your hair out of the way. Perhaps you are wearing gloves and putting some bread or rolls into a bag for a customer. Is there a queue in the shop? Are there cakes on display? Is it hot or cold in the shop? What is covering the floor? Are there flies buzzing around? Can you *see* yourself there? That's visualization.

Visualizing can be really useful to find out whether you can envisage yourself following through on a particular decision. For example, if you decide that you want to travel the world can you truly *see* yourself doing it? Can you see yourself packing your bags, getting on planes, seeing new places, staying in different hostels around the place? If you *can* see yourself doing it, how does it feel? Exciting? Daunting? Does if feel like the right thing to do or do your gut feelings say that you would not really enjoy it?

Using visualization is a little like daydreaming; but it is day-dreaming with a focus and a goal. It is like saying to yourself: 'What if ... then what?' Many people find it a good way of making a decision.

Gaining experience

Gaining experience of something is a great way of deciding if it is what you really want to do. Much like trying on a pair of jeans before you buy them, you would actually be trying the options before making your final decision. Work experience is a great example of this. If you think you might like to be, for example, a personal trainer, shadowing one while he or she works is the perfect way of helping you to finalize your decision.

Gaining experience ... View from Charlotte

I always try to get a bit of first-hand experience of anything I think I might want to do. Even when I was looking for a Saturday job I spent a morning shadowing one of the others in the shop to see if I'd like it. I'd hate to get myself into something I couldn't wait to get out of and this helps me to avoid that.

Facing fears

Sometimes we stop ourselves from even considering something because we have fears about what might happen. Facing up to those fears can really help to show us that we actually have more options than we once thought. For example, if you'd like to work for the European Parliament but are afraid of travelling overseas, you could either settle for a job that is unlikely to take you out of the UK or do something about your fear to enable you to choose from a far wider range of jobs.

There are many ways of getting help for your fears. Sometimes just talking to someone else and verbalizing what you have been holding inside is enough to make the fear less powerful. Other times, professional counselling may be more appropriate. Hypnotherapy can help too.

Information point

If you think that you might have some fears that are stopping you from making certain decisions, talk to your family or trusted friends. Your teachers or tutors at school or college may be able to help and so can your doctor.

Pretending that you are someone looking on

What if you were someone else *watching* you as you are now going through the anguish of making a decision? From your position on the outside, what advice would you give yourself? Imagining this can be a really effective way of helping us to see a course of action especially when we feel paralysed by the choice. Imagine stepping outside your situation and looking on with a clear mind and the right course of action just might come into you head.

A word of warning

Sometimes, we just need to give ourselves a nudge to actually take the plunge and make that decision. If you think this might apply to you, don't let procrastination (purposely delaying action) get in your way. If it does, you may drift along avoiding the decision-making process, missing opportunities all along the way.

If you are guilty of procrastinating, you are not alone by any means! Most people know that they can do this at some stage of their lives, but recognizing it and not allowing it to take hold are important. Do not delay decision making endlessly. If you think it would help, give yourself a deadline and aim not to go over it. This does not mean you have to rush at the decision, but there comes a point when you just do not need to think about something any longer!

Where to go for help

If you feel that you need outside help with any decisions you have to make in your life right now, remember that the following people in particular may be a great source of advice.

Your parents

Your parents or other adults who are like parents to you are likely to know you better than anyone else and may be able to point out a few 'home truths' as well as being there to bounce ideas off. They have watched you through your life so far and will probably have followed your changing likes and dislikes, preferences and desires more closely than their own. You may not feel that you always want to ask for the help of your parents when you are making decisions but they will have a perspective that is at least worth considering, if not fully taking on board!

Your brothers and sisters

Your brothers and sisters, especially if they are older than you, may well have been through experiences that you can learn from. What did they choose to do? What advice have they got for you? How about your younger siblings? How do they see you? Do they have any wise observations to make about, for example, the kind of career they see you doing well in? Maybe they have an opinion that can help you.

Your extended family

Do you have cousins, aunts, uncles, grandparents, godparents, even friends of the family? How close are you to them? Can you talk to them about the decisions that you face? What can you learn from their experiences? What perceptions of you do they have?

Your teachers

Like your parents, your teachers will have tracked your development over a period of time. Are there any who you get on with particularly well? What have they said to you over the years? Have any of them been particularly inspiring? Are any really easy to talk to about the things that are concerning you? Most students at school or college can think of at least one teacher who they could turn to in moments of indecision. Who is this for you?

Connexions

Connexions is *the* place to go for everything to do with education, careers and much, much more for everyone between the ages of 13 and 19.

Connexions Direct offers a whole range of advice and support for young people through an easy to navigate website. You can speak to a Connexions Direct adviser on the telephone or through web chat, e-mail or text.

Connexions Service is a network of Connexions offices that you can drop into for information, advice and practical help about pretty much anything and everything from relationships to careers, drugs to jobs. You can do this anonymously if that would make you feel more comfortable so you do not need to give your name and address. The people at Connexions do not share what you tell them with anyone unless they think that you may be in danger.

Information point

- *The main website for Connexions is www.connexions.gov.uk.*
- *You can telephone to speak to a Connexions adviser on 080 800 13 2 19.*

- *You can text Connexions on 07766 4 13 2 19.*
- *You can e-mail Connexions anonymously via the website.*
- *To find your local Connexions Service look in your* Yellow Pages *or search for the details on the website.*

Above all else, never feel that you have to make choices and decisions in your life alone; you don't. There are people out there who can help you, whether they are from within your family or not. You are not alone.

Summary

The key points from this chapter include:

- If you are reading this book it is likely that you are facing a turning point in your life. What will you do next?
- Making decisions can be difficult for all sorts of reasons, particularly if you tend to be a perfectionist.
- There are tools that you can use to help you to make effective decisions that you can stick to. These tools include: brainstorming, gathering information, writing a list of pros and cons, visualization, gaining direct experience and facing your fears.
- There are many sources of help for you when you face important decisions including: your parents, your siblings, your extended family and friends, your teachers, Connexions.

3 Career planning

This chapter looks at:

- planning your career and next steps;
- tracking progress.

While you cannot possibly know at the moment exactly how things are going to turn out for you as the years go by, it is important to have some idea of the direction you would like your life to take. These plans that we make for ourselves cannot be set in stone. We have to be willing and able to change our minds and direction as new opportunities present themselves. But without *any* plan at all, we could risk drifting without purpose, and this could be a waste of valuable time.

Planning your career and next steps

When deciding what you want to do with your life you need to keep these factors in mind:

- your strengths;
- the opportunities that are open to you;
- the limitations that you see yourself having.

Your strengths

Throughout your decision-making process, you should always remember what your strengths are. You will probably have done some work on identifying these at school. If you have not, you might like to draw up a list to remind yourself about them.

Action

Use a large sheet of paper and just blast out your thoughts and your strengths, scattering them on the page. Don't aim to sort them out into logical categories at first; you can do that later on. The following ideas may help you:

- Think about what you are good at. Don't just limit yourself to what you do at school – this is just a part of who you are!
- What were your best subjects at school? Are these your favourites (sometimes what we are best at is not necessarily what we enjoy the most)?
- Think about your hobbies. What do you do in your spare time? What are your real passions? Is there anything that you can't imagine life without (for example, were you born to play football, paint, run and so on)?
- What do you read, watch on TV, listen to? This will give you an idea about what your interests are.
- Think about your preferences. Are you an indoor type or an outdoor type? Are you fashion-conscious or not? Are you easy-going or serious?
- How do you spend your school holidays? Are there any activities that you nearly always do when you have a break from school? Is there anything you would like to do more of?
- What skills do you have in addition to any qualifications you have from school? Can you swim? Drive a car? Ride a bike? Juggle? Paint? The list is endless. It doesn't matter how frivolous you think the skill may be, add it to your list.
- Talk to your teachers, parents, siblings, other adults in your life. What do they say your strengths are? How do they see you?
- What dreams, goals and desires do you have?

Once you have written your ideas out on to a sheet of paper (be bold, don't limit yourself), aim to organize them into groups. You are free to make up your own category headings. Ideas that may help you are listed here, but don't let these headings limit you.

Add your own or leave some of these out; whatever is most useful to you and the list of strengths that you have devised:

- indoor strengths and outdoor strengths;
- literacy strengths;
- numeracy strengths;
- science strengths;
- key skills (such as communication, information technology and so on);
- specialist knowledge (for example, are you an ace bee-keeper or hotshot software designer?);
- personality traits (such as being helpful, considerate, having a sense of humour, being focused and so on).

These headings need to be devised to fit in best with your particular strengths. Have as many category headings as you need.

Now you have an excellent resource to use whenever you need to identify your main strengths.

Opportunities open to you

There will be certain opportunities facing you that you can take advantage of *right now*. It would be foolish to say that anyone can do anything, but there will be opportunities that you can go for, or at least consider going for. This book will tell you what those opportunities are but you should also talk to your careers adviser at school and your local Connexions service. Even if you are *sure* about what your next move will be, always look around to see if there is an opportunity you did not know existed or had not even thought of.

Remember, when you are looking at the opportunities that may be open to you, be realistic. You have to take your limitations into consideration. If you are terrified of water, training to be a lifeguard on the beach is not a realistic opportunity!

Realistic opportunities ... View from Naila

I always had this vague idea that I wanted to be a dentist. I was always fascinated whenever I went to the dentist and thought it would be a great job to do. But actually when I sat down to write out some thoughts about my career possibilities there were lots of things that came out that didn't fit with being a dentist. If I'm honest I sometimes dread going to the dentist myself especially if I have to have treatment. That wouldn't make me a good dentist! I also realized that I think I'd rather work outside if I can, at least for part of each day. The final thing that did it was that I hadn't realized just how much science I'd have to study to be a dentist. That's not a strong point for me. Realistically, it might have seemed like a good idea in the past but I can think of loads of other things that would be much more suitable for me. Being a dentist is not really an opportunity that's open to me if I'm totally honest with myself.

Limitations

If we are honest, we may feel that we do have certain limitations facing us. Someone who has a tendency to put on weight is not likely to make a prima ballerina or dancer, but need not abandon his or her dreams of a career in dance altogether. What other dance styles would be more suitable for this person? How about an ancillary role? It takes far more than just dancers to put on a performance! The team needs specialist make-up artists, lighting technicians, choreographers, costume designers – the list is long – and all of these people work in the world of dance.

However, there are sometimes real limitations that we have to take into consideration. For example, some medical conditions mean that certain careers are not possible, and some learning needs can limit our choices. Sometimes *people* can limit us if they have strong opinions about what we should or should not be doing. One famous example of this involves Robbie Williams, who was apparently told that he would never make it as a singer!

Are there any limitations facing you? But remember, you never know what you *cannot* do until you have given it your best shot!

As you read further into this book, just keep in the back of your mind all your strengths, opportunities and perceived limitations. Be open to the suggestions that you read and follow the pointers to further information about anything that sounds interesting. The most important thing you can do for yourself right now is to *believe that you can achieve*!

Tracking progress

You may well have been given information on ways that you can track your progress through education and work experience, especially as you work towards your qualifications and start thinking about moving into more study, travel or work. Most schools will have a method of helping you to gather information on what you have achieved to date and what you want to work towards next. This will usually involve some goal-setting exercises.

Often it is up to you to decide whether or not to track your progress in this way and, unless you are already doing this in your own manner, it is definitely going to be worth following your school's suggestions. Organizing your thoughts and plans, not to mention all of your achievements such as exam results, and non-academic successes such as swimming certificates or other hobbies pursued, is a great way of keeping important information in one place and of helping to track where you have been and where you want to go.

One way of starting this process, if you are not given guidance on it at school, is to think about the following:

- What likes and dislikes do you have? How do you learn?
- What are you good at? What skills do you have?
- What are your successes? What have been your most important learning experiences and achievements?
- What do you want to achieve? What changes and improvements do you want to make and what goals do you want to reach?
- How will you achieve? What action plans do you have? Do you have SMART (specific, measurable, achievable, realistic and time-related) targets?

- Who has helped you to achieve? Who can help you in the future?

You might like to start recording your thoughts on those questions in a notebook or folder. Some kind of box or pocket file is useful for gathering certificates and other evidence of achievements together in one place. Adopting this approach helps you to get and stay organized, and to be in charge of your plans for the future.

As you progress through your later years at school or college you may want to start thinking about:

- Your personal development – what personal qualities, attitudes and interests do you have?
- Your experiences of work – what work skills, enterprise activities and work placements have you experienced?
- Career planning – what are your career management skills like? How do you apply your plans?

Once you get started, make sure you get in the habit of updating what you write in your file. This should be a living, breathing project, not a once in a lifetime effort! It is particularly important to do this to reflect your changing interests, skills and achievements. Obviously, what you were really keen on in Year 7 might not do it for you in Year 11 and having some way of tracking your progress is an excellent way of making sure that you acknowledge these developments. Think of it as a 'working file' – in a way, it is a work in progress, and always will be as you go through your life.

One word of caution: don't use this as a way of recording what goes on at school. The idea is that it should represent the whole you. In other words, what you do and achieve outside school should be recorded too.

As you get older, you can use this progress tracker to:

- build up your confidence to make the most of yourself – understand yourself better, set goals and targets, develop your study and other skills, keep a record of all your achievements and so on;
- make the most of opportunities – manage your learning, make successful applications to further education (FE) or higher education (HE) or employment with training;

- make your experience count – give others the best possible description of yourself, your achievements and your potential.

Why track your progress?

It isn't compulsory to keep a record of your progress and future plans but there are many reasons why it is a good idea to get into the habit. Tracking your progress can help you to:

- become more organized;
- achieve higher grades or the qualifications you want;
- make more informed decisions on the options facing you;
- see how what you have done in the past and what you are doing right now fits in with what you hope to do in the future – to understand how aspects and dimensions of your life interlock;
- work through a personal crisis or simply to change some aspect of yourself for the better;
- focus on improving your skills;
- ensure that you can make the most use out of the feedback you receive all the way through your education and into work, where you are likely to be appraised on how well you are doing.

Summary

The key points from this chapter include:

- Career plans should not be set in stone – allow yourself to change your mind as your skills and goals alter over time.
- Writing down your strengths will help to focus your mind on what you might like to do with your life, or for your next steps at least.
- You should explore the opportunities open to you even if you think you know what to do next.
- Not everyone can do everything, but we all have opportunities and options facing us.
- Even if we think we have limitations we do not have to abandon our dreams altogether.

- Keeping a file to track your progress can be an excellent way of planning your development and recording your achievements.
- It is not compulsory to do track your progress in this way but it is useful for many reasons.

Part Two
Education

4 Looking at education

This chapter looks at:

- how education is likely to change for 14- to 19-year-olds;
- thinking about further education (FE).

14–19 reform

The very first thing to say about education choices facing 16-year-olds is that a lot is about to change. At the time of writing, the exact details of these changes, and when they will be implemented, are not yet known, but we do know what has been proposed.

Proposals for reform

In February 2004 the Working Group on 14–19 Reform announced its proposals for change. They made quite radical recommendations using some parts of our existing education and training system and bringing in new aspects that we have not seen before.

Building on those proposals, the Department for Education and Skills published a White Paper on 23 February 2005 describing the ways that it wants to reform education for 14- to 19-year-olds. (A White Paper is a document that the Government publishes which contains changes it proposes to make.) The Government has several aims that it wants to achieve, including:

- increasing the number of young people who take part in post-16 education;
- making sure that every young person has good skills in English and mathematics;

- offering better vocational routes, which will give young people the knowledge and skills they need for employment or further learning.

There are some important proposals that will change the way that young people aged 14–19 are taught in schools and colleges if it is agreed that the proposals should come into effect. These include the introduction of a general (GCSE) Diploma and a system of specialized diplomas that will cover every occupational sector of the economy. These diplomas will be available at three levels:

- level 1 (foundation);
- level 2 (GCSE);
- level 3 (advanced).

At the time of writing, it is thought that these major reforms will take until 2013 to achieve.

There has been talk that GCSEs and A levels might be abolished but that isn't the plan at the time of writing. The Government says that it will make improvements to them where necessary, but these changes don't mean the end of exams!

● Information point

If you would like to find out more about the changes to education for 14- to 19-year-olds you can visit the 14–19 website: www.dcsf. gov.uk/14-19.

For information about the rest of the UK, visit the following websites:

Scotland: www.scotland.gov.uk/Topics/Education;
Wales: www.learning.wales.gov.uk/;
Northern Ireland: www.dfes.gov.uk/14-19/n_ireland.cfm.

Thinking about further education

The education choices that you make at the age of 16 are important ones. They can affect your entire future. That is why it is really important to know exactly what is on offer to you, whether in the form of so-called academic qualifications or vocational ones, so that you can make an informed decision.

Staying on in FE is one of the best things that most young people can do for themselves. It offers the opportunity to gain valuable qualifications and skills that help directly with future career goals. Besides, there is real evidence to show that the longer you stay in education, the more money you will earn when you enter the workplace (see page 53 for more details).

For many, the choice is made easily and is a natural progression from their time at school but for others it can be a difficult decision to make. Which category do you fall into?

Action

If you are really undecided about what to do when you finish school at 16, think about your answers to the following questions. It can help to write your responses down so that you have something to read over. This also helps to make sure that you don't forget any of your thoughts. The aim here is not to reach any mind-blowing conclusions but rather just to get you thinking about your attitude to going into FE. There is no need to show your answers to anyone unless they bring up further questions that you would like to discuss with someone.

- Did you enjoy school?
- Did you enjoy the process of learning?
- Do you want to learn new subjects and skills?
- Was there anything that you didn't enjoy about being at school?
- Is there anything that you don't enjoy about learning?
- Do you think you would be best doing academic subjects in FE or vocational subjects? Or perhaps a mixture of these?
- Do you feel that you really can't study any more and need to get out and go to work?
- How do you feel about the prospect of staying on to study? Generally positive or generally reluctant?

Reaching your conclusions

There is one very important thing to remember when you are thinking about the possibility of staying on for FE and that is that studying at the post-16 level is nothing like being at secondary school. Even if you will literally be in the same school or on the same campus as you have been so far in your school career, you will find that the attitude of your teachers will be quite different from how it was when you were doing your GCSEs. You will have passed an important turning point in your life and will be seen more as a young adult than a child. You will have new freedoms and different treatment but there will be certain expectations of you. In return for all this, your teachers will expect you to take more responsibility for your learning. This means excellent attendance, commitment to your studies and, it goes without saying, being cooperative and switched on in class!

Even if you would say that you do not exactly love studying, you will see that there are many new and exciting opportunities for you in FE that are unlike anything you have done so far. Keep an open mind as you make your decisions and you will not miss out.

Information point

Did you know there are over 500,000 courses on offer around the country? There is bound to be something that grabs your interest from all of those! It is obviously not practical to list all of these courses here – there are far too many – but if you want to browse a courses database log on to the Connexions website: www.connexions.gov.uk.

Other sources of information are:

www.direct.gov.uk for details on all the different kinds of vocational and academic courses;
www.bbc.co.uk/schools/16guide for the BBC's pages on post-16 education and training;
www.cove.lsc.gov.uk to see if there is a Centre of Vocational Excellence near to you.

Don't forget that you can always contact Connexions if you would like to talk to someone about your education choices at age 16 or 18: 080 800 13 2 19.

If you still conclude that going to work really would be the best thing for you, do read through the following chapter on education first just in case there is something there that can change your mind. The following chapters in this book will also be of great help in organizing your next steps to find a job or some work-based training.

Making decisions ... View from Mack

I always thought that I wanted to leave school as soon as I could but everyone around me told me I was mad. I was fed up with being in classes and having to be indoors most of the day. It's just not me.

But I hadn't looked into exactly what I could do at college and to be honest hadn't taken that much notice of all those careers talks at school. I just knew I wanted to get out. My mum went to the local colleges and picked up prospectuses for me to read through and I found out that I could do agricultural courses really close to where I live. This seemed to be a great solution as I wouldn't be stuck indoors all day and could learn real skills that I could use as soon as I left college. I knew that realistically it would open up more opportunities for me and that I'd be crazy not to go.

Luckily I wasn't too late to apply and I did get on the courses I wanted to do. Looking back now it was the best thing I could have done. I was pretty determined not to listen to anyone's advice but I'm really glad I did in the end. I wouldn't be in anything like such a good position if I'd just left school and tried to get a job that suited me. I think I'd probably be unemployed and getting depressed about never having any money!

Summary

The key points from this chapter include:

- Education for 14- to 19-year-olds is about to change, but these changes may not affect you.
- Going into FE is one of the best things that young people can do for themselves.
- It is very useful to think about your attitude to going into FE to see if this can help you to make your decisions.
- Studying in FE is very different from what you have known at school so far.

5 Choices in further education (FE)

This chapter looks at:

- what to study in FE;
- the main qualification groups;
- where to study in FE;
- choosing a college.

If you have been reading this book from its first few pages, you will know by now that it emphasizes that there are many decisions to be made. But the more information you have available to you, the easier these decisions will be. Just take it one step at a time and don't rush at anything; it is essential that you are happy with, and committed to, the decisions that you make.

Information point
Education or training?

There is information on work experience and apprenticeships on page 78. While these do still involve learning and education, this is done alongside your work in a particular company or organization (although you usually would spend some time on day release at a local college). For this reason work-based training schemes are covered in the sections on work in this book.

What to study in FE

Before you can make a decision on what to study you need to know the full range of courses out there. You can find this information out by talking to your careers teacher at school and also by browsing the careers library at your local Connexions office. Most schools and colleges of FE have prospectuses of post-16 learning opportunities too, so it is worth gathering these to work your way through.

You will need to ask your careers teacher and other teachers at your school for advice on what type of qualification you would be best suited to. They will be able to help you by talking to you about your current levels of attainment in school and what you both feel would be a good level to go for in FE.

Remember, it is up to you whether you want to apply for academic and/or vocational courses. Both will give you valuable skills for the workplace and with the ever-increasing emphasis on skills they are likely to ensure that you have the edge in the job market when you are ready for work.

Don't forget that it is possible to mix and match your studies at post-16 so that you can develop a programme that is just right for you. For example, you could combine A levels with NVQ units to build a programme of study that best suits your plans for the future.

Information point

Your school may use an online or paper method of tracking your progress through school and beyond. You can use this to focus on organizing your skills, achievements and goals. Find out from your tutor or careers adviser if your school has such a thing for you to work with. Tracking your progress in this way can help you to:

- *organize your time so that you don't miss any opportunities;*
- *record your achievements and track your progress against your goals;*
- *practise putting together a CV and applications for jobs and courses.*

The main qualification groups

Basically, if you want to study in FE, you can choose from the following main qualification types for 14–19-year-olds. This is not a list of *courses*, just a list of the *groups* of qualification you may be able to choose from:

- GCE and VCE A levels;
- AEAs (Advanced Extension Awards);
- basic and Key Skills qualifications;
- GCSEs;
- entry level;
- NVQs;
- vocational qualifications.

GCE A level

The GCE A level is split into two parts: the AS and the A2. The AS (or Advanced subsidiary) is a qualification that can stand alone in its own right. It is the equivalent of half a full A level qualification and has three units that are assessed as though the student is half-way through an A level course.

The A2 is the second, more demanding part of a full A level. Like the AS it has three units and students are assessed as though they are at the end of a full A level. Again it is worth half of the full A level qualification but the A2 is not a stand-alone qualification in its own right.

The six units of an A level are usually assessed by examination, but some are assessed by coursework, which can account for between 20 and 30 per cent of the marks.

Information point

Even if you know that you do not want to go on into higher education (HE), gaining A levels is still a wise move as they are so widely known and understood by employers and recruiters.

VCE A levels

These are vocational A levels, which are designed to enable students to learn the skills, knowledge and understanding that they need in a particular vocational area. If you opt for vocational A levels you will probably be doing quite active learning and there will be some employer and professional input from outside your school or college.

●Information point

Since September 2005 VCE A levels have matched GCE A levels in that they will have AS units that are assessed half-way through the course. You can find out more about this by asking at your school or college or by visiting the Qualifications and Curriculum Authority website: www.qca.org.uk.

AEAs

If you are a very bright and able A level student you may have the opportunity to take an AEA. They are designed to be challenging to the very brightest students and may be useful if you are planning to apply to a university that is likely to have many students with a clutch of A grade A levels applying alongside you. If you can handle studying for these qualifications, they will help you to stand out from the crowd.

It is now possible to mix and match post-16 qualifications to suit your needs. If you have a clear idea of where you are now, where you want to go and what you need to get there, you will be more able to build up a picture of the courses you should study (enlist the help of others if necessary).

If you choose to do A levels in their various forms it is likely that you:

- have at least five GCSEs grades A*–C;
- are comfortable with exams;
- probably want to go on to HE;
- have the support of teachers who think you can do it;
- have a real interest in the subjects you are studying.

Basic and Key Skills

There are certain skills that are needed for success in study, work and life in general. These are known as Key Skills and it is possible to take Key Skills qualifications which explore the way that you apply the skills in different contexts. The Key Skills areas are:

- communication;
- application of number;
- information technology;
- working with others;
- improving own learning and performance;
- problem solving.

If you take a Key Skills qualification you will be assessed by test and a portfolio of evidence.

GCSEs

Although these are what you do at the end of your school career at the age of 16, you can still study them post-16 (particularly if you want to go on to do A levels or other qualifications that require you to have achieved a certain number of GCSEs and you need to resit any that you did not get the required grade in). GCSEs can be taken in over 45 subjects.

Information point

The QCA website carries a Student GCSE Guide. You can find it here: www.qca.org.uk/qca_6217.aspx.

Entry level

This is the first level of the National Qualifications Framework (NQF) – see below – and entry level qualifications are pitched below GCSE grade G, NVQ level 1 or vocational qualifications at level 1.

Entry level is subdivided into three levels: entry 1, entry 2 and entry 3 (the highest). From entry level 3 it is hoped that students would go on to level 1 qualifications (such as GCSEs) that appeal to them. If you opt for entry level qualifications it is probably because you have a learning need in a particular area, such as numeracy or literacy.

Information point

The National Qualifications Framework (NQF) for England, Wales and Northern Ireland sets out the levels at which qualifications are recognized. There are nine levels: entry level to level 8. GCSEs grades A*–C are level 2 qualifications and A levels are level 3 qualifications.

There is also a Framework for Higher Education Qualification levels that run from C (certificate), I (intermediate), H (Honours), M (Masters) to D (doctoral).

NVQs

NVQs are work-related qualifications. They focus on the skills, knowledge and competences that you need to do a particular job really well. There are national occupational standards that NVQs are based on. These standards tell us what people in certain jobs or professions do and the standards that they do them to.

There is no specified time in which NVQs have to be completed, although they do have to be completed within a 'reasonable' amount of time. This is so that you could combine part-time work with study for NVQs. There are no entry requirements and no age limits. You get NVQs through a combination of assessment and training.

NVQs have five levels. Most 14–19 learners achieve levels 1–3. Getting to level 4 in that age group would be extremely rare, but it is certainly something to aim for!

Vocational qualifications

There are almost countless vocational qualifications that are linked in to the NQF at every level. You can really let your imagination run wild when thinking about what vocational qualifications you might like to have because there is one to cover just about *every* industry sector you could imagine, from beauty to catering, secretarial skills to journalism.

There is a real push right now to get more young people to go for vocational qualifications so if you are at all tempted, ask for details at your local Connexions office or from your careers teacher. As there are so many vocational qualifications being provided by so many different organizations, they vary in length, level and assessment arrangements.

Information point

There are also other qualifications that you might like to look into and your careers teacher or local Connexions office can help you to do this. One such example is the Free-standing Mathematics Qualification. It is part of the NQF and is for post-16 students. There are three levels: foundation, intermediate and advanced, and they are not attached to any other qualifications.

Scotland

Scotland has a different education system from the rest of the UK and if you want to find out about FE there you should talk to your careers teacher at school or college as well as having a good look through the following website: www.learndirectscotland.com.

In short, Scotland's SVQs are equivalent to NVQs elsewhere in the UK, Standard Grades are equivalent to GCSEs and Highers are equivalent to A levels.

Information point

You can also get information about careers and education in Scotland from the following websites:

www.careers-scotland.org.uk;
www.bbc.co.uk/scotland/education/.

Where to study in FE

You may know that you definitely want to stay on for FE but you still have decisions to make if you are not just staying on at school! Here are some of your options:

- stay on at school if yours has a sixth form attached;
- go to the sixth form in another school;
- go to a local college of FE;
- go to a sixth form college;

- attend a specialist college (for example one devoted to agriculture or aviation);
- go to a private fee-charging college;
- attend an HE college that offers some FE courses.

Sixth forms and sixth form colleges

Sixth forms are attached to, or part of, a school and sixth form colleges are separate establishments. You can take a range of courses at sixth forms but they do tend, still, to specialize in A levels and GCSE resits (although not exclusively by any means). Sixth forms in schools can offer you the potential benefit of being taught by teachers that you already know – but for some students this is a distinct disadvantage and they prefer the opportunity to go somewhere new and start afresh!

Regardless of whether you entered a sixth form or a sixth form college, you would be expected to manage your own studies, time and deadlines.

Other colleges

Other colleges of FE vary tremendously and this is usually dependent on the quality of the alternatives on offer or the size of the town that you live in. If there are very good sixth forms around it is likely that other colleges will specialize in more vocational courses. Here you would have the option of studying full- or part-time and this may help to sway your decision.

Choosing a college ... View from Andy

I knew that I wanted to do A levels but when I went round the colleges on their open days I just didn't like the local sixth form college. Most of my friends were going there but I still felt that it wasn't right for me. The local college of FE had a really strong art department and as that was one of my best subjects I really wanted to go there. They do higher education courses at the FE college so it meant that I had the benefit of using the resources and equipment that the degree students were using while studying my A levels. In the end there was no competition – I couldn't throw away that opportunity, so chose the college of FE over the sixth form college.

Choosing a college

There are approximately 476 colleges of FE in the UK of which about 102 are sixth form colleges, but for many students it is obvious which college they should attend, particularly if they want to take a particular course that is only taught in one local college. However, if you have a choice to make, these ideas may help you. Ask these questions about any college you are considering attending:

● Can you do the combinations of courses and subjects that you are interested in?
● Does it have a good reputation for the kind of subjects you want to study?
● Find out what the results are like there. Are they good? Do people achieve well there?
● Could you imagine being happy there?
● Do you know others who are going there? Would it matter to you if you don't?
● What is the atmosphere like? Do you think you could study there?
● What are the facilities like? Does it have strengths that you would be able to take advantage of?
● Are there any sporting opportunities? Does it matter to you if there aren't?
● What are the student welfare facilities like? Is there plenty of advice on offer?
● What's your gut instinct? Could you be happy and do well there?

The only really effective way of choosing where you are going to continue your studies in FE is to visit all the options that are open to you. All the colleges will have open days where you can look around, meet staff and students, try out taster sessions and chat to others who are thinking of going there. Your local paper will publish details of open days at the relevant times and your local Connexions office will have the details too. Even if you think you know where you want to go, take the time to look at the other options in your town, or within commutable distance.

Action

It is a good idea to keep notes on the various colleges that you visit. This way, if you are stuck between a choice of two, you can use your notes to help you reach a decision.

Once you know where you would like to study, obviously you will need to apply for a place. The best advice here is to follow the guidance of your school or the Connexions service. You will need to fill in application forms and they may also ask you to attend for an interview.

Colleges want to be as sure as they can about two main things before offering places: that potential students will stay on their courses and not drop out; and that the students will get the best results they possibly can.

No college wants dropouts and flunkers as students so convince them that you will stay and will achieve the best you can!

You can get all the forms you need direct from the college itself if not from your school. Make sure that you meet all the deadlines you need to and ask for help if you are struggling with the application form. Most careers teachers and Connexions staff will be able to guide you through this process.

Information point

The section on work will have some useful advice for you on making applications generally, which you will be able to apply to any applications you make. There is also advice on interviews there too, which will be useful if you have to have one to get into the college of your choice. See page 104 for more information.

Summary

The key points from this chapter include:

- It is up to you whether you study academic or vocational subjects in FE. Some people choose to study a combination of the two.
- There are around eight main qualification groups.
- There are several ways of studying in FE. You may be able to stay on at school, go to a separate sixth form college or go to your local college of FE – these are just some of the options you may have.
- It is important to choose the college that is right for you and there are many factors to take into consideration.

6 Choices in higher education (HE)

This chapter will look at:

- what to study in HE;
- the main qualification groups in HE;
- choosing a university;
- applying through UCAS;
- starting your course.

HE is what you progress to after completing FE (post-16) courses should you so decide (assuming you have the necessary entry requirements). HE courses can last anything from one to four or five years or more and there is a variety of qualifications you can gain.

Going into HE is not just a matter of doing a degree or nothing. There are several options open to you, so you will need to do a little research to make sure that you take the path most suited to you.

Information point

There is a 'gateway to higher education' on the internet that can be found at www.hero.ac.uk. HERO stands for Higher Education and Research Opportunities in the UK. It is well worth a visit, especially for access to online prospectuses and a wealth of other inside information on getting the most out of your time in HE.

Before you research HE courses, just take a moment to think about why you are even considering going into HE. Is it to put off getting a job or to study something you are genuinely interested in and/or to further your career? Make sure that you know what your motivations are and then read the following points:

- Just under 15 per cent of students flunk university. That's more than one in seven.
- Estimates of student debt suggest that you could expect to graduate with around £15,000 of debt and possibly even more than that.

Are you still interested?

However, there are definite advantages to think about:

- Although you will almost certainly end university with a debt to repay, some estimates suggest that over their working life some graduates can expect to earn an extra £400,000 for having a degree (this is an estimate, not a promise!).
- The chances of you being unemployed are thought to be cut by half when you have a degree.
- You can expect your salary to rise faster with a degree – when compared with non-graduates estimates suggest that you can expect to be earning as much as 30 per cent more for men and 46 per cent more for women 10 years after graduating.
- University-goers develop marketable transferable skills.
- The opportunity for an 'all-round' education is open for all at university – the social and cultural life that's to be had helps to develop all-rounders who are not just fixated on their subjects!
- You get letters after your name!

Has that recaptured your interest?

Information point

For information about student life in the UK, log on to www. studentuk.com. Also check out www.uni360.com, providing virtual tours of universities and much more, and the National Union of Students website www.nusonline.co.uk.

What to study in HE

Not only do you need to know the full range of courses out there before you can make a decision on what you want to study in HE, but you also need to think about the following considerations:

- What courses are open to you with your current qualifications?
- What courses are you most interested in?
- Do you need a vocational degree to achieve your goals (for example, to be a vet or a doctor)?
- Are you studying anything at the moment that you want to continue with?
- Does it look like you will get the results you need to do the course that you are interested in? Do you have a plan B in case you don't get enough points/grades?
- Do you have the relevant work experience you need (if this is a requirement)?
- Do you actually *need* to go to university for the career you want to pursue?

Even if you get on your perfect course, there will be times when the work seems too much (or you have put it off for too long and are now facing all-nighters to get your essays done!). Just imagine how this would feel if you have allowed yourself to be persuaded to do a course that other people want you to do or that you thought sounded fun at the time but did not really have a burning passion for!

Information point

Not all courses run to the same pattern. Some are modular (meaning that you can choose certain self-contained modules to study), others are sandwich (meaning that you will spend a year out either abroad or in industry), combined (two or more subjects making up a single course of study) and so on. Make sure that you find out exactly what kind of course it is that you are interested in. If you are unsure of any of the terms used your local Connexions office can help you. There is a huge amount of advice on the Aimhigher website too: www. aimhigher.ac.uk. This website aims to give all the information you need to get started on the road to HE.

If you do not have a career path in mind, it is particularly important, essential even, to choose a course that will grab you and hold your attention until you take the final exam. University life will hold much to tempt you away from your studies so if your heart is not completely in it you are more likely to fall behind. Do something you get a kick out of and the chances are you will stick with it to the end.

Information point

UCAS is the central organization that processes applications for full-time undergraduate courses at UK universities and colleges. You can do a full course search on the UCAS website: www.ucas.com.

The UCAS website also carries invaluable advice on how to apply for HE courses. Applications must be made online. If you don't have access to the internet at home and you have to compete to use it at school, you may want to use one of the online centres which have teamed up with UCAS to give students access to work on their applications. To find out more, visit www.ucas.com/apply/online_centres/.

Other websites that can help in the search for a course are: www.ukcoursefinder.co.uk and www.hotcourses.com.

The main qualification groups

Basically, if you want to study in HE, you can choose from the following main qualification types. This is not a list of *courses*, just a list of the *groups* of qualification you may be able to choose from:

- H (Honours) – Bachelors degrees, graduate certificates and diplomas;
- I (intermediate) – Diplomas of Higher Education and Further Education, foundation degrees, Higher National Diplomas (HNDs);
- C (certificate) – Certificates of Higher Education.

Honours degrees

These are the most common HE qualifications. They are called Bachelors degrees and are either arts-based (the BA, or Bachelor of Arts) or science-based (the BSc or Bachelor of Science). They take between three and five years of full-time study to complete. Honours degrees tend to be subject-based rather than linked to specific careers or professions.

Foundation degrees

Foundation degrees are employment-related qualifications. They have been designed with employers and aim to put an end to skills shortages. They combine vocational and general learning. They have flexible methods of study. Full-time foundation degrees take two years to study and part-time ones usually three or four years pro rata. There are no set entry requirements so you can apply even if you do not have other qualifications; it is up to the university or college to decide whether you are a suitable candidate or not. If you successfully complete a foundation degree you may be able to add a further 12–15 months' study to what you have done so far and convert it to an Honours degree. It is possible to study a foundation degree course while working.

Information point

You can find out more about foundation degrees from the following website: www.foundationdegree.co.uk.

HNCs/HNDs

Higher National Certificates or Diplomas can be done in a wide range of subjects, usually linked to specific careers. Often, HNCs and HNDs are studied part-time by people who are also working. They take two or more years to complete. Having an HNC can mean you can enter the second year of a suitable Honours degree while having an HND can mean you can enter the second or third year.

Certificates/Diplomas of Higher Education

The Certificate of Higher Education is a one-year course that can be done if you feel you need to gain some confidence before starting further HE studies. The diploma is a two-year (three-year part-time) course often linked to specific careers. It is like a degree but has less content. It is sometimes possible to add a year of study to the diploma to convert it into a degree.

Information point

You can find the contact details of universities and HE colleges at www.hero.ac.uk/sites/hero/uk/universities___colleges/index.cfm.

Choosing a university

There are many factors to consider when choosing a university, not least, does it offer exactly the kind of course you want to do? University is about much more than the studying you will do there. It is about meeting new people, having new experiences and widening your horizons, as much as anything else. So, with this in mind, when it comes to choosing where you want to apply to, think about these considerations:

- Does it offer the course that interests and motivates you most?
- Can you meet the entry requirements for the course you want to do there?
- Will it give you the opportunity to build on your past achievements and strengths?
- Is it close enough to home (if you will be living at home through HE) or within a distance you are happy travelling (if you will be moving away)?
- What reputation does the university have?
- What reputation does the course have?
- Does the university excel in any particular area? Would your course be sidelined in favour of its 'pet' courses or are all treated equally?

- Would you be able to study in a way that suits you? How many lectures would you have to attend and how much private study would be expected? Is there any practical work to do? Would you get a year out in industry or abroad?
- Would you get any one-to-one tutoring?
- What weighting do exams have on the course? Is any coursework taken into consideration?
- If you have any particular special needs, can the university cater for you?
- Would you get a chance to learn skills that would make you more employable than other graduates?
- Would you get a chance to do some work experience?
- Does the university have an active student union? What entertainments would there be on offer? Does it offer a good social life?
- How good are the sports facilities?
- Is it a campus university (where most of the university buildings, including halls of residence, are in one area, often with green space in between) or are the buildings spread out across a town or city?
- What kind of student accommodation is there? Would you be guaranteed a place in a hall of residence for your first year at least?
- What is your instinctive feeling about the place?

Information point

Apparently, 87 per cent of students say that going to university is a good investment! Also, by 2010, it is thought that the number of jobs needing the skills learned in HE will rise by 1.73 million. That's an awful lot of jobs!

Open days

The only way to know if you will be happy at a particular university is to visit it and have a look round. All universities have open days and you should definitely attend any at universities you are thinking of applying to. Even if the journey seems like a hassle, do it!

Information point

Your local Connexions office will have a booklet called 'The Sixth Formers' Guide to Open Days' and it is well worth having a read of this. You should also visit www.opendays.com for the detailed information that you need. This website also allows you to book online.

Information point

For a student-written 'alternative' guide to UK universities visit www.realuni.com.

The online 'Push' guide to university is an independent guide to finding the right university for you. It can be found at www.push.co.uk.

You might find www.unofficial-guides.com of interest too.

Applying – UCAS

UCAS, pronounced 'you-cass', is the Universities and Colleges Admissions Service. It is responsible for handling nearly all the applications for HE courses.

Information point

To get a clear idea of the application process you need to log on to the UCAS website: www.ucas.com, where you will find detailed guidance. It is a good idea to note key dates in your diary so that you don't miss any important deadlines.

Applications to UCAS are made online via the UCAS website. You can apply for up to five courses in five different institutions (but you can just apply to one if there is only one course in the whole country that you want to do – alternatively you can apply to five courses at one university if you are sure that you want to go there and are not too bothered about what you study).

The UCAS application asks for details about your qualifications so far and grades achieved. You will also need to complete a personal statement to sell yourself! Your school or college can help with this, as can Connexions, and there is even a website: www. personalstatement.info, although writing from your own ideas and own 'voice' will always be best.

Your school or college will help you through the UCAS application process. There are some important deadlines so make sure that you don't miss them. If you are applying to Oxford, Cambridge or for medicine, dentistry or veterinary science/medicine you will need to submit your application by 15 October of your final year of FE. Other applications need to be submitted by 15 January of the year of expected entry to HE.

Information point

UCAS has a tariff that compares all the different qualifications that can get you into HE. Points are assigned to each type of qualification and grade. It can seem quite daunting to go through at first, but it is not that bad if you get the help of your tutor at school or college. The Connexions service can help with this too.

To find out more about the UCAS tariff visit www.ucas.com.

- There is a fee to pay. As an example, the fee for students starting university in 2008 is £15 (£5 for those who apply to one course at one university).
- Once your application has been submitted, UCAS will send an acknowledgement back as well as sending your application to the admissions tutors in the institutions you have chosen.
- UCAS will inform you if you have been successful in your application.
- You may be called for an interview (see the section on page 104 for general advice on interviews).
- If you are offered a place this will probably be conditional on you achieving certain results in your exams. If you already know your results (for example, if you have taken a year out) any offers of places are likely to be unconditional.

- If, when your results come out in August, you do not have exactly the grades you needed, the institution may agree to take you anyway.
- If you do not get offered a place when your results are known, you can enter the 'clearing' system. This is basically when all the courses that are not yet filled and all the students who do not yet have a place try to match up with each other! It's a busy time as courses have to be filled between the end of August and the start of term. If you need to go through clearing, your school or college will be able to help you through the process. Basically, you will have to keep a close eye on the broadsheet newspapers and the internet to find out what courses still have places. Do not be tempted to leap at the first thing that looks vaguely interesting. Not surprisingly, of all the students who do not make it through to the end of their HE courses there is a higher proportion who have entered through clearing than who got on to the course of their choice. This is worth keeping in mind.

Information point

ucasextra enables students who find themselves without an offer of a course to have an additional choice through UCAS. If you take the ucasextra route, you don't have to wait until clearing to carry on with the search for a place.

You can apply via ucasextra from mid-March to early July in the year of intended entry to HE. So, for example, if you aim to start a course in the autumn of 2009, you would go through ucasextra from mid-March of that year. You would be eligible to apply if:

- *all five of your choices have been used up;*
- *you have not had any success with any of your choices;*
- *you have cancelled your choices and have no offers of places;*
- *you have declined all offers made to you.*

You can find further information about ucasextra here: www.ucas. com/getting/after/extra.html.

Information point

The Nursing and Midwifery Admissions Service (NMAS) processes nursing training applications (apart from those for nursing degrees, which are processed by UCAS). Find out more by telephoning 0870 112 2206 or looking at the NMAS website: www.nmas.ac.uk.

Starting your course

Congratulations! You are off to university! Whether you are actually leaving home or staying put, this is a good opportunity to get yourself sorted before launching into your next phase of studying. These ideas may help:

- How prepared are you emotionally? Is there anything you want to talk about before you take the plunge? Have you got any concerns or anxieties?
- Make sure that you read Part Six of this book, especially the sections on finding somewhere to live and money.
- Is there a chance you could take a holiday before your course starts? This will give you a chance to gather your thoughts about what is ahead.
- Do you need anything new to take with you? Do you have enough clothes and shoes?
- Have you got plenty of paper (for note-taking) and change (for the passport photo machines you are bound to need to use to get things like a union card and library card)?
- Is there a book list you need to be looking at? It might be worth scouring some second-hand bookshops to see if you can get some bargains. Some online bookshops sell second-hand copies of books too, but check that you get the right editions.
- Do you know how you are going to get you and all your stuff to university?
- Spare a thought for your parents and close relatives as you are getting ready to leave. It might be incredibly exciting for you, but the chances are they will really miss you. Make a promise to keep in touch and stick to it!

- Set off with a really positive attitude about what is ahead of you. Aim to really enjoy it. After all, you deserve to after all your hard work so far!

Leaving home ... View from Ashley

It wasn't until I had graduated that my mum told me how upset she'd been the day she and dad drove me to university for the first time. Apparently she had cried most of the way home that day! I really appreciated the fact that she didn't tell me at the time as I would have thought it was a really big deal. I'm glad I made the effort to stay in touch with my family and friends when I went away and I made sure that I didn't go more than six weeks without going home for the weekend so that we could all catch up with each other. It was quite a learning curve for me – we don't always realize what an impact we have on other people and I think we have to be sensitive to what others close to us might be feeling at such turning points in our lives.

Summary

The key points from this chapter are:

- There are distinct advantages to studying in HE, not least that graduates typically earn considerably more than those who have not studied in HE.
- It is essential to make the right choice over what to study in HE to give yourself the best chance of success, especially if you do not have a career choice in mind.
- Choosing a university is easier said than done – there are many factors to take into consideration.
- It is a good idea to go to the open days for the universities that you are interested in.
- Applications for most places on HE courses are handled by UCAS.

Part Three
Work

School can teach you some important life lessons.

But you might find you get your best results outside the classroom.

Apprenticeship Programme

Tesco is the UK's number one retailer – and the country's biggest employer in the private sector. As our business continues to expand and enjoy even greater success, we need people who will grow with us. That's why we're so committed to offering fantastic training and development opportunities, and encouraging everyone who works with us to reach their full potential.

Take our Apprenticeship Programme. Designed to give our people the chance to gain a nationally recognised vocational qualification on the job, it's the perfect foundation for a career in retail.

Developed in collaboration with City and Guilds, at the end of this year-long programme, you'll not only have gained an NVQ in Retail Skills, but also Key Skills in Communication and Application of Number and a Technical Certificate in Retail. You'll also have learned invaluable life skills such as team-working, customer service and time management.

And, once you've completed the programme, you'll find there are plenty more opportunities to undertake additional training which could take you even further still. There really are no limits to what you can achieve here, so, if you're looking for a career in a fast-paced, constantly changing, highly stimulating and fun environment, exactly what you're looking for might be right on your doorstep.

To find out more, visit **www.tesco-careers.com**

www.tesco-careers.com

Tesco is an equal opportunities employer.

TESCO | *Every little helps*

7 Types of work

This chapter looks at:

- getting work at 16;
- getting work at 18;
- types of work that you can do.

Getting a job is not just about going for a cosy 9–5 with one of the major employers (if there is such a thing as a 'cosy' job!). There are many types of job out there, not to mention the on-the-job training and apprenticeships, and work experience that you can undertake.

Getting work at 16

As you read through the next few chapters you'll find out about some of the options that are open to you if you want to find work at the age of 16 (after you have left school). For example, you may start work on an apprenticeship scheme, which means that you will be working and training at the same time.

Information point

Initially, the places to go for advice if you are thinking of getting a job straight after leaving school are: your school's careers teacher; your local Connexions office. Visit www.connexions-direct.com for further information or telephone 080 800 13 2 19.

While the decisions you make in your life are ultimately for your benefit, it is a really good idea to get on to an apprenticeship or training scheme. You will be able to gain vocational qualifications as you are working and earning money and keep up with the competition in the workplace. If you leave school and go straight into a job that offers you no further training, education or development you could find yourself falling behind the others in your age group who you will be competing with for jobs throughout your life.

What to do next

If you know that you are going to try to get a job at 16 rather than stay on in FE, these steps might help you:

- Ask your form tutor and careers teacher about work experience. He or she may be able to arrange something for you to do after school or in one of the school holidays in your final year to give you that little extra advantage on the job market.
- Attend every session that your school runs on careers. They may have a careers fair where local employers come to your school to talk to students about the world of work from their perspective. If your school runs a careers fair make sure that you go – you could make really useful contacts and find out about options that you had not ever thought of.
- Ask your careers teacher about work-based training schemes and apprenticeships. He or she will be able to give you all the latest details and tell you about any local schemes that may exist.
- Get a notebook and write down all the information you gather. Even if it is not useful now you never know when it might come in handy! Make sure that you read through these notes frequently to remind yourself of what tips and information you have picked up.
- Do not be tempted to take just *any* job, particularly if it doesn't offer you any future prospects. Always think about what you can progress to. It is important to think about your working life as a series of steps or stages and to get stuck in a dead-end job at such a young age will not be good for you.

- Do not take a job that you know is too easy for you. You will get bored very quickly and that will destroy your chances of getting any job satisfaction at all.
- Make sure that you know exactly *why* you want to get a job and not stay on in FE. Perhaps reread the first few sections of this book to see what choices you have, particularly in FE.
- If your final decision is to go for work, make sure that you read this chapter thoroughly. Your CV and letter-writing skills will need to be excellent and the chapter on going to an interview will be very useful too.

Getting work at 18

If you want to get a job at the age of 18 you can still use the Connexions service for advice as well as your local Jobcentre Plus. You may also want to consider doing a training scheme so that you learn additional skills alongside your job. This would be the best idea for most 18-year-olds who decide not to go into HE.

What to do next

If you know that you are going to try to get a job at 18 rather than stay on in HE, these steps might help you:

- Talk to as many teachers and tutors at your school or college as you can. Use their expertise and advice. In particular, make use of the careers library and any specialist careers help that might be on offer.
- Get into the habit of visiting your local Connexions office as often as you can. Ask about the vacancies that they know about and any training schemes that you might be suitable for. You are not too old for a training scheme such as an apprenticeship and there just might be the perfect opportunity for you!
- Aim to get your next move sorted out before you leave school or college so that you do not have any periods when you have nothing to do.

Choices. Choices. Choices.

You can join us after University or you can join us now.

Your choice.

A-level Options Programme

Not everyone leaving school wants to go on to university before getting their career up and running. And why should you when Tesco offers a 12 month development programme that could lead to a management position within 6 months.

Offering exceptional on- and off-the-job training, the level of exposure and responsibility you get will depend, in part, on the store format in which you train. For example, Express and Metro stores will see you develop to a Duty Management position. In our bigger stores (Superstores and Extras) you'll develop to manage your own department. We also offer the option of working across the different range of stores we have.

You'll also have the opportunity to specialise in a particular area – so, if you have a real passion for people you could train as a HR Resource Manager or, if it's finance that really pushes your buttons, you might want to train as a Compliance Manager.

You'll start the programme as a Team Leader in a local store on a competitive salary and benefits package. This will give you an excellent grounding in how the store environment works and experience of coaching, communicating and co-ordinating others. You'll attend workshops, devise a development plan with your manager and start to build your 5 year career path.

In fact, however far you want to go, we'll help you identify what you need to do to get there – it's all here for the taking. All we ask of you is a real hunger to succeed, a real customer focus, bags of energy, plenty of commitment, at least 3 A levels (grade A-D or equivalent) and GCSE Maths and English (grade A-C).

We will be recruiting for this programme on our website from March 2008 to begin in September 2008. To find out more about this exciting opportunity with the UK's number one retailer, visit **www.tesco-careers.com**

- Use the careers library at your local Connexions office. Ask for support and guidance – there may be someone there who can spend some time going over possibilities with you.
- Ask at your local Jobcentre Plus if they have an adviser who specializes in your age group. Ask if you can make an appointment to see him or her.
- Do not reject any ideas without fully considering them. You may not have thought of them as possibilities before but could they be for you?
- Read all the information in this book about how to find vacancies, apply for jobs and attend interviews.

Types of work

It would be impossible to list here all the possibilities that exist in the world of work today. The Information Age is helping to ensure that the pace of change is rapid and we all need to make sure that we can remain employable by:

- getting the qualifications we need to be able to thrive and compete in the working world;
- developing our skills and looking out for new opportunities and experiences;
- having high standards in certain key skills such as ICT, communication, numeracy and literacy;
- being willing and able to cope with change;
- being willing to look at the possibility of pursuing several careers through our lifetime.

With the right attitude and a commitment to show employers that you have what it takes and that you have the qualities that are needed in the workplace, there's every chance that you can succeed in getting a job if that is what you want.

The different sectors

The world of work can be split into three main sectors: the private and public sectors, and a new non-governmental 'Third Sector'. They all have quite different approaches and philosophies, and they feel very different to work in. You may feel that you are naturally more suited to one than another, depending on your personality and nature.

The public sector

There are certain organizations that belong to the state (this means that we all 'own' them). These include:

- the National Health Service;
- the maintained education system (state schools, local education authorities, the inspection service and so on);
- the Civil Service;
- the police;
- fire and rescue services;
- central government;
- local government;
- a wide range of other organizations.

The public sector exists to provide a service rather than to make money (although there is a drive for the public services to *save* money by being more cost effective). The wages of people working in the public sector are paid out of money that the Government has collected in tax.

The private sector

This sector includes all companies that are not owned by the state and that provide goods and services. For example, manufacturing companies, retailers like high street shops, the hotel industry, banks, insurance companies and so on. This sector exists to make a profit and the wages of people working in this sector are paid out of this profit and not by the Government out of taxes.

The 'Third Sector'

The 'Third Sector' is the name given to the group of organizations that can be described as being non-governmental and that typically use their profits to reinvest in social, cultural and environmental projects. These organizations might be charities, voluntary and community organizations, social enterprises, not-for-profit organizations, cooperatives or mutuals. The 'Third Sector' is growing in the UK and makes a huge contribution to society as well as to the economy and the environment.

Information point

You can find out much more about the 'Third Sector' and the job opportunities that it might hold for you from the following websites:

- *www.cabinetoffice.gov.uk/third_sector/ – This is the website of the government department with responsibilities for the 'Third Sector'. Here you'll find information on the Prime Minister's 10-year vision to support the 'Third Sector' as well as other information on the sector and a dedicated newsletter.*
- *www.thirdsector.co.uk/ – This is the website of a UK publication for the voluntary and not-for-profit sector. You will find information about the sector, latest news and job opportunities here.*

Other ways of viewing the world of work

As well as splitting the world of work into the public, private and Third sectors, it can also be split into the following:

- the leisure industry (including hotels, sports centres, leisure centres, holiday companies and so on);
- the financial sector (including banks, building societies, accountants, insurance companies and so on);
- the health sector (including the NHS, private hospitals, private healthcare practitioners, the world of complementary and alternative medicine and so on);
- the so-called 'invisible' sector (including tourism, imports and exports and foreign students);
- the farming industry (including farms, dairies and so on);
- the manufacturing industry (including companies that produce goods such as cars to sell in the UK and abroad);
- the construction industry (including building contractors, engineers, architects and so on).

Table 7.1

Sector	A few examples of types of work/jobs in each sector
Agriculture and food	Farming, food preparation, food science
Construction	Bricklaying and plastering, surveying, civil engineering
Health and medical	Doctor, dentist, pharmacist, homeopath, osteopath, nurse
Scientific	Zoology, botany, horticulture
Computing	Software engineer, database manager, hardware technician
Architecture and planning	Town planning, environmental technologies
Environment	Sustainability, conservation, ecology, pollution
Sport and leisure	Sports coaching, leisure management
Civil Service, politics and government	Social worker, tax inspector, administrator, clerical officer
Business administration	Marketing, human resources, land and property management
Education	Teacher, nursery nurse, classroom assistant
Financial services	Bank and building society work, insurance, sales and so on
Forces	The armed forces, police work
Librarianship	Librarian, information service
Creative arts	Design, music, drama, beauty and hairdressing
Media	Journalism, PR, publishing and so on
Entertainment	TV work, actor, writer
Retail	Sales assistant, manager, personnel
Self-employment	Anything at all!

There are, of course, other sectors that could be added to this list, but this is just to give you an idea of the range that exists.

Job categories

The table on the previous page shows some of the jobs that you might consider going into. It is not a definitive list by any means but will offer you some ideas.

• Information point

To find out more about work categories and the kinds of jobs they include, take a look at www.jobs.ac.uk. If you are interested in eco-friendly employment, visit www.environmentjob.co.uk/ which lists jobs and volunteering opportunities in the environmental sector. There is also a 'definitive guide to careers with a conscience' called 'The Ethical Careers Guide' which can be found here: www.ethical careersguide.co.uk.

The armed forces

One option open to school leavers at both 16 and 18 is to enter one of the armed forces. The armed forces in the UK are the British Army, the Royal Navy and the Royal Air Force. There is an incredible array of jobs on offer in the forces and in the Ministry of Defence civilian careers (take a look at the websites below for more information).

Being in the armed forces is also an opportunity to undertake FE. Welbeck – The Defence Sixth Form College – admits students 'with a career ambition' to join the Royal Navy, the British Army or the Royal Air Force or to become Ministry of Defence Civil Service Engineers (see the website listed below for further information).

Working in the armed forces is not all about active service by any means. There are amazing opportunities to be had if you like the idea of seeing the world, or pushing your body to its ultimate in fitness. It is not for everyone though, and if you think a career as a Royal Marine commando is up your street, remember what the advertisements say: 99.99 per cent need not apply! But the armed forces are not all like the Royal Marines and if you think you might be tempted, do spend some time browsing the relevant websites to see exactly what opportunities are out there for you.

Information point

For more info about a career in the armed forces take a look at the following websites:

www.welbeck.mod.uk
www.mod.uk
www.rafcareers.com
www.armyjobs.mod.uk
www.royal-navy.mod.uk

Action

Take a few moments to think about the kind of work environment that you would like to work in. Here are some examples of the kinds of possibilities there are – you could work:

- alone;
- with others in a team;
- in a building;
- outside;
- in a factory;
- in a shop;
- in an office;
- on a ship;
- in the air;
- above ground;
- underground;
- with others of your age;
- with others of various ages;
- with people of the same level of education as you;
- with people of various degrees of education;
- at night;
- in the daytime;
- in uniform;
- in your own clothes;
- in smart clothes;
- in casual clothes.

These are just some ideas, but they should help to trigger your own thoughts on the kind of environment in which you would like to work.

Aim to draw up a shortlist of possibilities. Do also pay attention to anything that you really would not like to do. For example, if you hate being on an aeroplane, a career as an air steward is probably not for you. Use your conclusions to help you in your job hunt.

Summary

The key points from this chapter include:

- You need to spend time researching your job prospects if you want to leave school at age 16.
- Work-based training schemes are a very good idea for many 16- and 18-year-old school and college leavers.
- The world of work can be subdivided into many different sectors. One way is to split it into the public sector, the private sector and the 'Third Sector'.
- There is an enormous range of jobs that school leavers can do.
- You need to think about what kind of job would suit you best of all.
- The armed forces is another possibility for 16- and 18-year-old school and college leavers.

Work experience, job shadowing and work-based training

This chapter looks at:

- doing work experience and job shadowing;
- apprenticeships;
- Entry to Employment;
- the Connexions Card.

Work experience

Rather than offer help to organizations as you do when volunteering, work experience and job shadowing are purely for your own benefit. That said, many companies are keen to take on young people for work experience. You never know, if they like you and you like them there may be a job for you at the end of it!

Taking someone on for work experience or job shadowing does entail a fair amount of work on the part of the organization so they do want to see quite a high level of commitment in return. Effective work experience programmes usually involve planned and supervised activities so that you can really get a taste of what it might be like to work in that company or industry.

Work experience ... View from Neil

Doing work experience was one of the best things I have ever done. I always thought that I wanted to be an accountant and when I was at college I got the chance to spend one afternoon a week in a local accountant's office. It was so amazingly boring! I'm not saying that accountants are boring, but for me the time went so slowly and I hadn't really understood how much fine detail the job involves. I got really impatient and it really taught me that the job's not for me.

I love maths and want to make sure that I can use the maths I've learned when I'm working and I thought that accountancy was the obvious option. But I was glad to have had the opportunity to find out that it wasn't before I started the training process. I was talking to one of the accountants in the office about what other options I might have and she had some really good ideas for me to follow up. So, it was definitely a worthwhile thing for me to do.

You will almost certainly have done some work experience while at school. If this is the case, think back over your experiences. What did you learn? How did you learn? If you are yet to do work experience, think carefully about what you would like to do and where. Is this something you can arrange by yourself in your own spare time?

Arranging your own work experience

If you want to try out what it might be like to work in a particular place, you can arrange your own work experience to carry out in your spare time. Even if you cannot offer full days because of study commitments, you could perhaps do some hours after school or college or spend a week or more somewhere in your holidays. You can use your initiative over this and arrange whatever would fit in with your schedule.

Opposite is a sample letter that you might like to use when approaching companies direct to ask for work experience.

Your address here:

2 Orchard Street
Worksworth
West Shire
WW2 4HY

Date here

Address of the person you are writing to here:
  (Make sure you find out the name of the person you need
to write to)

Mrs B Short
Human Resources Manager
Worksworth Electronics
Worksworth
West Shire
WW3 7RT

Dear Mrs Short

I am writing to request a period of work experience at
Worksworth Electronics. I have just completed my GCSEs and
I am very interested in working in the electronics
industry.

Ideally I would like to spend two weeks with your company
and I would be particularly interested in experiencing the
manufacturing side of your business, but I would be very
grateful for any time and experience you are able to offer
me. I am very willing to learn and to undertake whatever
tasks you think it appropriate for me to do.

I have enclosed my CV, which contains my full contact
details, and I look forward to hearing from you.

Yours sincerely,

Your name here

If you do not hear anything within about 10 days of sending your letter, you can always ring up to check that it arrived and to see if it is possible to make arrangements over the phone. Try to be as accommodating as you can. If the organization offers you a day's work experience when you really want a week, take it; one day is better than nothing.

Once you are doing work experience try to identify the transferable skills (more on this on page 166) that you are learning. At the end of each day it is a good idea to jot down what you have done and what you have learned. You will be really grateful for this when you come to write job applications or apply for a place at college or university.

Work experience ... View from Caz

I didn't get the work experience I wanted when I was at school so I decided to arrange my own in the summer holiday after I finished my GCSEs. I've always wanted to be a hairdresser but thought I should really get some experience first before making a commitment to a course.

I wrote to the manager of my local branch of a hairdressing chain. I wanted to go for one of the bigger salons in my town so that I could see a whole range of cuts, colours and treatments. I'm also really interested in hair fashion and styling so I thought the bigger the salon the better.

The manager invited me in for a week and asked one of the senior stylists to look after me. I was dreading it being cliquey but it wasn't at all. They were all really friendly and even got me washing hair by the end of the week. I learned how to mix colours (although they didn't let me loose on the customers!) and how to answer the phone and make bookings on the computer. I absolutely loved it and definitely want to go into the profession.

To anyone thinking of arranging their own work experience, go for it. You've nothing to lose and you might have as much fun as I had. At the end of the week I really didn't want to leave and I still go in there if I have a spare afternoon. You have to be willing to get stuck in; I swept up so much hair that week it's untrue! But overall I found it a great experience.

Just as Caz found, there may well be certain tasks that are too difficult or technical for you to do on your work experience. If this is the case, the chances are that you will 'job shadow'. This simply means watching closely while someone else does the job. This is not as tedious as it might sound, especially if you give yourself mini tests on how things are done and what techniques are used. Remember, when you are job shadowing, to ask if there is anything you do not understand. And if it looks like there is something you can do (like Caz when she learned to wash clients' hair) ask if you can do it. They can only say 'no' and just might say 'yes'.

Information point

The National Council for Work Experience (NCWE) is an organization which aims to provide young people and employers with everything they need to know about work experience and work-related learning. They can help students to:

- *put theory learning into practice;*
- *consider career options;*
- *find out what they like or do not like doing;*
- *get some practical experience/start to develop 'employability' skills.*

You can find NCWE's website at www.work-experience.org. The site has a great resource centre too, which is well worth checking out. You can also telephone NCWE on 0845 6015510. As NCWE is not a placement agency, they do not accept CVs.

The website carries a really useful list of links for young people wanting to do work experience. Click on the '15–18-year-olds' button for more information.

Apprenticeships

If you intend to leave school at 16 you may be able to get a place on an apprenticeship scheme. These schemes offer the opportunity to learn on the job and to build up the knowledge and skills that you need while also gaining qualifications and earning money at the same time. Can't be bad!

There are no set entry requirements for apprenticeships apart from the following conditions:

● you need to be living in England (see the Information point below for details for people living in Scotland, Wales and Northern Ireland);
● you must be aged between 16 and 24;
● you must not be in full-time education.

There are different kinds of apprenticeship available and it depends on your experience and the opportunities in your areas as to which one you go for. All apprenticeships lead to NVQs, Key Skills qualifications and usually a technical certificate such as a City and Guilds, and possibly other qualifications specific to the particular occupation.

Apprenticeships usually take between 12 and 24 months although they have no set time limit. On an apprenticeship you would be paid a wage by your employer (that reflected your age, skills and abilities) and receive targeted on-the-job training. You would also spend time at a local college or other learning provider gaining all the valuable skills you would need really to understand the job and succeed in that field.

Employment rights and responsibilities

Employment rights and responsibilities are an important part of apprenticeships. The reason for this is to help apprentices to learn all about:

- the rights and responsibilities of workers/employees;
- how workers/employees are affected by public law and policies;
- issues such as discipline, representation and the organization of the relevant industry.

Information point

To find out more about apprenticeships in England visit www. apprenticeships.org.uk or telephone 08000 150 600 or Connexions on 080 800 13 2 19.

If you live in Wales visit http://new.wales.gov.uk/topics/educa tionandskills/learning_and_qualifications/?lang=en. If you live in Scotland the website to look at is www.scottish-enterprise.com/ modernapprenticeships. Those living in Northern Ireland should visit www.delni.gov.uk.

Apprenticeships and Advanced Apprenticeships

These are for young people aged 16–24. They involve working and training while studying for qualifications at the same time. They lead to NVQs, Key Skills qualifications and, usually, a technical certificate, and can last for between one and five years depending on the employment and type of apprenticeship.

Entry to Employment – E2E

E2E is a scheme for people who are not yet ready or able to start an apprenticeship. It is a work-based programme that will have been devised to match individuals' particular needs but the schemes do have a focus on improving motivation, personal effectiveness and employability. At the end of E2E you would go through a transition programme that would help you to progress either into employment (with training), apprenticeship, FE or training.

Information point

To find out more about E2E e-mail E2Einfo@lsc.gov.uk or telephone 0870 900 6800.

Action

New projects designed to help young people get into work seem to be quite common so it is always a good idea to call into your local Connexions office to see if there is anything, whether it be a local or a national initiative, that you can take advantage of. If you are not 'in the know' you may be missing out on some great opportunities.

Summary

The key points of this chapter include:

- Work experience is an excellent way of finding out whether a particular job is for you.
- You can arrange your own work experience to do in your spare time.
- Apprenticeships offer school and college leavers a chance to learn and work at the same time.
- E2E is a scheme that people who are not yet ready to do an apprenticeship can do.

9 Finding and applying for jobs

This chapter looks at:

- finding out what you want to do;
- where to look for vacancies;
- researching jobs;
- applying for jobs;
- filling in application forms;
- writing a CV;
- writing a covering letter;
- writing a letter of application;
- making speculative applications.

Knowing that you really should get a job is one thing, knowing exactly where to look for what you want is another. This chapter should help to make sure that you do not miss out on the perfect vacancy for you.

What do you want to do?

The level of success we have in our working lives does seem to be linked to the attitude we have to our work. We are unlikely to have a positive attitude to it if what we do for a living is far removed from our hobbies and interests. Before you can even start looking for jobs, you have to have some idea of what it is that you would be happy doing. As well as the information in this chapter, the following activity may help to give you some ideas.

Action

This activity will help you to work out what it is that grabs you and what you might like to do for a job.

Answer the following questions by writing your responses down on a sheet of paper. Your answers can be as detailed as you like. They are for your eyes only so make them as useful as they can be for you.

- What interests you?
- What are your hobbies?
- Do you have a career plan? What is it?
- Would you describe yourself as an indoor or an outdoor person?
- What are your skills? (Remember: skills are not the same as interests.)
- What are your abilities? (For example, can you drive? Do you have any vocational qualifications?)

Some careers experts split job activities into four categories: working with objects, information, concepts and people.

- Are you an 'objects' person? Do you want to work with goods, building them perhaps, or designing or selling them?
- Are you an 'information' person? Do you want to analyse, gather, manipulate, record or publish information?
- Are you a 'concepts' person? Do you want to communicate, create, debate, market or teach concepts?
- Are you a 'people' person? Do you want to represent, manage, direct, guide, share with or motivate people?

These are just a few ideas. There is information in Parts Four and Five that will also help you to find out what motivates you.

Information point

Your local careers or Connexions office will be able to offer more information and ideas on what you might like to do next. You can find the contact details for your local office in the Yellow Pages *or at your library.*

Where to look for vacancies

You have to be good at research if you are to find the right job for you. Knowing where to look for job vacancies is critical, and that does not just mean flicking through the jobs pages of your local paper. To give yourself the best chance possible your job hunt will need to be far reaching, covering newspapers and the internet, your personal contacts and your local Jobcentre to name but a few. Get your vacancy radar tuned so you do not miss out! The table overleaf will help you to focus your search.

Stay positive as you look for vacancies. Even if the job market seems dead, you have to be creative and use your initiative. Is there something that you can apply for that will take you one step closer to what you really want to do? Might it open up opportunities for you once you are in post?

When to look

Vacancies occur all through the year, but some may be seasonal. You will need to do some research into the kind of job that you are interested in to see if vacancies are more likely at certain times of the year than others. Even if you find that this is the case, it is still worth looking all the time anyway. You never know when the perfect job might turn up and if you are not looking in the right place you will miss out on it.

Researching the job

For every job advertisement you see that you would like to apply for you need to ask yourself a few key questions:

Table 9.1

Where to look	What to look for
Your local library	Local and national newspapers, specialist magazines, local jobs bulletins, careers books, local business directories
Your local Jobcentre Plus	Vacancy cards, leaflets, one-to-one advice, website, books
Your local career/Connexions service	Careers libary, one-to-one advice
Your school or college	Careers section of library, careers adviser, one-to-one advice
The internet	There are literally hundreds of jobs advertised online. It is best to do a search for what you are looking for but these are good for starters: www.worktrain.gov.uk www.workthing.co.uk www.jobsite.co.uk www.fish4jobs.co.uk
Job agencies	There is almost certainly at least one job agency on your local high street. Call in or make an appointment for some one-to-one advice about whether they can help you. Most will have job vacancies displayed in the office too
Your local radio station	Most local radio stations have a jobs slot. Ring up to find out when it is
Your local community	Shop windows, Post Offices, information points and so on often have posters, leaflets and postcards about job opportunities
Friends, family and acquaintances	Make use of all your contacts

- Does it look like the kind of job you could do? This is not as obvious as it sounds – some job advertisements give very little away about what is involved. Do you need to find out further information before you would be in a position to apply?
- Do you have the appropriate skills and qualifications needed?
- Do you need to be knowledgeable about any current affairs or industry inside information in order to get through the application stage? Should you look at any trade publications?
- Is the job with the kind of company you would like to work for? Can you find anything out about the company before applying for the job? Does it have a website? Do you know anyone who works there who can give you some inside information?
- Would you be able to get to work if you got the job? Could you drive there or travel by public transport? Would you have to move or could you stay living where you are now?
- Does the job offer any training opportunities?
- Is the pay good enough? Would it allow you to pay your living expenses as well as have some left over for spending money or savings?
- Do the prospects of the job look interesting?

Applying for jobs

Everything you have read, thought about and acted on so far should help you to understand that it is best not to just go for any vacancy you see advertised. It helps tremendously if, first, you know a little about what you want to do and where you want to do it. Do not bother even applying if you cannot do it with enthusiasm and *intent*. You need to intend to get any job you go for. If you don't, your lack of drive and enthusiasm will shine through far brighter than any of your great selling points. You need to show that you are hungry for *that* job, not *any* job.

Once you have found an appropriate vacancy to go for you need to start the process of actually applying. There are usually two stages to this process: the written application stage and the interview stage. This means that you will have to be good at presenting yourself on paper as well as in person. It is not enough to be good at one and not the other.

Every application you make (whether for a job or a college place), will require you to follow certain instructions. It goes without saying that you need to follow these exactly. If you are required to fill in an application form, do not send in your CV instead, however wonderful it may be! Always do exactly what is asked, otherwise you risk your application going straight in the bin without even being considered.

It is well worth stocking up on some good quality A4 writing paper and matching envelopes and blue or black ink pens that will not splodge or smudge. If you are asked to complete an application form you will find A4 envelopes useful too so that you do not have to fold the form to send it.

Before even making the first mark on your paper, think carefully about exactly what you have to offer. All job applications require a fair amount of 'selling' so do not go any further without establishing what it is that you have to sell.

Action
Your unique selling points

While many of the activities in this book are optional (you only need to do them if you think they will help you) this one really is important. Write your answers down and use them to refer to when you are making applications.

- What have you got to offer a company?
- Why should they employ you?
- What are your unique selling points? (Think of skills, achievements, accomplishments and so on.)

These questions are deliberately open-ended so that you are not restricted in your thinking or limited by any suggestions that could have been listed here. Think as widely as you can; you will be trying to sell yourself on the job market so make yourself as attractive as possible.

Selling skills ... View from Jas

I hate doing this kind of stuff. It seems a bit phoney to me. But then my mum told me that it's just a process you have to go through. Once you've got your job you don't have to keep selling yourself unless you want to go for promotions really quickly. In a way it's like a game but it's one that everyone's playing so if you don't want to be left out you have to join in. My advice would be to always be honest though. Putting a positive spin on stuff is one thing, but lying is completely different! If you lie about your skills you'll quickly be found out.

Mistakes to avoid

Always bear in mind that most employers won't even look at any applications that are:

- not exactly what they asked for (for example, a CV instead of their application form);
- not appropriate for the job (for example, it is a job that requires catering qualifications and you do not have any);
- messy, untidy or illegible;
- lacking in vital information such as your contact details;
- not unique to that job – no prospective employer wants to read an application that has obviously gone off to loads of different companies.

Filling in application forms

Many jobs require candidates to complete application forms. This is usually so that they can be sure they get the information they need and can judge candidates equally. Although the whole form-filling process can be time consuming, the advice here may help it to go without hitch:

- Find out when the closing date is and do not miss this deadline.

- Before doing anything, take several photocopies of the form so that you can have practice runs, but remember that you can only send in the original.
- If you have to download the form from the internet, make sure that you have the right one before starting.
- Gather together all the information you might need. For example, your schools and the years you attended them, qualifications and exam results, the names of your referees, your full contact details, your National Insurance number and so on.
- Always follow the instructions you are given exactly. Some ask you to use blue ink and some black. If this is not specified, use blue or black, but no other colour. Even in the so-called creative industries, pink or green ink would probably be frowned upon!
- If you make a mistake, start again. If you are using the original form, simply cross out the error with one neat line. Do not use liquid paper or multiple scribbles over the mistake.
- Answer every question. If a question does not apply to you put 'n/a' (not applicable) in the box rather than leaving it blank.
- Be scrupulously honest. That said, do not be shy about your achievements.
- Aim to show what each experience has taught you. If you have spent time volunteering on a play scheme, state what transferable skills that has given you (see page 166).
- Look carefully at the person specification for the job. You will almost always be given an outline of the kind of person they are looking for. For example, job details might say, 'must be motivated, honest and reasonably fit' in which case you would need to show specifically in your application that you are all of those things, preferably with examples for each.
- Always get someone to check over your rough version first, before taking the plunge and doing it neatly. Ask the person to look out for spelling mistakes, grammatical errors, inconsistencies, potentially negative points and areas that simply do not come over well. If he or she helps you to do any rewrites, make sure that the language is what you would use yourself.
- Make sure that you have practised fitting your writing into the space available.

- Write a covering letter to go with the application form. This need not be lengthy, but should be on good quality A4 paper, and laid out as you would lay out any formal letter. Make sure you have the name of the person you should send it to and underneath where you write 'Dear X', write the title of the post that you are applying for. Underline this if you are writing the letter by hand or type it in bold if you are using a word processor. Include any reference numbers the job may have too. Do not repeat any of the information you have included on the application form but simply say, 'Please find enclosed my application for the post of XYZ.' You may also like to add, 'I look forward to hearing from you.' You then need to add something that will encourage the reader to look at your application (see the section on writing covering letters below). End your letter formally with 'Yours sincerely' (assuming that you know the name of the person you are writing to). Do not attach the letter to the form in any way. As long as your name is on both (which it should be), the recipient will be able to tie them up together. (See more tips on covering letters in the section below: Writing a covering letter).
- Take a photocopy of all the forms and letters that you send.
- How does the form need to be returned? Can it be e-mailed (in which case you will have completed an electronic version of it)? Or should it be posted? Or can you deliver it by hand?
- Make sure that you get the form in on time. Most companies will not consider any applications that arrive after the closing date.
- If you want acknowledgement that they have received your application, include a stamped addressed plain postcard that can be posted back to you. You may like to write on the postcard something like, 'confirmation of receipt of application to XYZ company'.
- Be sure to make a note of when you send in your application.

Referees

Many application forms ask you to give the names of one or two people who would be willing to act as referees for you. This means that these people will be contacted by the company (should the company want to interview or employ you) and asked to provide a character reference about you.

Most employers will look carefully at the status of the people you appoint as referees so it is best not to list your best mate! Choose referees who will be in a position to sell your skills to the prospective employer by matching your qualities to the job's requirements. You want them to be as supportive as possible too, so *always* ask their permission first before putting their name down on the form. Good choices for referees might be a family friend who has known you for some time (especially if he or she is in business or a member of a profession) and your school or college tutor. If you have had a job already then your current or previous employer might be willing to act as a referee.

What if you do not hear anything?

You may need to follow up your application if you do not hear anything within a few weeks of sending it in. Usually, all you need to do is make a quick telephone call. Look up the name of the person you need to speak to and call from somewhere quiet and private. Have with you the date that you sent the application and the exact title of the job you applied for.

You should be told what stage your application is at, but if you are not, ask if it is possible to know when you might be told. Do not telephone again unless you do not hear anything by the time the person has said you will.

What if you get turned down?

It is not a disaster if you do not get invited for an interview. It may be very disappointing but it is best to cultivate the attitude that the job obviously was not meant for you and that something better will come along in the future. That is not to say that you can sit back and wait! As soon as possible get back out there, make another application and get some more possibilities in the pipeline.

One positive thing to remember is that each time you apply for a job you are gaining valuable experience. If you do not get called for an interview, look back over what you sent in and see if you would do anything differently with hindsight. Some employers will offer feedback on unsuccessful applications. If this is offered to you, take it. If it is not, ask for it. Information like this can be invaluable when it comes to applying for jobs in the future.

Writing a CV

CVs, or curricula vitae, are essential in the world of job hunting. Even if you are not looking for a job it is important to have one prepared and up to date so that when you do come to apply for jobs you have a CV ready to go.

It is easy to procrastinate about preparing a CV. It can take time to get together and can be difficult to get looking just right. It helps a lot if you have access to a computer so that you can manipulate the information on screen. In the end, though, you just have to take the plunge and get stuck into it!

Why have a CV?

Your CV is your summary of your life and achievements. It is an important part of job hunting but it will not get you a job on its own. You should see it more as a useful tool.

Once you have written your CV you can either send it to prospective employers in response to a job advertisement or you can use it to make speculative applications. Even if you are asked to apply by completing an application form, the fact that most of the information that you need is gathered together in one document will be really helpful when it comes to filling in the form.

How to write a CV

There is no single format for writing a CV but the way in which you present the information is critical. Research has shown that it can take the average reader less than 10 seconds to glance over a CV and make a judgement. It is critical that your CV captures the interest of its reader immediately so that he or she reads it long enough to be captivated!

Your CV may have a difficult job to do in seducing readers into employing you, but that does not mean that you can misrepresent yourself in it. Honesty is *always* the best policy. Besides, you never know when those little white lies are going to get you!

Some people choose to head their CV with 'Curriculum Vitae'; this isn't strictly necessary as it should be obvious what the document is, but you won't lose points if you decide to do this. Then you will need to divide your CV into sections under the following headings:

- personal details (in which your name, address and contact details go – whether you include your date of birth is up to you);
- education and training (in order, starting with your secondary school(s) and including the qualifications and grades gained);
- employment (starting with your most recent experience first). Make sure that you add a little detail about your roles and responsibilities. You may also like to add work experience here but be sure to make it clear that it is your paid work you are describing;
- voluntary work;
- hobbies and interests (aim to show all aspects of your personality but do be honest! Remember that this section should support your job application);
- additional information (sometimes called a 'skills summary' – this is basically your best bits!);
- referees (usually two – make sure that you have already asked their permission).

There are some 'dos and don'ts' when it comes to preparing a CV. These ideas may help:

- Do type your CV or print it out from a computer. Always make sure that you have a few copies handy. Use good quality paper and stick to one typeface.
- Don't bind or staple your CV in any way. It does not need clipart or borders and should be on plain paper. Selectors want to see your skills and achievements, not your artistic talents.
- Do take care over the layout. Make sure that the type is well spaced yet does not cover more pages than it needs to. No more than two sides of A4 is adequate for most people.

- Do not include any salary information. That can all be discussed at interview.
- Do not include personal details such as height, weight, marital status, parenthood status and so on. Age is optional but strictly not necessary. If age restrictions apply to a job the application form will give details. Photos should not be included either.
- Don't include testimonials from other people.
- Do remember that skills are more important than experience and accomplishments are more important than responsibilities.
- Do use short bulleted statements rather than long, flowery sentences.
- Do remember that your CV will develop over time. Keep it up to date and vibrant.

There are many books and websites that can help you to create a winning CV. One of the books is *Preparing the Perfect CV* by Rebecca Corfield (see Appendix 1 for details).

Writing a covering letter

Covering letters are essential in the job application process. Whether you are sending in a CV or an application form, you will need to send a covering letter with it. Your covering letter does need to state that there is a CV or application form enclosed, but it also needs to grab the reader enough to make sure that he or she looks at what you have sent.

Use these tips when writing a covering letter:

- Always find out the name of the person you need to write to. Do not use 'sir' or 'madam'.
- Include a sentence or short paragraph that explains why you are enthusiastic about the job.
- Include a sentence that shows how appropriate you are for the job.
- End with an expectation of a reply ('I look forward to hearing from you').
- Always write a fresh covering letter for each job you apply for. Never be tempted to send generic letters as the employer will not feel that you have made an effort.

- Remember that your covering letter is likely to be the first representation of you that a prospective employer will see. Make sure that it is concise, structured and faultless.
- Always keep a copy of the covering letters you send out.

Writing a letter of application

Sometimes you may be asked to send a CV with a letter of application rather than fill in an application form. This can be a daunting task as you really have to sell yourself, but not having the restrictions of an application form does have its benefits.

Your main goal when writing such a letter is to make sure that you can fit the profile of yourself with the profile of the person the company wants to employ. Whatever they are looking for, show that that person is you!

Selling your skills

Think about this for a moment: you have unique selling points that no other person in the world has. What you can offer an employer will not be repeated in anyone else.

Follow these ideas when writing a letter of application:

- Write a list of key points that you know about the job. What sort of person are they looking for?
- Make a list of the unique selling points that you would like to include (use your responses from the activity on page 90 to help you here).
- Make sure that your first sentence really grabs the attention of the reader. Try to end with something memorable too.
- Aim to convey a sense of your personality – let you shine through from the page. For example, what motivates you?
- Write about your qualities. These ideas may inspire you:
  - friendly;
  - approachable;
  - thoughtful;
  - supportive;
  - energetic;
  - enthusiastic;

- open to learning new things;
- fit and healthy;
- non-smoker;
- punctual;
- neat;
- hard working;
- keen for challenges.

- Make sure the main body of the letter is filled with your *skills* and *achievements*.

- Do not include anything negative, or use potentially negative language. Always emphasize positive things about yourself.

- Lay the letter out as you would any formal letter, with your address and the address of the person you are writing to at the top, the date and a reference to the job you are applying for. End with 'Yours sincerely' if you know the name of the person you are writing to.

- Write in concise sentences rather than lengthy scrawls. Avoid over-using 'I did' and go for 'action' words instead. These examples may help you:

accomplished	effected	invented
achieved	eliminated	launched
arranged	enacted	led
assessed	engaged	maintained
compiled	established	managed
composed	evaluated	modernized
concluded	expanded	monitored
conducted	formulated	observed
consolidated	generated	organized
created	implemented	originated
cultivated	improved	performed
defined	improvised	prevented
delivered	incorporated	produced
demonstrated	initiated	promoted
designed	inspired	proposed
developed	instigated	provided
devised	instructed	recommended
documented	introduced	redesigned

reduced	revitalized	tightened
regulated	shaped	uncovered
renegotiated	simplified	unravelled
reorganized	streamlined	utilized
resolved	strengthened	visualized
reviewed	structured	vitalized
revised	supported	volunteered

- Write about what your experiences have taught you so far.
- If you have travelled, done voluntary work or have any hobbies that may be relevant then mention this too. Always link back to why this makes you great for the job.
- Never be tempted to reuse the same letter of application for different jobs. Always tweak it or rewrite it completely so that it fits the requirements of each application.
- End your letter of application with the expectation of a reply.

Making speculative applications

You may not have seen a job vacancy but know that you want to work for a particular company. If this is the case, then make a speculative application. This means sending in your CV with a covering letter explaining why you want to work for that company and a little about yourself and your main selling points. End your letter by asking if you can visit the company to look around or even attend for an interview. There may not be a vacancy for you to fill immediately, but most companies will keep letters and CVs sent in speculatively and look through them when a vacancy arises. Look at it this way, it is pretty flattering for most companies!

Here are some points to remember when making speculative applications:

- Always telephone the company first to get the name of the person your letter should be addressed to.
- Include a stamped addressed envelope for a response.
- Plan your covering letter carefully. You need to include your achievements and outstanding skills so refer to your responses to the activity on page 91 to help you out.

- In your first paragraph state what you want. For example, 'I am particularly interested in working for your company. I understand that there are no vacancies at present but I would like to be considered for any that arise in the near future.'

- Then add a paragraph detailing your main achievements and skills. This need not be very long; it is best to make every word count and refer readers to your CV for further information.

- End by asking for an interview. You can even give broad suggestions of when this might be (for example, 'I am available to attend for an interview on most days and can be available at short notice').

- Say something that indicates that you expect a reply. For example, 'I look forward to hearing from you and enclose a stamped addressed envelope.'

- Keep your letter concise and punchy. If they want to know more they will invite you for an interview.

- Use good quality paper. Always check for errors (getting someone else to as well is a good idea – two brains are better than one and it is easy to miss your own mistakes).

- If you do not hear back within about 10 days, it is perfectly reasonable to make a follow-up call asking to speak to the person you wrote to in order to find out if your letter has been received.

Speculative applications ... View from Nick

I really wanted a job in my local bookshop. It's a really good one and one of the few independent ones left. There wasn't anywhere else that I wanted to work at the time and I was so frustrated that they never seemed to advertise job vacancies. Then I decided to send in a letter to the manager just to see if they had anything going. I explained in my letter that I was really keen to work there and why and actually asked if I could have an interview in case anything came up in the future. I included my CV too. It felt a bit pushy but I knew I didn't have anything to lose.

About a week later I had a phone call from the manager offering me a job! I couldn't believe it! I asked him if he wanted to interview me and he said no, he liked my handwriting and was happy to offer me the job! He told me when to turn up for my first day and that was that.

When I started work there I found out that every person employed there had written in speculatively. It's obviously how the manager found his staff. I really loved my time there and only left when I moved away. Since then I've got two more jobs by writing speculative applications so I know that it works. Sometimes your letter hits the right desk at the right time and you're in luck. I'd definitely recommend trying to get a job in this way.

Summary

The key points from this chapter include:

- Success in life can be linked to the attitude we have to life.
- Job vacancies are advertised in a wide range of places. You have to make sure that you look at as many sources as possible so that you do not risk missing out on your ideal opportunity.
- Don't just go for *any* job vacancy. Make sure that you research each possible vacancy to see if it is suitable for you to go ahead and apply.
- You have to sell your skills in every job application you make.
- A CV is a summary of your life and achievements. It is a vital part of the job application process.
- Even if you don't see a vacancy advertised for a particular company you can still make a speculative application, asking if they have any jobs going and if they would consider you for an interview.

10 Interviews

This chapter looks at:

- what interviews are;
- how to prepare for an interview;
- what to do on the day of an interview;
- psychometric testing;
- starting work.

What are interviews?

Interviews are simply an opportunity for an employer to decide who they want to employ for a job. They are also an opportunity for candidates to decide whether they want to work for that company or organization. It is most definitely a two-way thing!

It is a good idea to think of interviews as fun. OK, that may not sound very realistic when you are nervous about being interviewed, but the more you can think about interviews as opportunities to meet people and find out about a new work place the better.

Regardless of the outcome, an interview is *always* a positive experience. Even if it goes so badly that you do not have a hope of getting the job, or you realize that the place is a dump that you could never work in, you will have learned valuable things about the whole process. For this reason, it is a good idea to jot down a few of your thoughts *after* an interview. For example, how did it go? Would you do or say the same things again? What would you change? And so on.

Preparing for the big day

If, after sending in your application for a job, you are invited for an interview, you will usually be given some notice. This can be valuable time to prepare for the big day. A word of warning though: try not to get too wound up about your preparation or you will get too stressed out to perform to the best of your ability.

When preparing for an interview make sure that you:

- Confirm that you will be attending for the interview as soon as possible. You can do this by letter or telephone (or e-mail if the company has given you an e-mail address for correspondence).
- Find out all you can about the company.
- Work out how you will get to the interview. If possible, do a dry run so you know exactly how long it will take you to get there. Always leave extra time for traffic jams or train or bus cancellations. Some organizations will pay travel expenses but others will not, so it is worth checking in advance. If you need to stay overnight the night before in order to be there on time then make the necessary arrangements in good time. Again, check whether these expenses will be paid and what sort of budget you have to keep to. Remember to get receipts for everything that you will be claiming for.
- Sort out your outfit as early as possible. Make sure that it is comfortable, clean and appropriate for the job. If in doubt, wear a suit and tie, or smart jacket and trousers/skirt. Nothing too baggy, skimpy, flesh-revealing or bright! Remove piercings. Whether it is right or wrong, instant judgements will be made about you based on your appearance so give yourself the best chance possible. Clean your shoes too. If you are not sure about your outfit, ask the opinion of someone you trust.
- Do not smoke or drink alcohol anywhere near your interview clothes; the interviewers will be able to smell it a mile off!
- Write the name and telephone number of the contact person on a piece of paper to take with you just in case you get held up and need to ring them.
- Gather together any exam certificates you may be asked for.
- Read through your application form and CV to remind yourself what you wrote.

- Get an early night before the interview. The last thing the interviewers want to see is bags under your eyes.
- Be positive about the interview. If you go into it thinking 'I'll never get this', you probably won't! A positive mental attitude is one of the most effective ways of standing out from the crowd.

The day of the interview

Even though you may be nervous, make sure that you have a good breakfast so that you have the energy you need to get you through the day. Drink plenty of water too, as this will help you to keep a clear mind.

There is no real way of knowing exactly what the day will bring unless the company gives you a detailed breakdown of events in advance. However, most interviews follow this pattern:

- They take place in a meeting room or private office. There may be a desk between you and the interviewer(s) or you may be seated on comfortable chairs around a coffee table, or any number of scenarios.
- There may be one or more people interviewing you.
- These people should be introduced to you.
- They may start by asking you simple questions to break the ice: something like 'did you find the place OK'? Or, 'how was your journey?'
- There will be a period of questioning about a variety of things to do with you, the job and possibly other issues too.
- You will be asked if you have any questions (make sure that you have thought of some. If you really cannot think of anything, say 'no, I think all of my questions have already been answered, thank you').
- You may find that you are interviewed at the same time as other candidates in a group interview.
- You may be asked to do some psychometric tests (see below).
- You may be shown around the workplace either before or after the formal interview (although remember, even when you are being shown around you are being interviewed).

- You may be offered the job there and then or they may say that they will write to you when they have made up their minds.

What interviewers are looking for

The person or people who interview you are looking for key things. They want to make sure that the person they eventually employ will be:

- able to match the job specification;
- able to fit in with the existing staff;
- willing to make a positive contribution to the organization;
- respectful of the management;
- motivated and conscientious;
- able to do the job;
- willing to learn;
- very likely to stay in the job if employed.

All of this will be far easier for them to find out if you answer all the questions as fully as possible. If a question could have more than a yes or no answer, give it. They want to see that you are comfortable talking and engaging in conversation. If there is anything you do not understand, ask them to repeat the question. If you still don't get it, say so, don't guess at an answer!

Possible questions

It is impossible to know what you will be asked at an interview, but the following could come up:

- What can you offer this organization?
- Why should we employ you?
- Why do you want to work here?
- What are your strengths?
- What are your weaknesses?
- How have your past experiences prepared you for this job?
- What did you enjoy most about school/college?
- What are your goals and aspirations?
- Where do you see yourself in two years' time?

Sometimes you may be asked about your likes and dislikes, hobbies, what films you enjoy and what books you read. All of this can help an interviewer to build up a picture of what you are really like. It can also help him or her to make a decision over whether you would fit in well and make a positive contribution to the organization.

Touring the premises

A tour of the premises, whether that be an office, factory, shop or whatever, will usually be a feature of any interview. If it is not, it is well worth asking if you can be shown around. You will probably find that certain questions come to mind as the tour progresses and it is fine to ask these as they arise. You may be shown around by yourself or with the other candidates.

There are certain things to look out for and think about when looking round a potential place of work:

- Does it *feel* like a place you could happily go to every day to work?
- How are people working? Is the place in silence? Can you hear chatting? Are people working hard? Does it seem like a relaxed atmosphere?
- Are people talking to you as you go around? Does it seem friendly?
- Does it look safe? Does it feel like there is fresh air and enough light? Is it too warm or too cold?
- Are you shown round the whole workplace? Do you see where you would be working?
- Do you get to meet your potential work colleagues? The person you would be reporting to? The boss? Do you get to speak to them and ask any questions that you have?
- Can you visualize yourself working there?

As you take your tour, keep all of these questions in mind. There is no need to make written responses, but it is really important to take notice of any gut feelings that you have about a potential place of work.

Body language

It has been said that body language can shout louder than any words you may use. Body language is the non-verbal communication that we use. Without realizing it, we reveal our thoughts through body language as well as reading the thoughts of others through theirs. These tips will help you in interviews:

- Smile. It shows that you are not hostile.
- Give a firm handshake. It shows that you are not timid.
- Make eye contact. It shows that you are sincere.
- Nod. It shows that you are listening and 'with' the speaker.
- Sit up straight. It shows that you mean business.

Whatever you do, don't:

- turn you body away from the speaker;
- cross your arms and legs;
- slouch;
- jig about or swing your leg;
- touch your face, hair or any other part of your body.

What if things go wrong?

Once you are at an interview don't worry if things seem to go wrong; it really doesn't matter. Just do the best you can. If you forget your train of thought when you are half-way through an answer just stop, smile and say something like: 'I think I'll start again.' You are only human, and so is the interviewer. The chances are that he or she will know exactly how you are feeling. Remember that it is not so much the 'mess' you get yourself into (if you do that is!) as the way you get yourself out of it that counts!

Whatever happens at the end of an interview, don't forget to thank your interviewer(s) as you leave.

If you find that you are attending interview after interview and not getting anywhere, ask someone you trust to give you a mock interview. You may be able to get advice on this at your local Connexions office. You might also like to read a specialist book on interviews (see Appendix 1 for further information).

Psychometric testing

Some employers do what is known as psychometric testing on candidates for jobs. Psychometric testing falls into three main categories:

- ability testing (testing people's potential);
- aptitude testing (similar to the ability testing although aptitude testing looks at a person's job-related abilities);
- personality questionnaires (testing a person's characteristics, in particular those that may be relevant to the job).

Probably the most common of these are aptitude tests, so for the purposes of this book we will focus on these.

Aptitude tests

Aptitude tests are a way of testing a person's general intelligence as well as specific abilities such as reasoning skills and thinking skills. The tests are objective, meaning that the results should not be influenced by the personal feelings and interpretations of the employer using them. The most often used tests aim to assess verbal and numerical logical reasoning skills – in other words, how well you understand and manipulate language and numbers.

Many organizations, both large and small, use aptitude tests to help them recruit new staff. The tests give them a broader picture of each candidate than a simple application form can give them. Although it might seem like a big hassle to have to go through these tests, they will almost certainly work in your favour. Many interviewers are pretty biased people. They can make snap decisions based on their first impressions of your appearance and general feeling that you give off. Aptitude tests help them to make sure that the first impressions they had of you were not wrong.

If you are going for an interview as either a potential student or employee, you should be told in advance if you will have to sit a test as part of the interview process. It should not be sprung on you at the last minute.

It is possible to prepare for taking aptitude tests. You will not know exactly what you will be faced with when attending an interview but you will at least be familiar with the style of question that is likely to be asked and this can really put you at an advantage.

It is quite easy to obtain sample tests. There are several on the internet and Appendix 1 of this book contains some useful book titles to look out for. There is also a test for you to try out. No checking the answers in advance! Practising aptitude tests is a really good idea. Research suggests that about 3 out of every 10 people invited to sit an aptitude test do not bother to turn up on the day. It is always worth turning up – you never know, you may pass with flying colours!

Aptitude test questions tend to follow particular patterns. They usually (but not always) ask you to:

- find a missing word;
- spell;
- check for mistakes in printed text;
- identify the odd word out;
- continue a number sequence;
- perform mathematical calculations;
- fit shapes together;
- match symbols;
- ask how strongly you agree with certain statements (such as 'I like helping people').

Each test is usually designed to cover a broad range of skills and aptitudes. Some of the questions will have right or wrong answers, others will be more open to interpretation. Usually, these tests are not marked in terms of passing or failing but it could be that you turn out to be too different from the intelligence or personality profile that they are looking for, so your application goes no further. For example, if your test scores show that you are quite shy and introverted, despite being really good at verbal reasoning, it is unlikely you will get into training as a flight attendant.

If English is not your first language, these tests can be more difficult, especially if they are testing quite high levels of language understanding. If this applies to you, make sure that you read through the section on discrimination on page 218.

Action

Turn to Appendix 2 and try your hand at the example recruitment tests.

Aptitude tests ... View from Pete

The first aptitude test I had to take went really badly. I hadn't done any preparation and just wasn't into how to do them. I didn't finish in time and probably did hopelessly. I didn't get the job anyway! After that I went to the library and got some books out and did practice tests. You can soon get to work out the kinds of questions they ask and it gets easier to see what each question is asking you to do. The more you practise the easier it is when you are faced with one at an interview.

I'm on my third job now since leaving school and I've had to do an aptitude test at every interview. Not everywhere uses them but you have to do them for a lot of office-based jobs.

It really pays to focus on your weak areas. I was never that happy with the numeracy-type questions but the verbal reasoning ones were fine. I had to force myself to sit down and practise the number sequences and so on until I felt reasonably happy. I've done a few of the online tests too and they're really good.

My advice to anyone who hasn't yet done an aptitude test is don't be afraid of them. They're not as bad as they sound!

Graphology

Some companies employ a graphologist to assess the handwriting of candidates who apply for jobs. Graphology is the study of personality and character that might be revealed in a person's handwriting. It is thought that only around 10 per cent of companies are using the services of a graphologist so you may never come across this throughout your entire working life, but it is still worth making sure that Word, text and e-mail do not destroy your handwriting skills for good.

If you want to know more about graphology visit www. britishgraphology.org or www.handwriting.org.

Safety

When attending interviews, keep your safety in mind. Make sure that:

- the interview is being held on the organization's premises or, at least, in a public place like a hotel (not in a car or car park or some other location that could affect your safety);
- you tell someone where you are going and what time you expect to be finished;
- you never accept a lift from your interviewer, even if you think he or she can be trusted (better to be safe than sorry);
- you do not answer questions of a personal nature (politely say 'I don't want to answer that', and leave if you are at all unsure).

Possible outcomes

You have found a job vacancy, applied for it, got through the first stage of selection, been invited for an interview and had the interview. So, what are the possible outcomes?

- You are offered the job. Congratulations! Accept it if you know that you want to work at that organization and you want that job. Then make sure that you ask what the next arrangements will be. Will they send you a letter of confirmation? Will they send you a contract? Do they need to receive your acceptance in writing?
- You are invited back for another interview. This is a second chance for both sides to see if having you do this job would be the right thing. Prepare for, and treat, a second interview in exactly the same way as you would a first interview but make sure that you have thought of some specific questions to ask. Be prepared for second interviews to be quite different from first interviews.

- You are not offered the job. Don't worry! This will have been an excellent experience and something that you will undoubtedly learn from. However disappointed you are, make sure that you look for another job to apply for as soon as possible. (See page 218 for information on discrimination.) Don't let failure hold you back.

Pay

It probably goes without saying that you'll be paid according to what you do and that different jobs offer different salaries. Generally (although this is not always the case), you will get paid more if you are:

- well qualified;
- experienced;
- able to prove you have a good track record with a particular company;
- good at what you do;
- reliable;
- flexible;
- successful in promoting the cause of the company or organization;
- able to negotiate a rise!

Some jobs will pay you according to where you are on a pay scale that will be relatively fixed, whereas others will have less formal pay structures with salaries being negotiated as and when appropriate.

Information point

For further details on money, taxation and the National Minimum Wage, see the chapter on money on page 191).

Action

How important is money to you? Of course everyone needs to earn money in order to pay their way, but do you want to earn enough or far more than that? Take a moment or two to think about how important money is to you and what your financial goals are. Do you want to be as rich as possible or is job satisfaction, regardless of how much you earn, the most important thing to you?

Location

Where do you want to work? Would you be happy moving away from your family and friends? Or do you want to stay in the area in which you grew up? Or perhaps you would be happy to work abroad? Depending on where you live it may be that there are greater opportunities open to you if you move away. However, this is not necessarily the best thing to do if you end up homesick or feeling socially isolated and lonely. If you are thinking about moving away do consider how this might make you feel. A bit of mental preparation will really help you to make a success of it.

Do also consider whether you want to take a job that would mean a journey into work. If you are losing an hour in the morning and an hour in the evening just in getting to and from work, will you be happy about this? Or would you rather live closer to your work (or your work be closer to where you live)?

Information point

The Trades Union Congress (TUC) has published a guide on employment rights for young people. The guide, called Workwise, can be downloaded free of charge from: www.tuc.org.uk/extras/YMN WorkWise.pdf.

Starting work

When you are offered a job it can feel like that is the goal achieved! In a way it is, but you have still got to go through the following stages: signing a contract and starting work on your first day.

Before you actually start work you should have been told all about the terms and conditions of your employment. These will usually be explained in a written contract that you will have to sign. Terms and conditions are what is expected from you and what you can expect from your employer. They cover things like the hours that you must be in attendance at work, what paid holidays you are entitled to, your job role and description, sick pay entitlements, the notice period required on both sides, your salary and so on. If you have not received a contract and the first day of the job is looming, get in touch with the person who interviewed you and ask if a contract has been sent to you. Some companies cover this kind of thing on your first day at work as they 'induct' you into your new workplace.

Before you start work make sure that you know:

- when to arrive;
- where to arrive;
- what to wear (especially if there is a uniform);
- what to bring (is there a canteen there where you can buy lunch or can you leave to go to local shops? Would you have to take your own lunch with you?).

On your first day:

- Look around to see how other people of your level dress. Do you fit in? If you are in any way unsure about how you look at work, ask the person you are working with if your clothing is OK. It is better to be safe than sorry and if you have asked someone's opinion they will know that you are serious about wanting to make a good impression.
- It goes without saying that personal hygiene should be excellent and your clothing should be clean and tidy.
- It is a good idea to take a notebook and pen with you so that you can make a note of anything you need to remember but are likely to forget.
- Go in with a positive attitude. Show that you are keen to do well and committed to the job and the company or organization.
- Talk to people and make an effort to introduce yourself. The people you meet early on are likely to be those that you befriend as time goes on.

- You can expect someone to spend time with you on the first day going over all the information that you need to know such as health and safety considerations and practical things like where the toilets are. This is often known as 'induction' and can last anything from a few minutes to several days.
- Expect to be pretty tired by the end of the day. It might be a longer working day than you are used to and the tension of starting a new job can be pretty draining too.

It is a good idea to keep a mini-diary of your first few weeks at work as it is likely that your boss will want to know how you are getting on after you have been there for a month or so. If there is anything that you are not enjoying, do not quit until you have really given it a good chance. You never know, there may be an opportunity to change some aspects of your work after you have been there for a while and remember, there are aspects of any job that can be gritty and unenjoyable! It is just a question of making the most of things and if after a few months you know that you will never be able to settle there, maybe that's the time to start looking around for something else.

For many people, starting work is an exciting time in their lives offering more advantages and opportunities than anything else. Let's hope that this will be your experience too.

Information point

Your local Connexions office or Citizens' Advice Bureau can tell you all about your rights at work. If there is anything you are not sure about in your contract you can ask someone there to read through it for you and explain the parts that you don't understand.

Summary

The key points from this chapter include:

- Interviews are a two-way process for employers to see if they want to employ you and for you to see if you want to work for the organization.
- It is essential to prepare for interviews to enhance your chances of success when interviewed.

- Interviews can take a variety of formats.
- To improve your chances during interviews, you will need to answer all the questions you are asked as fully as possible.
- Some interviews include psychometric tests. It is possible to prepare yourself for these.
- Body language can give away your inner thoughts. It is important to be aware of how you sit, stand and generally conduct yourself.
- Most jobs offer some form of induction for new employees.

Part Four

Travel

11 Studying and working abroad

This chapter looks at:

- whether travelling is right for you;
- studying abroad;
- funding studies abroad;
- working abroad.

Travel – is it right for you?

It can be easy to get swept along with the tide of opinion among your friends about travelling. In some groups it will be seen as *the* thing to do and anyone not jetting off to slum it in some far-flung corner of the planet might be viewed as playing it just a little too safe for comfort. There is no doubt that travelling can be a valuable and worthwhile experience but not everyone feels the need or the desire to do it. Don't even think about surfing the internet for great travel deals until you have sat down and thought about whether or not travelling is really for you.

Action

When thinking about whether travel might be the right thing for you to do, consider the following points. You may like to make a note of your responses to help you to clarify your thinking:

- Do you definitely want to do it; you have no doubts at all?

- Would you like to do it in an ideal world but at present have too many concerns?
- Do you envisage difficulties but nothing that will stand in your way?
- Can you not see the point of it?
- Would you do it if you had the money but not otherwise?
- Do you see travel as a way to contribute to the world or a way to see the world, or perhaps both?
- Do you associate travel with holidays or working opportunities?
- Do you associate these working opportunities with volunteering or with earning money?

Aim to get to the core of why you do, or do not, want to travel. Be totally honest with yourself. There are no right or wrong answers, but you do need to work out what lies at the heart of your personal motivations before taking any further steps.

If you have written your responses down, put them away for a few days and then reread them. Do you still feel the same way? Is there anything you would like to add to your responses?

Studying abroad

There are many opportunities out there for young people to study abroad. You can use the services of one of the many dedicated companies and organizations offering opportunities to study abroad or you can organize your own studies. You may even find that if you do a course in HE you get to study abroad through an exchange system or a placement abroad.

The European Economic Area (EEA) agreement came into force on 1 January 1994. This agreement is concerned mainly with four freedoms:

- movement of goods;
- movement of persons;

- movement of services;
- movement of capital.

This has helped to create many opportunities for people belonging to European Union (EU) member states such as the United Kingdom. With the barriers to movement around the EEA breaking down and the EU ever-expanding, you might want to look into the opportunities for studying, as well as working, abroad that this may offer you.

Information point

At the time of writing there are 27 member states of the EU: Austria; Belgium; Bulgaria; Cyprus; Czech Republic; Denmark; Estonia; Finland; France; Germany; Greece; Hungary; Ireland; Italy; Latvia; Lithuania; Luxembourg; Malta; Netherlands; Poland; Portugal; Romania; Slovakia; Slovenia; Spain; Sweden; and the United Kingdom. There are also three countries that are candidates to become members of the EU: Croatia; Former Yugoslav Republic of Macedonia; and Turkey.

Studying abroad is not the 'be all and end all' – there are plenty of young people who choose to stay in the UK for their studies – but there are certain advantages in taking this step if you think that it is a good idea for you:

- It would help you to start to understand another country – this could be a distinct advantage if ever you wanted to apply to work there.
- It would undoubtedly show you new approaches and techniques in your chosen area of study
- You would learn another language as it is spoken by its people – invaluable in today's economic climate.
- You would certainly be attractive to any UK business that may want to expand further into mainland Europe.
- It would give you invaluable experience if you think you may want to be self-employed in the future, seeking to take advantage of the markets that Europe offers.

As an EU citizen you can apply for any HE course in the whole of the EU. That said, it would only really be wise to do this if you were fluent in the language of your chosen country and, most likely, if you had pre-existing links with that country (for example, if you have lived there for some time in the past or have relatives there).

You can also apply to HE institutions around the world outside the EU, but would need to satisfy visa requirements and have sufficient funds to pay for what could be comparatively expensive course fees. Do not forget, too, that many UK HE institutions offer the opportunity to go abroad for at least part of a course, allowing you to live and study in another country usually for about a year, sometimes less.

Studying abroad ... View from Mike

I was offered the chance to spend a term in Sweden on an exchange programme and leapt at the opportunity. I was in my second year of a nursing degree course and couldn't wait to see how things were done in a different country, especially one that's got such a great reputation for healthcare. A small group of us went over there and we lived in nurses' accommodation in Stockholm. We weren't that far from the city centre and took every opportunity to get out and about and see what life in Sweden is really like. As well as the actual practical experience in hospitals there, which I'd say was invaluable, I found the whole thing such good grounding in so many ways. It was the longest I'd been away from the UK and I learned a lot about myself during that term; probably more than in any other term at university. I'd say to anyone who's given the chance, do it! It doesn't matter what you may be missing at home and on your course, the chances are you'll be getting far more from the experience of going away than you would from staying put.

The EU Lifelong Learning Programme

The EU Lifelong Learning Programme is made up of four main sectoral programmes, meaning that there is one for each of the main sectors of education. The Comenius programme is for school education, Erasmus is for higher education, Leonardo da Vinci is for vocational training and Grundtvig is for adult education. These programmes have the aim of promoting lifelong learning as well as fostering 'interaction, cooperation and mobility between education and training systems within the EU'.

Information point

If you think you might be interested in taking part in one of the opportunities offered by the EU Lifelong Learning Programme, you can contact the British Council on 0161 957 7755 or general.enquiries@ britishcouncil.org. There is also a website you might find useful: www.lifelonglearningprogramme.org.uk.

The Youth in Action Programme

The Youth in Action Programme encourages the involvement of all young people, including those with fewer opportunities and those aged between 13 and 30. It has five key actions:

- Action 1 – Youth for Europe: supporting exchanges and youth initiatives and encouraging young people's participation in democratic life.
- Action 2 – European Voluntary Service: encouraging young people to take part in a voluntary activity abroad that benefits the general public.
- Action 3 – Youth in the World: encouraging cooperation with partner countries by building networks, promoting the exchange of information and assisting with cross-border activities.
- Action 4 – Youth Support Systems: promoting the development of exchange, training and information schemes.
- Action 5 – European cooperation in the youth field contributing to the development of policy cooperation in the youth field.

Information point

If you would like further information on the Youth in Action Programme and how it may benefit you, or if you want to become involved in the programme, you can e-mail eac-youthinaction@ ec.europa.eu. You can also find out more at the programme's website: http://ec.europa.eu/youth/index_en.html

IAESTE

IAESTE is the International Association for the Exchange of Students for Technical Experience. It allows science, technology and engineering students to do paid work placements abroad (as long as they are course related) lasting 8–12 weeks. These placements take place in the long summer break.

Information point

To find out more about IAESTE, log on to www.iaeste.org.uk or e-mail United_Kingdom@iaeste.org.uk; tel: 020 7389 4771.

Information point

You can find out more about the opportunities that exist for you to study abroad from the following websites (don't forget that as well as doing your own searches on the internet it's also worth talking to your careers teacher/adviser – there are lots of opportunities out there for you):

www.britishcouncil.org/home – The British Council;
www.acu.ac.uk – the Association of Commonwealth Universities;
www.careerseurope.co.uk – for general advice;
www.studylink.com – particularly for opportunities in Australia.

Your local Connexions office will also be able to give you more information on studying overseas. Ask if they have the Exodus database for you to browse. This can also be accessed via the Careers Europe website (see above).

Funding studies abroad

If you do decide to pursue the idea of studying abroad you will need to think carefully about how you will fund yourself. Studying in a foreign institute of HE or a university will almost certainly mean paying course and tuition fees as well as your living expenses while you are abroad and this could be more expensive than staying in the UK.

There are organizations that can help with the financial aspects of your plans to study abroad. Grants and loans are available, so talk to your college's career adviser and also to Connexions. Do also take a good look through Appendix 1 in this book, as well as your local library, for further ideas and information. Do be aware of the timescales involved in applying for study places abroad. Meet all the relevant deadlines and you will not find yourself having to kill time.

Working abroad

There are almost countless opportunities for young people who want to gain some experience working abroad. For example, you could:

- teach English as a foreign language almost anywhere in the non-English-speaking world (a TEFL qualification is nearly always needed);
- do childcare or domestic work, for example as an au pair (although there are age limitations and requirements can vary from country to country);
- do catering work, particularly in the popular tourist areas of countries;
- go for seasonal work in a ski resort in the French, Swiss, Austrian, German and Italian Alps, Andorra, Spain, Scotland and elsewhere;
- work on a kibbutz or moshav in Israel;
- do farm labouring and fruit picking (particularly in hot countries);
- go for summer camp work as a counsellor (particularly in the United States and Canada);
- work as a representative for a package tour operator;
- work in a theme park, for example in Florida.

There are many organizations that can help you to find suitable work abroad. It is well worth talking to as many people as you can who have done it, spending some time browsing the shelves of your local library and settling in to a few hours online. Good starting points on the internet are: www.ciee.org/representatives/; www.gapwork.com.

If you want to work outside the EU, you will probably need a work permit and visa. The relevant country's embassy in London will be able to tell you more. You can find the addresses and contact details of embassies at the Foreign and Commonwealth Office website: www.fco.gov.uk.

Your local Jobcentre Plus will have a Euro adviser who will be able to offer you advice on working within the EU as well as information about the European Employment Service (EURES). To find your local Jobcentre Plus office visit www.jobcentreplus.gov.uk and to find out more information about the European Employment Service visit www.europa.eu.int/eures/index.jsp.

Working abroad ... View from Natasha

OK, I know it wasn't the most glamorous of jobs but I loved the time I spent working in a ski resort in Switzerland. The pay wasn't exactly fantastic and it's incredibly labour-intensive work especially if you're working in the chalets, preparing food for guests, cleaning and sometimes entertaining. But the whole experience was so good for me and I did get my accommodation and board thrown in. I met young people from all over, especially Europe and Australia, and I'm still in touch with many of them. I really improved my skiing too, which was an added bonus.

I wasn't tempted to stay there forever, and by the end of the season I was ready to return home. I missed my own bed, my friends and family, but wouldn't have given up my time there for anything. One of the great things about working within Europe was that you don't have the hassle of having to get work permits or visas. It really is quite easy to organize, I think.

A friend of the family got me in touch with the company that I worked for but I know that there is plenty of information on the internet about working abroad, especially in the skiing industry. Now I've done it in Europe, I might try somewhere further away in the future – who knows! But for now I'm going to get into my course and try to forget about the freedom of the slopes!

I'd recommend spending some time working abroad to anyone. You're never going to make your millions out of it but it's usually a pretty 'casual' way of seeing somewhere new, learning some new skills and earning enough money to get by. Although it was hard work, I found it relatively low-pressure, which meant I had plenty of time and energy to make the most of it.

Action
Is working abroad for you?

It's all very tempting when you hear about the experiences of others and their jaunts around the world, but working abroad is not all about holidaying (although it's usually possible to fit a fair amount of that in!). Think about your answers to these questions when deciding if working abroad is for you:

- How do you feel about possibly knowing little about the country and culture that you would be working in?
- How happy are you to 'learn on the job'?
- Are you open to fairly menial or manual work?
- Do you like to make new friends and get to know strangers possibly from totally different cultures than yours?
- How happy are you to learn a different language?
- Are you likely to feel homesick? What strategies have you learned to deal with this?
- Are you happy in your own company? You may have to spend time alone.
- What about your religious beliefs? Would you be happy working in a country that has differing beliefs?
- Are you open to learning new customs?
- Are you open to new culinary experiences?
- What would you do if you really wanted to come home? What contingency plans would you make for this?

Aim to answer these questions in as much detail as possible. Note your answers down if that would help you. Add any other thoughts and reflections you have as you think about it all.

Summary

The key points from this chapter include:

- It is important to take time to think about whether you want to go travelling and, if so, what you hope to achieve by travelling.
- There are many opportunities for young people to study abroad. Some of the programmes include: Erasmus, Leonardo da Vinci, Youth in Action and IAESTE.
- It is possible to get grants and financial help to study abroad.
- There is a wide range of jobs that young people can do abroad.

12 Taking a gap year and volunteering

This chapter looks at:

- what gap years are;
- what gap years can give you and why you might want to take a gap year;
- gap year guides;
- travel precautions;
- volunteering abroad and in the UK;
- Millennium Volunteers;
- coming home.

A gap year

Taking a gap year simply means taking time out from your life plans to do some other activity, either paid or voluntary, or to take an extended holiday. Although the majority of people taking a gap year do it after university, a significant number do it before university. Each year, it is estimated that around 50,000 18-year-olds take a gap year, each spending an average of £3,000 to £4,000 on their trip. Most stay away from the UK for around four months.

If you decide to take a gap year, be really clear in your mind about what it is that you want to achieve. It is all too easy to let the time, which usually runs to a full academic year plus a few summer months, slip away if you are not focused and committed to making the most of it.

Want an Amazing Gap Year?
Investigate *Africa and Asia Venture*

Africa and Asia Venture work hard to find those areas most in need to send their volunteers. If you're after a foreign city experience with mod cons and conveniences to enjoy, we're not for you. If you want total immersion in a culture that will teach you to appreciate the really important things in life, perhaps we can help.

Try working in some of the world's poorest communities to discover what many have learnt before you – that rural people who own very little are the most generous and welcoming…and have the broadest smiles ☺☺☺☺. They will also teach you far more than you can imagine but you have to experience it to know truly what we mean!

 We offer **teaching, sports coaching and community and environment placements** for groups of up to thirty 18-24 year-olds in Africa, Asia and Mexico. Call **01380-729009. www.aventure.co.uk**

What can a gap year give you?

- The chance to save money for your time in HE – even if you have managed to finish college without having any debts, the chances are that if you go into HE you will need to take out student loans and an overdraft. Although you can start to repay these loans only when you are earning a certain amount (there is more on this subject in Part Six), obviously the more you borrow the longer it will take you to repay, despite the fact that student loan interest rates are relatively low. The more money you have saved to begin with, the easier your financial situation will be. That said, the other side of this argument is that you should be able to earn more money when you have left HE than before you start your course, so some may say that should be taken into consideration. However, many students do report that the more money they have in the bank before starting in HE, the more secure they feel. This depends entirely on the kind of person you are and how comfortable (or otherwise) you feel about being in debt.
- A break from formal education while you recharge your batteries – completing A levels can leave some students pretty exhausted and in need of a decent break from studying. This does not mean that you will not go back to studying the following year, but taking a gap year can allow you to indulge in some interests that you are not going to be tested on! If you're interested in doing this, the Universities and Colleges Admissions Service (UCAS – www.ucas.com) has further information for you on deferring entry to HE.
- The chance to 'see the world' – think about it! You could travel by train, yacht, aeroplane, car, bike or foot! The opportunities are seemingly endless. And being of student age, there are amazingly good value deals to be had. However, do not fall into the trap of thinking that this is the only chance you will get to travel. At present, the fastest growing group of 'gappers' is people from the 25–35 age bracket seeking a break from their careers.
- A way of helping others through voluntary work – doing something useful will nearly always lead to a sense of satisfaction. You do not need to jet off half-way round the world to achieve this, although of course if that is what you fancy there are plenty of

opportunities out there for you. Just remember that voluntary work can start at home too. Employers will generally be impressed by time spent doing voluntary work and there is no doubt that this can help you to gain invaluable life skills too.

- An opportunity to gain work experience to kick-start your career – there is a developing trend, particularly in some professions, for employers to want prospective employees to have gained some practical experience in the field before wanting to take them on. In some professions, like teaching, practical experience is pretty essential before even getting on a training course. Taking time out to gain this, either in a paid capacity or as a volunteer, is invaluable for those who know exactly in what direction they want their career to head.

- The chance to taste the world of work before continuing your plans – whether you want to go into HE or straight into work, taking time out to try different kinds of workplace can help you to decide where you really want to be. There are some organizations that sponsor students through their degrees and they often want them to spend some time working in the field before committing to a course. Getting stuck in is the only way really to know whether the job will be right for you. Leaping in one particular direction could see you feeling trapped and wanting to backtrack to take a different path; work experience can help you avoid that.

- Time to think about what direction you truly want to take in life – for some people, taking a year out can give them the time and space they need to make some long-term plans about their lives. The pace of life up to the age of 18 can be so fast that this is the only chance to think clearly about the future. If this is the case for you, it is really important that you take steps to make your decision rather than putting it off indefinitely. If you know you want to study but you are unsure about what course to go for, take some advice from your school or college. You could even start with making a list of what you do not want. That can sometimes help you to focus on exactly what it is that you do want.

Who is impressed by gap years?

Generally, employers and institutes of FE and HE are pretty impressed by those who have taken a gap year to do a structured and specific activity, even if that activity is travelling on an extended holiday. It helps if you can answer questions on why you did it, what you got out of it, the changes you think it brought about in you and the benefits you could bring to a university, say, or a company because of it.

Action

If you have taken, or are considering taking, a gap year, make sure that you can answer the questions mentioned above. Ultimately, you need to be able to explain to an admissions tutor or employer precisely what your gap year gave you. Here are some ideas to get you started:

- knowledge of different communities;
- increased confidence;
- physical fitness;
- valuable work experience;
- specific skills such as keyboard skills;
- a greater understanding of yourself.

Make sure that you think as widely as you can about your gap year so that you can paint the picture of it in the best colours possible.

Gap years ... View from Alice

I definitely knew that I wanted to take a gap year but I just wasn't sure when. In the end I decided to take one after my A levels and before going to university.

I knew that many universities run taster courses but I decided that I wanted to have a break from academic study. My long-term plan is to be a teacher so to me it was important to give

GREENFORCE
GLOBAL ADVENTURES

gap years that make a difference

www.greenforce.org
Call 020 7470 8888 or email
info@greenforce.org for a brochure.

Conservation, community, teaching English, scuba diving,
animal welfare and working abroad programmes.

Greenforce is a non-profit organisation which arranges overseas volunteering projects for anyone taking a gap year, or adventure break.

Whether it's marine conservation with tropical fish in the sapphire waters of the South Pacific, or caring for majestic pandas in the bamboo forests of central China, Greenforce has an opportunity for every interest.

With over 15 years of expedition experience, Greenforce has worked with the Red Cross, WWF, UNESCO and the UN to name but a few. Exciting world locations and excellent overseas staff are two of the reasons the organisation continues to offer inspiring and educational adventures with an outstanding reputation and the best safety record in the business.

For those of you who want to earn money on your gap year Greenforce also offers paid internships, guaranteed jobs in Australian outback, and paid jobs teaching English abroad.

The organisation is also carbon neutral and offsets the carbon footprint of both its staff and volunteers.

GREENFORCE
THE NON-PROFIT ADVENTURE SPECIALISTS

myself the opportunity to see different parts of the world and have a bit of fun before getting back down to work and three years at university followed by another for my PGCE. I didn't want to go from school to college to university and then back to school as a teacher without ever taking a year out.

My cousin and I decided to go travelling for six months. This gave us time to work and save up some money. I worked in a day nursery during the day and at my local theatre in the front of house team in the evenings. I didn't have much spare time but I wanted to be focused on saving as much money as possible. Sometimes it was hard but you have to keep your mind on what you're going to be doing later in the year! We didn't want to have to work while we were travelling and this seemed to be the best way of achieving that.

There were key places that we wanted to see. Mostly these were in Europe so we decided to plan a roughly circular train trip taking in all that we wanted to see. This took us six weeks, and then, after a brief visit home to get our stuff washed and to repack, we flew out to Australia. We have family out there so we were able to stay and sample real Australian life rather than just the backpackers' trails, which was an amazing experience. From there we went to New Zealand and then back home via Malaysia.

It cost more than we'd anticipated, but once you're out there you may as well take advantage of the opportunities you've got. I think it was the best thing I could have done with that year. Working in the nursery really confirmed to me that I definitely want to be a teacher, and seeing so many places abroad not only helped me feel a little more 'worldly' but also helped me to realize that I love living in this country!

Action

Before you even start planning a gap year, think carefully about your answers to the following questions. Jot down your responses if you think it will help you to make your decision:

- Will I be able to get the most out of a gap year?
- Can I afford to take a gap year?
- Am I motivated enough to plan it and save for it if necessary?
- Do I know what I want to do when I return from whatever gap year activity I choose to do?
- Can I create a gap year that will fit in with my plans for the future?
- Overall, will my life be enhanced by taking a gap year or will I just be killing time?
- Do I *want* to do this with all my heart?

Gap year guides

Gap years need meticulous planning if you are to get the most out of them. There are many sources of information on this for young people now and most broadsheet newspapers such as *The Times*, the *Independent* and the *Guardian* run stories about gap years in the summer months following exams. A list of gap year guides can be found in Appendix 1.

Information point

There are a number of excellent websites that can help you to learn about, plan and prepare for taking a gap year. While it is usually a good idea to do an internet search on the kinds of activities you are specifically interested in, the following websites will also be helpful:

www.gapadvice.org
www.statravel.co.uk/gapyear
www.gapyear.com
www.gapyearjobs.co.uk
www.gap-year.com

www.gap.org.uk
www.yearoutgroup.org

Travel precautions

Plan any travel that you do in your gap year very carefully. There are many books and websites available to help you to do this. Talk to the adults in your life about your plans too. Those close to you are bound to have concerns about you jetting off and if you talk through your plans and all the precautions you have in place they will feel happier and more able to support you. Remember, this plan may be as new for them as it is for you!

Wherever you decide to travel to, make sure that you have a passport that will be valid right through to *after* you plan to return to the UK and adequate insurance, including health insurance. There have been some reports recently of Britons abroad who were not given the medical treatment they needed until they could prove that they had insurance to cover the cost. Make sure that you carry all the relevant documents with you at all times and have photocopies of them in your luggage as well as leaving copies behind at home. It's an old cliché, but it's better to be safe than sorry!

A search on the internet will bring up companies to approach for insurance quotes. Always read the small print; cheapest is not necessarily best.

You may be feeling daring but there is little point in putting yourself in undue danger. The Foreign and Commonwealth Office (FCO) website is packed with current information on where not to travel in the world because of political instability and, although you literally may be able to get to these places, you'd be well advised to heed what the FCO says; besides, if you did travel to one of the countries currently off limits, your travel insurance may well be invalidated.

Personal safety

Whatever you do in your life and whenever you do it, being aware of your personal safety is really important. Although attacks on travellers are relatively rare, some countries are deemed more dangerous than others, and it will always be worth knowing how to look after yourself and others in the event of trouble. Be realistic about it: in all likelihood you will be perfectly safe, but it can be all too easy to throw caution to the wind when you're away from home and having a great time. This isn't about not having fun – it's about going about it as safely as possible. As the Ultimate Gap Year website (www.ultimate gapyear.co.uk) says, 'Travel is not without risk. The risk needs to be kept to a minimum acceptable level without eliminating the sense of fulfilment for individuals.'

There are several courses which would-be travellers can attend to learn all about staying safe while taking a gap year. You can find out about these from the website mentioned above, and your school may also run sessions on how to stay safe while travelling. There is essential safety advice and knowledge that you should have before setting out so be sure to find out as much as you can. Don't assume that you are streetwise and know all there is to know, and likewise don't let fears about safety put you off from travelling at all! To find out more about travel safety try these sites for starters:

www.ultimategapyear.co.uk
www.safetrek.co.uk
www.suzylamplugh.org/home/index.shtml

Information point

For further information on this visit www.fco.gov.uk or telephone 0845 850 2829 for travel advice and 020 7008 1500 for general enquiries.

Books and websites (particularly those listed in Appendix 1) will be invaluable in planning your gap year. Taking the time to focus on exactly what it is you want to achieve from your year out will help to ensure that you reach your goals, even if they are simply to relax and have fun.

The Year in Industry scheme

If you think you may want to work for a full year before starting HE, consider taking part in The Year in Industry. This is a scheme, administered by the Engineering Development Trust, for gap-year students to gain pre-university experience of industry backed by comprehensive 'off-the-job' training. The main features of The Year in Industry are that it:

- is tried and tested;
- is available nationwide;
- targets the most able young people;
- matches students to companies' needs;
- arranges real work in industry;
- selects students pre-degree, at their most receptive and enthusiastic;
- fosters continuing links between companies and undergraduates.

Students taking part in The Year in Industry agree to:

- follow the company's terms and conditions of employment;
- show initiative and self-motivation;
- be present for all training sessions offered.

In return, the company agrees to:

- employ the student between September and July;
- offer 'useful and challenging' work;
- free students up to attend The Year in Industry training courses;
- pay students a wage, typically from £8,000 to £12,000.

Each year approximately 600 students are placed with over 250 companies throughout the UK. Interestingly, 25 per cent of those taking part have gone on to get a first-class Honours degree and 35 per cent get upper seconds.

Information point

For further information on The Year in Industry, visit www.yini.org.uk, or telephone 023 8059 7061 or e-mail enquiries@yini.org.uk.

Volunteering

If taking an extended holiday for your gap year does not quite do it for you, there are plenty of opportunities to take part in volunteer projects all around the world. Many agencies exist to help young people find suitable voluntary work, for example, Camp America (recruiting people to work with children on summer camps in the United States), GAP Activity Projects or au pair agencies (looking for people to work in families looking after children and generally helping in the house). With these kinds of projects you may need to supply the money for your air fares.

Information point

www.worldwidevolunteering.org.uk is an enormous database of organizations and volunteer placements. Your local Connexions office may have access to it so it is well worth asking if volunteering is for you.

There are also opportunities to volunteer closer to home. Volunteering England and Community Service Volunteers are just two of the organizations in the UK that help find placements for would-be volunteers. There are many conservation organizations, too, and these are often seeking volunteers. This is a great way of getting involved in helping to preserve nature or your local heritage as well as making sure that you are not going to be stuck behind a desk from nine to five!

Information point

Community Service Volunteers (CSV) offer what they describe as high quality volunteering and training opportunities. Through taking part in a CSV project, you would have the chance to help real people, significantly improving their lives. Check out www.csv.org. uk for more information.

Millennium Volunteers

Millennium Volunteers is a Government initiative offering great volunteering opportunities to 16- to 24-year-olds. The voluntary work you do would be based on your interests as closely as possible. Since it started, Millennium Volunteers has helped well over 111,000 young people to become involved in voluntary projects.

The organizers of Millennium Volunteers say that there are many advantages open to young people who involve themselves. For example:

- You can develop the skills and interests that you have.
- You can develop new skills and interests.
- You get a nationally recognized and accredited award.
- You get travel and other expenses.
- There are training opportunities that you can take advantage of.
- You can have fun and make new friends.
- You can put 'MV' on your CV!

There are MV projects all over the UK so there is bound to be something going on near you that you can get involved in. If you complete 200 hours of volunteering in a year you will receive an Award of Excellence! Over 40,000 MVs have already received one.

Information point

To find out more about Millennium Volunteers take a look at www.wearev.com.

Coming home ... View from Jon

I was so excited about getting away from my village that I didn't put any thought into what it would be like when I got back. I got really depressed and demoralized because I'd been working on a kibbutz among other things, it'd been fantastically hot and a totally new experience for me. I got back to my quaintly English village in the middle of winter and everything felt wrong. I know

I upset my family and I felt really bad about that. It wasn't their fault – they'd always supported me.

Looking back I can see that I was just kicking out because I didn't want to face up to the fact that I needed to get on with the rest of my life. It really helps if you can get something organized *before* you leave so you don't end up in the state I was in. The lower I felt the harder it was to get up off my backside and make future plans. I ended up wasting a year when I got back from travelling just trying to get my head around what course I wanted to do and where I wanted to be. I don't recommend that to anyone.

If you're not careful, all the benefits you gain from travelling and working abroad can be lost in a second if you just go home and coast. Get it sorted! Just make sure that even if you're not exactly sure about what you want to do next you're at least *thinking* about it and not putting off the decision making until some point in the future. If you're not careful, that point will never arrive and then what?

Coming home

If you are planning to spend any time away from home during your gap year, or as part of your studies, make sure that you do some mental preparation about returning home. The chances are you will have had some amazing experiences – possibly even life-changing experiences – and you may have a slightly altered perception of your home life as a result. Before you even start packing your rucksack for your outward journey, make sure that you have firm plans for what you are going to do when you return, even if these plans are simply to spend a fortnight fully researching your options and re-evaluating your life after the experiences that you will have had. Above all else, you want to avoid coming back to an apparently empty life as this could lead to huge feelings of anti-climax.

Having said that, you should be aware that what you thought you wanted to do before you ever set foot on the plane may be very different from what you now want to do having spent six months in the Australian Outback! Be open to the changes and personal developments that take place and do not try to squeeze yourself into plans that no longer fit you. The pitfall you need to avoid is drifting on your return until something as exciting as what you have just been doing turns up. With that frame of mind, it probably never will!

Summary

The key points from this chapter include:

- Each year, around 50,000 18-year-olds take a gap year.
- Gap years can give you a wide variety of experiences and opportunities.
- It is essential to plan your gap year as much as possible. Don't drift into it or you may fritter the time away.
- Employers and university admissions tutors are generally impressed by people who take a gap year.
- There is a tremendous amount of advice out there for young people who are thinking of taking a gap year.
- Voluntary work can be an excellent way of spending all, or at least part, of a gap year.
- Millennium Volunteers is a Government initiative to encourage young people to get involved in voluntary projects.
- If you are planning to spend any time abroad you must think first about what you plan to do on your return – don't drift!

Part Five

Other options

13 Self-employment and beyond

This chapter looks at:

- all you need to know about self-employment;
- other options such as franchises and cooperatives;
- job sharing;
- portfolio working;
- work/life balance.

Leaving school at the age of 16 or 18 means that you face many choices. The obvious ones are either to go into FE or HE, or to get a job, but there are other options that you may not have thought of. Self-employment is something that many people consider at some point in their lives. It would be relatively unusual for someone to go into it straight from school, but if you think that it might be something you would like to explore later on in your life then you could bear this in mind when making choices now. Voluntary work or unpaid work such as job shadowing are two other choices. It is important to take time to make sure that you opt for what is best for you at the moment. Above all else, think about your options in the broadest way possible. So-called 'conventional employment' is not all that is open to you.

Let's just get real for a moment though. Doing anything other than getting a job can lead to periods of what some may describe as 'intense poverty'. Unless they have a private income from a loaded family, probably every student, entrepreneur, volunteer and self-employed person has been through it. Opting for one of the alternatives can mean risk taking and insecurity; it takes guts and commitment. That said, the benefits are potentially immense. Are you up for that?

Self-employment

Not many school leavers go straight into self-employment and even at graduate level the figure stands at only about 2 per cent, although this is thought to be rising. But self-employment shows all the signs of being a growth area of the UK economy. You may have long-term plans of self-employment so this chapter could offer you some useful ideas.

What is self-employment?

Self-employment literally means employing yourself – being your own boss. Whether this is a *lifetime* choice or a *lifestyle* choice, that is either permanent or temporary, is down to you.

Most self-employed people get work (or contracts or customers/clients) from many sources, yet no single company or client is responsible for them. This has its advantages and disadvantages but one thing to keep firmly in mind is that as a self-employed person you do not get sick-pay, paid holidays, a regular salary, or any of the other benefits or bonuses associated with being employed such as medical insurance and access to a company pension scheme.

As a self-employed person, your income would come from work completed that you then invoice your customer for. You would need a steady flow of contracts to ensure that you do not have any periods with nothing to do. This will also ensure that your cash flow remains healthy.

Being self-employed means having to be responsible for your tax and National Insurance. When you are employed by a company, this would be taken 'at source', meaning that tax and National Insurance are collected before your wages reach you. Consequently, all the money you earn is yours to spend (once all your bills are paid!). When you are self-employed, you have to make sure you save some money from each cheque received to pay for tax and National Insurance (in two lump sums through each year).

Any profits you have left when your bills are paid (including any savings and pension contributions you may be making) could be put back into your business. For example, you may need to buy a newer vehicle or rent larger premises.

Types of self-owned business

If you start up your own business (as opposed to simply working for yourself on a freelance basis) you will probably choose to run your business either as a sole trader, a partnership or a limited company.

Sole trader

This is a business in which just one person is the owner. As a sole trader, it is still possible to employ other people, but you do not need to go into the complexities of setting up a formal business. Another term for a sole trader is an 'unincorporated business'. Any profits made belong to the sole trader (although they will be subject to tax as appropriate).

Partnership

A partnership is a relationship between two or more (usually up to 20) people for the purposes of running a business and making a profit. Profits are split between all the partners and taxed as appropriate.

Limited company

Limited companies must have at least one shareholder, at least one director and a company secretary. If you run a limited company you will need to submit certain documents to the Registrar of Companies as well as produce accounts and file an annual report.

It is probably best, if you are thinking of self-employment as an option, to start out as a sole trader or partnership.

Why be self-employed?

There are many reasons for being self-employed. For many people, the example of their family has a large influence. If self-employment is a way of life for your parents or siblings, you are more likely to view it as a viable option for yourself; providing they run successful businesses that is!

In addition, some people are just better suited to it than others. Whether this is known from early on or learned as a result of work experience, you will know whether self-employment is a way of life that you could thrive in.

Certain types of work are typically more usual for the self-employed. For example, jobs in the media seem increasingly so as are many artistic and design-based jobs.

Pros and cons of self-employment

Pros	Cons
You can be your own boss.	You are the only one in charge.
You can set your own hours.	You need strong motivation and drive.
You can promote your own ideas.	Your ideas and concept may be 'stolen'.
You may be able to work from home.	If working from home, you can never get away from your home office.
You can build up many sources of income.	You have to deal with job insecurity.
It may not matter where you live in the country.	You can end up feeling socially isolated.
You can decide when to take time off.	You do not get holiday and sick pay (nor the time to have a break!).
You have greater control of your life.	You have to stay on top of your business' direction.
You can dictate what your prices are.	Clients rarely pay on time.
You get to use a wide range of skills.	You do not have time to update your skills.
The profits you make are yours to keep.	You will have no retirement income if you do not make your own arrangements for a private pension.

Is self-employment for you?

To be self-employed you need to offer a product or a service; preferably something that is not commonly being offered already (or that has a unique selling point). If nothing springs automatically to mind, think about your skills and aptitudes, hobbies and talents. Is there anything in that lot that you can market as being unique?

Remember, too, that if you take the plunge and go self-employed you will need to become expert at finance, sales and marketing, advertising, management, administration, human resources (if you employ others), ICT, the law as it relates to your business and much, much more. Your levels of self-motivation will need to be so honed and so reliable that you will be able to ride out every storm as it strikes. You will need excellent support to draw on as and when necessary and a very friendly bank manager!

Above all else, your vision must be realistic, yet ambitious. There has to be a genuine need for what you want to offer and a willingness in you to reach the prize you desire through creativity, honesty and innovation. Does that sound like you?

Is self-employment for you? ... View from Neil

I've always known that I want to run my own business. I don't want to spend my entire working life being someone else's employee. But I've watched my dad run his own business and have seen how much work is involved. I knew I wasn't ready for that when I left school so I got a job with him and I'm earning money and learning about running a business now. At the moment I have fairly fixed hours so I can make the most of my time off too. But I will be starting my own business within the next five years. I don't want to leave it any later than that. I know what I want to offer and am in the process of doing some research into how viable my idea is. It's looking good at the moment so I won't reveal anything about it!

Help starting up

A quick search on the internet will confirm just how much support there is out there for young people wanting to start up their own businesses. In particular, contact:

- Livewire – www.shell-livewire.org;
- The Prince's Trust – Business – www.princes-trust.org.uk;
- the New Deal – www.jobcentreplus.gov.uk.

What if your business fails?

Many small businesses do not make it through their first two years so it is important to be prepared for possible failure. This in itself is not a reason to back out of your dream if you really want to be self-employed, but it is certainly something to be aware of. Success for the self-employed person is not a foregone conclusion.

There are sometimes wider factors that have an influence on how successful your business can be. Factors such as the state of the national and global economies, interest rates, house prices, domestic politics, international politics (such as wars and conflicts), trends and fads for and against the product or service you are providing and so on, all of which have an impact on the profits that businesses can make. Even if you are doing the best you can, working as hard as is humanly possible, these other factors could conspire to make your business fail.

As a self-employed person you need to be as forward-thinking as possible. Taking out relevant insurances and expanding at a sensible pace will help, as will seeking advice and support as soon as you detect problems, but there are still no guarantees that you will succeed. That said, the belief that self-employment is the riskiest way to earn money no longer holds true. Your income may be irregular and working hours long, but this can also apply when employed by another person or organization.

Alternatives

As well as being employed, or going for self-employment, there are still other options that you might want to consider.

Buying a franchise

Franchises are other people's business ideas, sold on. Rather than growing in the conventional way, some business owners (franchisers) choose to sell a licence for other people to use their idea, allowing the franchisee to trade under that company's name. Business outlets are owned by the individual franchisees while the franchiser retains control over key aspects such as marketing, quality and standards.

Franchises can be shops, restaurants, clubs – almost anything! Examples of franchises that you will have heard of (and may have used) include the following:

- Alldays Stores;
- Clarks Shoes;
- Domino's Pizza;
- Kall-Kwik Printing;
- Saks Hair and Beauty;
- Thorntons;
- Toni and Guy;
- Tumble Tots.

There are many advantages to buying a franchise, not least that it is a tried and tested business idea that is known to work. As you can see from the list above, many franchises are household names, and it is an opportunity to have a relatively independent role in a nationally recognized business. However, one potential disadvantage is the amount of money that would-be franchisees have to put up front. Franchises are not altogether risk-free either so, as with any business proposition, careful thought and planning would be required before proceeding.

Information point

For further information and all you need to know about taking out a franchise make sure that you visit the British Franchise Association website: www.thebfa.org.

Job sharing

There are many jobs that can be split and shared between two (or sometimes more) people. Even some headteacher posts in schools are shared between two people. Although job sharing is still pretty rare, it is on the increase and employers do generally seem to be quite supportive of the idea.

Job sharing is different from basic part-time work. When job sharing, although you would be working part-time, you would be contributing, with your job share partner, to a full-time post. This means that you are more likely to be able to do fairly 'high-level' work whereas if you were to take a part-time post it is less likely to be particularly high-flying. Getting promotions as a part-timer (as opposed to job sharer) does seem to be potentially difficult too.

There are pros and cons to job sharing; really, whether it appeals comes down to personal preference. Ultimately, people choose to job share if it means they can pursue other goals such as further study, building up their own business in their spare time or looking after a family or a sick relative.

Job sharers usually split the tasks of the role, pay, holiday and any other benefits that the job may have according to the hours each person works. Needless to say, job shares are as successful as the relationship between the job sharers. If that is based on trust, cooperation, support and respect, among other things, the job share has a far better chance of working.

There are several options open to job sharers when dividing out the work. The job could be shared by:

- working alternate weeks;
- splitting the week into two full days and one half day each;
- splitting the day into a morning and afternoon session;
- working two days one week and three days the next;
- working to an uneven split with salary and tasks reflecting this pro rata.

Action

Can you job share?

If you think you might like the opportunities that job sharing can offer you, take a moment to think about the questions below as to whether you fit the profile of an effective job sharer. In order to job share successfully, you need to be a particular type of person. Job sharing is no good for 'control freaks' who like everything to be just so! Could you job share in the future? To help job sharing arrangements work effectively, job sharers need, at the very least, the following:

- excellent communication skills;
- skills of cooperation rather than competition;
- flexibility;
- compatible, but not necessarily identical, methods of working;
- commitment to the arrangement;
- complementary knowledge and skills.

The question is: how well do you fit this profile?

Portfolio working

It is probably true to say that there is no longer any such thing as a 'job for life', if there ever was. Many people are now wanting to work to a different pattern than the traditional Monday to Friday, nine to five and employers are responding to this by offering a range of possible contracts. This means that one person may have a portfolio of several jobs. For example, you may be employed on a part-time contract for one company for 15 hours a week, do some freelance work for another 15 hours and teach an evening class for 5 hours a week.

'Outsourcing' has increased over recent years, meaning that freelance employees and contractors have to be relied upon. This has helped to change many people's views about work. We all need to make sure that we remain employable, whether on a short-term or permanent basis, by keeping our skills up to date and our minds tuned to the idea of lifelong learning. This can greatly help the portfolio worker.

Portfolio working may not suit everyone; some prefer the thought of being employed full-time by one company. But for others, it is the ideal way of working as it best suits their personality.

Portfolio working ... View from Dave

I think I'm pretty unusual among my friends because they've all got full-time jobs but I knew that wouldn't be right for me. My main interest is music. I love everything about it. I know that ultimately I'd love to record my own; not necessarily to be famous, but for the pure pleasure of creating something that I can keep forever. If I make anything out of it, that would be great!

I wanted to get a job in a record shop, not just for the discount! I work three days a week in a small independent shop and I get given a budget to order some of the stock. That's brilliant, seeing what deals I can get, trying to research stuff that I think will sell well, getting to know customers and their tastes and so on. It's fascinating being that bridge between musicians and record producers and listeners. You find out so much about the whole industry from that central point.

On my other two days I work (for peanuts!) in a recording studio. Again, I see it as a way of gaining valuable knowledge and insight into the way the music industry works. Sometimes I'm little more than tea boy but I have worked on some interesting projects and learned so much.

I also play the guitar and keyboard myself and am gaining in confidence as a singer. I play in a band and we often get gigs at the weekends so that also brings in extra money. I see everything that I'm doing now as a route to my ultimate goal. I've got a portfolio of jobs but they are all connected and are teaching me different skills from various angles of the same business. I've got no regrets at all about choosing to do things this way. And if I'm honest, many of my friends are quite jealous, even though I'm sure they're probably earning a bit more than me right now!

Short-term contracts

These contracts can have various names, for example, specific task contracts (where you would be employed to cover, for example, a maternity leave) or fixed-term (for example, to cover the busy Christmas season in a shop). The contracts have a fixed finishing date and help to allow employers to increase or decrease their workforce as and when they need to. Some people thrive on short-term contracts, liking the variety and flexibility that they offer. They can also mean the opportunity to gain experience in a wide variety of work settings, which can be particularly useful if you are not completely sure of what you want to do and where you want to do it.

Cooperatives

Cooperatives are democratic organizations, owned and run jointly by their members, that share their profits among themselves. These profits shares usually depend on an employees' level within the company (often linked to salary). People choose to work in cooperatives as a way of starting a new business while having the security of working with others.

There are many different types of cooperatives, from those offering transport services to a community to babysitting circles, building services to wholesale food supplies. Some even operate their own forms of currency as a way of trading skills within a group.

Information point

The Co-operative Group is an example of a large and successful cooperative in the UK. Infinity Foods is another example. Visit their respective websites for further information: www.co-operative.co.uk; – www.infinityfoods.co.uk.

Communes and communities

OK, it is just a relatively tiny percentage of people who live and work in communes, but rising numbers have passed through one at some stage of their lives. Communes appeal to those people who do not feel completely comfortable with the realities of the world of work, seeking to do things in an alternative way. Different communes have different reasons for being, but in general, members share accommodation and resources (to a certain extent) and work together on a common project such as making things or growing crops, to be self-sustaining or offering educational programmes.

●Information point

Two examples of successful communities are the Findhorn Community in Scotland, www.findhorn.org, and the Pilsdon Community in Dorset, www.pilsdon.org.uk.

Work/life balance

Rather shockingly, employees in the UK work the longest hours in Europe. In fact, only employees in the United States work longer hours out of the whole of the developed world! This, combined with the way that new technologies have impacted on our lives, means that personal time is being squeezed. There is no doubt about it, you will need to work hard at creating a division between work and leisure and ensuring that your life has a healthy work/life balance. Whether you live to work or work to live is up to you, but you will need to leave time to relax and pursue hobbies and leisure if you are to avoid the strains of negative stress.

Working hours

Full-time, permanent jobs used, in the main, to mean being in your place of work from nine to five, Monday to Friday. Now, flexible hours (flexitime), shift work, opportunities for part-time and term-time work, working from home and so-called hot desking (shared desks for employees such as sales representatives who are not in the office long enough to have a desk each) mean that there is far more variety in working hours to be had out there. Overall, it is estimated that over 2 million people work from home and the number of those who do at least some work at home is likely to be far higher. In fact some people estimate that as many as 60 per cent of us will be working from home, whether employed by a company or self-employed, by 2010. Do not get locked into thinking that you will be doing the same thing in the same place at the same time each day; working life does not need to be like that any more.

Summary

The key points in this chapter include:

- Self-employment means employing yourself, or being your own boss.
- Although not many school leavers go straight into self-employment, it is something that many people consider at some stage of their lives.
- There are several types of business that you can set up including being a sole trader, running a partnership or a limited company.
- There are pros and cons of self-employment that need to be fully considered before taking the plunge.
- There is plenty of help available to you if you want to start up your own business.
- If you have difficulties running your own business there are several sources of support.
- Buying a franchise can be one way of running your own business in a relatively safe way, although there are still risks attached.
- Job sharing is another possibility for young people who want some time spare to pursue their own interests or to continue studying.
- Portfolio working is when you have several jobs from different sources or employers.
- Cooperatives are democratic organizations that are owned and run jointly by their members.
- Whatever you decide to do, it is important to pay attention to your work/life balance.

14 Voluntary work

This chapter looks at:

- voluntary work as an alternative to paid work;
- reasons to be a volunteer;
- Millennium Volunteers;
- transferable skills.

The voluntary sector

Rather than getting a job or starting your own business, you may want to spend some time doing voluntary work. (For information on doing work experience and job shadowing see Chapter 8; for information on volunteering in a gap year see Chapter 12.) Although doing voluntary work would not provide you with an income (expenses may be paid) it does offer the chance to gain useful experience, to develop skills and to find out exactly what it is like to do a certain job. Many feel that it is worth going without an income for a period in return for these benefits.

The voluntary sector in the UK is huge and covers just about every area of society. The turnover of the voluntary sector is around £16 billion and there is every indication that this will only go one way – up. Around 5,000 new charities are registered each year, which add to the approximately 150,000 charities already in existence. Some can afford to have paid staff (such as Oxfam) and others are run almost entirely by unpaid volunteers.

International agencies make up by far the largest part of the voluntary sector. After that come the cancer charities and a little further down the list come animal protection charities (interestingly, above children's charities).

Working in the voluntary sector as an unpaid member of staff can be a great way of eventually getting a paid post there. Charities nearly always need administrators, fundraisers, project managers, press and PR staff and many more. If you have got your eye on any of those roles, starting out as a volunteer could be a wise career move.

Do you want to work for no pay?

Working unpaid is not such a weird concept, really. In fact, some people go as far as paying their own travel and living costs in order to work for free! It all depends on what the perceived benefits are. If you think about it there will be jobs and activities in your life that you will be happy to do for no immediate financial gain (it is important to remember that you may well end up earning slightly more because of your experience than you would have done had you not volunteered). Doing voluntary work is simply about expanding that outwards into your community to see if you can spend some time helping others and achieving an end goal.

Why be a volunteer?

There are many motivating reasons to choose to do a period of voluntary work. Have a think about these ideas. You could do voluntary work in order to:

- gain knowledge and skills that will be useful in the future;
- benefit society and your local community;
- try out new ways of working;
- be part of a team of people working together to achieve a common goal;
- gain a way into an organization;
- gain experience of a career you might like to enter;
- travel.

Why be a volunteer? ... View from Geraint

I've been working part-time in my local Oxfam shop for the past two years. It's not staffed entirely by old ladies! Most of the volunteers are about my age and we've all got our own areas of interest. Because the shop's in quite a wealthy area we get a lot of decent clothes to sort through. Some are vintage originals, which we have to get advice on, others aren't up to much but still sell. Any clothing we can't sell to customers can be sold to a recycling company. Nothing gets wasted.

My favourite part of the job is sorting through the books as they come in. We've had quite a few first editions and some really valuable titles. I'm getting far better at spotting the potentially valuable stuff but again, we can get advice on this.

Obviously I can't do this forever; I've got to earn enough money to live. But I've never wanted to be rich. I just want enough to get by. I hope I never have to give up doing some voluntary work as it really keeps me grounded. It's a great way of knowing that you're giving something back to your local community as well as learning first-hand about other people's experiences of life. It's easy to shut yourself off from the needs of others if you never give your time to a charitable cause. I don't want to preach about it, but for me, I need this kind of constant reminder.

Information point

There is information on volunteering in a gap year in Chapter 12 and you can also look for voluntary work at your local Volunteering England. You will find the contact details in the Yellow Pages. Alternatively, visit www.do-it.org.uk; www.volunteering.org.uk.

It is not necessary to commit to a full working week of voluntary work. Often there is the chance to do as much or as little as you like. You may want to fit volunteering around other commitments.

Don't forget the Community Service Volunteers website: www. csv.org.uk.

Millennium Volunteers

As mentioned in Chapter 12, Millennium Volunteers (MVs) are young people who give up some of their free time to help their local communities. The scheme is national, with 114 MV projects established around England, offering young people great volunteering opportunities. Although there are incentives for completing certain numbers of hours of voluntary work in a year, you do not have to devote whole weeks or months to the programme if you do not want to or cannot spare the time.

The organizers of Millennium Volunteers say that there are many advantages open to young people who involve themselves. With MV projects all over, there is bound to be something going on near you that you can get involved in.

Information point

To find out more about Millennium Volunteers take a look at www.wearev.com.

Young people who have joined MV projects are involved in an amazing range of activities. Take a look at the following list to see if there is anything that sounds interesting to you. Some of these projects have led to employment opportunities for the people involved. The projects include:

- being a DJ for community radio;
- designing a mural for a local residential area;
- learning sign language to work with a youth group for deaf people;
- getting involved in 'peer listening';
- building a waterfall in a sensory open-air theatre;
- being a reading assistant in a local primary school;
- volunteering in a drop-in centre for young people;
- coaching an under-15 football team.

This is just a small taster of the kind of activities you may be able to get involved in.

Transferable skills

Spending time working in any organization, whether paid or otherwise, will teach you skills that can be transferred to other jobs or placements. These skills are known as transferable skills. Some people believe that being able to identify the transferable skills that you have is one of the most important things that you can do when you are thinking about applying for jobs or courses.

Transferable skills can be divided into different categories. These categories can include: communication skills, interpersonal skills (relating to other people), organization skills and general work skills. Take a look at the list below for examples of all of these.

Communication skills include:

- speaking effectively to others;
- listening with attention;
- being able to express your ideas;
- being able to take part in group discussions;
- conveying information;
- being able to negotiate;
- being able to 'read' the non-verbal communication of others (such as body language);
- writing effectively and concisely;
- summarizing and editing;
- handling electronic communication such as e-mails;
- being able to communicate effectively on the telephone;
- skills of self-expression.

Interpersonal skills include:

- being sensitive to the needs of others;
- being able to express your own needs assertively;
- getting on with people and developing rapport;
- supporting others;
- motivating others;
- being able to cooperate;
- managing conflict;
- having skills of perception.

Organization skills include:

- being able to pace and organize your workload;
- noticing details;
- coordinating the tasks that you have to do;
- making decisions;
- solving problems;
- handling information and data;
- working to deadlines;
- leadership skills;
- goal-setting skills;
- goal-realization skills;
- being able to cope with change.

General work skills include:

- literacy and numeracy skills;
- being able to follow instructions;
- accepting responsibility;
- being able to implement decisions;
- punctuality;
- time-management skills;
- skills of self-motivation;
- creativity;
- commercial understanding;
- research and information-gathering skills;
- skills of analysis and evaluation.

The list is virtually endless – there are many more that could be added here. There is no way that a single employer or course admissions tutor would expect you have all of these skills under your belt, but you will almost certainly be very good at a few of them, reasonably good at others, have just a little knowledge of some and be ready to learn the rest. That's fine – as long as you can identify some of these skills in yourself you will have an excellent base on which to build in the future.

The thing to remember with transferable skills is that it is not necessarily what you are doing in a job or placement that matters. You might be washing glasses in a restaurant and may never again do that in your working life, but the experience will still have taught you how to take instructions, how to work in a team and how to work safely, to name just a few. These are all skills that will be useful in future jobs.

Action

Transferable skills

First of all add any transferable skills that you can think of that have been left off the lists above.

Now go through each one and think about what situations in your life may have taught you each skill. For example, you may have learned about team work through playing in a sports team or you may have learned some commercial understanding from your Saturday job in a clothes shop. Aim to think as widely as you can about it. Do not worry if there are some skills there that you just cannot account for; that does not matter. What you are aiming for is as long a list as possible of your own personal transferable skills (with examples of how and where you learned them) that you can refer to when you make your job applications.

You have probably realized by now that simply identifying transferable skills is not enough. A potential employer or course admissions tutor does not want to read that you have an array of transferable skills without them being related directly to the job or course that you want to do. Being able to facilitate group discussions is not necessarily going to help you in your application for a holiday job in a call centre! But being able to negotiate and listen attentively will. Transferable skills have to be applicable to the job, placement or course that you want to transfer them to. For every transferable skill, ask yourself: how will this help to support my application or future life direction?

Action

Look at the table below. It shows possible interview questions and the responses of two mythical candidates. Which one would you rather employ, a or b? Think about why you made that decision.

Table 14.1

Interview questions	Response from candidate A	Response from candidate B
You left school six months ago. What have you been doing since then?	Applying for jobs	As well as applying for jobs I've been working as a volunteer in my local library
Do you work well with other people?	I prefer to work on my own	Yes, I really enjoy working with others. I'm on the children's homework team at the library and we help them with their homework and coursework problems. It's good fun
Have you had experiences of working with the general public?	No, but I can learn	Yes, working at the library has given me lots of experience of working with the public expecially when it's really busy at the weekend and we have to deal with one question after another
Are you confident dealing with telephone and e-mail enquiries?	Yes, I've got my own mobile phone and computer so I know how they work	Yes, I was trained at the library so that I can take telephone enquiries and I help my Dad out answering the e-mails he gets for his business

Summary

The key points from this chapter include:

- Being a volunteer can give you many benefits such as useful experience, developing skills and knowledge of exactly what it is like to do a certain job or activity.
- The voluntary sector in the UK is huge and covers just about every area of society.
- There are many places to find information on volunteering.
- Millennium Volunteers offers great volunteering opportunities to 16- to 25-year-olds.
- Volunteering gives you valuable transferable skills.
- Transferable skills can be very useful to add depth to job and course applications.
- Being aware of what skills you are learning, and how and when you are learning them is crucial.

15 Being unemployed

This chapter looks at:

● unemployment statistics;
● what happens when you visit your local Jobcentre Plus office;
● the Jobseeker Direct telephone service;
● Income Support;
● Jobseeker's Allowance;
● New Deal;
● Work Trial and Employment on Trial.

Unemployment statistics

Being unemployed literally means not having a job. The latest unemployment figures (January–March 2007) show that there were 497,000 unemployed 18- to 24-year olds classified as unemployed. If you are facing unemployment for whatever reason, you are not alone. Sadly, it does seem that young people aged 16–25 are twice as likely to be unemployed compared to older age groups in the labour market (which is defined as men aged 16–64 and women aged 16–59).

There is a link to qualifications here. Surveys in the past have found that someone with no qualifications is 1.8 times more likely to be unemployed than someone with GCSEs (grades A*–C) and 4.6 times more likely to be unemployed than someone with A levels. For this reason alone it is best to stay on in FE if you possibly can.

Jobcentre Plus

If you are looking for work you will be familiar with your local Jobcentre Plus office. When you first visit one of these offices you will meet a personal adviser who will need to take some personal details and will probably want you to prove your identity, so it is worth taking some documents with you such as your passport. You will be told about the vacancies that suit you and arrangements will be made for you to be sent the relevant claim forms for any benefits that you are entitled to (see below).

Information point

Jobcentre Plus is part of the Department of Work and Pensions. It provides services to people who are of 'working age'. This means people between the ages of 16 and 65. The aims of Jobcentre Plus include:

- *helping to get more people into paid work;*
- *helping employers to fill their vacancies;*
- *giving people support if they cannot work.*

You can find out all about Jobcentre Plus by visiting www.jobcentre-plus.gov.uk.

Visiting your local Jobcentre Plus office

When you meet the personal adviser he or she will want to talk to you about the following:

- The work experience that you have so far. This could be paid work in the form of previous jobs including part-time ones, or unpaid in the form of work experience you did at school or college or have arranged for yourself.
- Your skills. This is why it is really important to have thought about what you have to offer. See the chapters on looking for a job in Part Three for more information.

- Any training and qualifications that you have. Your working file (if you are using Progress File) will be useful here as you will already have gathered all the relevant information together.
- The education and training opportunities that you are interested in taking up.
- The support that you might need in order to do a job or take part in further training and education (such as childcare or special help if you have a disability).

You will also get the chance to discuss what kind of jobs might suit you, the amount of money you can expect to earn and the support that Jobcentre Plus may be able to give you once you have started work.

Information point

Jobseeker Direct is a telephone service that can help you find a job. When you ring up, the advisers will be able to tell you about the vacancies that exist in your area. You can telephone Jobseeker Direct on 0845 6060 234. Lines are open between 8.00 am and 6.00 pm Monday to Friday and 9.00 am to 1.00 pm on Saturday. It is helpful if you have your full address, your National Insurance number, your date of birth and the vacancy job reference ready when you call.

Benefits

There are two main benefits that young unemployed people can claim: Income Support and Jobseeker's Allowance. There may be other benefits that you are entitled to and when you go to your local Connexions office or Jobcentre Plus office the advisers there will be able to go through exactly what you can claim.

Information point

For further information and a rough guide as to how much you may be able to claim, contact your local Jobcentre Plus or visit the Connexions website: www.connexions.gov.uk. The Jobcentre Plus website has useful information too: www.jobcentreplus.gov.uk.

New Deal for Young People

New Deal is designed to help unemployed people aged 18 upwards (16 for lone parents) to find employment by preparing them for work. It could be that they need further training, education or experience or simply need to brush up on the kinds of skills that employers are looking for. New Deal for Young People (18–24) offers the chance to work in the voluntary sector, the Environment Task Force or full-time education and training.

Everyone on New Deal gets a personal adviser who will help them to sort out their experiences, interests and goals and make a plan that suits them best to enable them to get a job. This adviser is the person to contact with any queries or concerns throughout the programme.

Information point

In order to qualify for New Deal you need to have been claiming Jobseeker's Allowance for six months or more. You can find out more about New Deal by telephoning 0845 606 2626 (lines are open from 7.00 am to 11.00 pm, seven days a week) or by visiting www.new deal.gov.uk.

Work Trial and Employment on Trial

The Jobcentre Plus Network runs several schemes to help people find jobs. One such scheme is Work Trial. This is usually open to people who are aged 25 years or over and who have been out of work for six months or more. However, there are exceptions to this rule so it is well worth checking with your local Jobcentre Plus office or Jobcentre to see whether you could benefit from this scheme.

During a work trial you would:

- fill an actual vacancy for up to 15 working days;
- continue to receive any benefits that you are entitled to;
- be paid travel expenses of up to £10 per day and meal expenses of up to £3 per day.

Employment on Trial gives you the opportunity to try out a job if you are not certain whether it is the right one for you. To be eligible for the scheme (which basically means you will not jeopardize any benefits you may be entitled to if the job does not work out) you have to stay in the job for over 4 weeks, but not more than 12, working at least 16 hours in each week. This is only open to those who have been out of work or full-time education for 13 weeks before the job starts.

Information point

For more information on these schemes visit: www.jobcentreplus. gov.uk.

If you are unemployed, it goes without saying that you should be doing everything you can to get a job. See Part Three of this book for all the information you need.

Information point

Do not forget that Jobseeker Direct can help you to find a job if you are aged 18 or over. You can telephone Jobseeker Direct on 0845 6060 234. Lines are open between 8.00 am and 6.00 pm Monday to Friday and 9.00 am to 1.00 pm on Saturdays.

Being unemployed ... View from Chris

Having been unemployed and now working I think I'm in a good position to say what's best. I thought that if I was unemployed I'd get loads of benefits and wouldn't have to bother working but it's not like that at all. You have to show all the time that you're actively seeking work and that's like a full-time job itself. I also got really bored because most of my mates got jobs really easily and all I was doing was looking for work (not very well) and getting more and more depressed about always being skint. I started to feel like I was wasting my life. Not having to get up in the mornings isn't fun for long when you know that other people are all going to work, having a laugh with their mates and earning money. That's what I wanted.

I was lucky that I got a job that gave me one day a week to go to college. I'm working towards an NVQ now and I'm earning money too (although I wish it was more!). I'm much happier now than I was this time last year.

The advisers I saw at the Jobcentre Plus office were good for me. They weren't really pushy – I hate that. But they do keep you thinking about what you want to do and the kinds of jobs you might be good at. I think that's important – to try to get something you're good at. After being unemployed you need something that will make you feel good about yourself. I'm really glad I've got that now.

Summary

The key points from this chapter include:

- Young people aged 16–25 are twice as likely to be unemployed than older age groups.
- Not having any qualifications further increases the likelihood of being unemployed.

- If you are aged 16 or over your local Jobcentre Plus office is the place to go for help if you are unemployed.
- If you are aged between 16 and 18 then you can also call in to your local Connexions office if you are unemployed.
- Jobseeker Direct is a telephone service that can help you to find a job.
- The two main benefits that you may be able to claim if you are unemployed are Income Support and Jobseeker's Allowance.
- New Deal for Young People offers 18- to 25-year-olds the chance to work in the voluntary sector, the Environment Task Force or full-time education and training, among others.
- Work Trial is a scheme that is usually open to people who are aged 25 years or over and who have been out of work for six months or more.
- Employment on Trial gives you the opportunity to try out a job if you are not certain whether it is the right one for you.

Part Six

Practical issues

16 Moving away from home

This chapter looks at:

- living away from home;
- going to university;
- finding accommodation;
- moving away for work;
- making new friends.

Living away from home

Whatever you decide to do when you leave school, there is a possibility that you will have to live away from home, for at least part of the time, to do it.

Going to university

Going to university is an amazing experience for many students. It is exciting and challenging, new and yet daunting all at once. There is a lot to think about though. For most students this is their first time away from home and the thought of being responsible for all the things you have had help with up until now can be scary! If you are leaving home, there will be no one to do your washing and ironing, no one to do the food shopping, no free taxi service and no one to remind you to get on with your work. But on the positive side, you will be leaving home in a relatively gentle and safe way, and will probably still go home for the holidays!

Although increasing numbers of students are choosing to live at home while they study at university (usually to save money), you may be one of those who decides to leave home. If this is the case, the first thing you will need to do is to find somewhere to live.

Finding accommodation

You should be given advice from your university on how to go about getting accommodation. You will probably be faced with two choices: living in a university-owned hall of residence; or renting a room in a house or a flat close to where you will be studying. This house or flat may be university-owned or leased or it may be on the private rental market.

As soon as you have your place confirmed, get in touch with the university's accommodation office. They will be able to give you all the information you need. If you want to apply for university accommodation, make sure that you get your forms in on time. You may want to visit the university again to look round some of the accommodation options open to you. If you do this, be sure to talk to as many students as you can for some first-hand opinions.

If you apply for university accommodation but do not get a place, ask to go on a waiting list. There are bound to be would-be students dropping out before the first term starts so you never know, you may be lucky!

Information point

Take a look at your university's website for more information about finding somewhere to live. The site might include some students' experiences to help you decide what you want to go for.

Making new friends

When you start at university it is really important to make new friends. You will be taking part in new experiences and so many opportunities will be open to you (not just related to studying either!). Unless you are happy to integrate with others you could be in for a lonely and isolated time. Sure, it is wise to remember that you are at university to study, but being there also gives you a chance to take part in non-academic activities, even if that is just a prolonged chat over coffee with your mates.

Friendships are often made early on in the term – even in the first week. You will probably find that those you befriend in your first few days will stay friends throughout your course. It goes without saying that you need to trust your instincts when making friends at university. Make sure that the people you befriend want you purely for your friendship and that they have no ulterior motives (such as getting you to join a club or organization that you are simply not interested in).

If you are living at home and going to university, as increasing numbers of students are choosing to do now, be sure to make friends with other students who are doing the same. Perhaps there is someone you can travel in with or share lifts with? Your experience of university will be slightly different from that of students who are living in halls of residence or house and flat shares around campus, so it will be important to make friends with those who are having a similar experience as you as well as other students.

Making new friends ... View from Al

When I first went to university I lived in a hall of residence. It's fairly easy to make friends as you're all together, all in the same circumstances. You naturally have quite a bit in common with each other. I found that the older students were pretty good at making sure that all the freshers were looked after and within no time at all people had formed friendship groups. Certain corridors got certain reputations too! There were some people who seemed to prefer to be on their own rather than part of a big group. In a strange way, these people kind of found each other too.

I was really surprised when one girl along my corridor suddenly left hall. Apparently she hadn't been happy living like that and wanted to live in a family group. So she left and rented a room in a local family's house. I guess hall isn't for everyone.

Even though being in hall means that you have loads of people around you really close by, it's still important to make friends with people on your course and from other halls. Join societies and get out there so you don't just rely on your mates from hall. It can get pretty intense living and socializing with the same people so you need to be willing to take part in other activities. I joined the countryside conservers so we often went out on Sundays to do conservation work. I was also in the rowing club so that took up quite a bit of time but I did make great friends through it.

I think making friends at uni is just like anything else: the more you put into it the more you get out of it.

The friends that you make at university could well be friends you keep for life. They will certainly be an important dimension of your enjoyment while studying so it is worth putting as much into your friendships as you can (providing you have the time that is!).

Not making friends can leave you feeling isolated and lonely and may even have an impact on the way in which you settle into your course. Some people even leave because they have not managed to settle in. If you are having trouble settling in, there will be help available. All universities have student welfare counsellors who can talk things through with you and help you to see a way forward. Whatever you do, don't attempt to get through these feelings alone; you don't have to. There will always be help out there for you. It is usually a good idea to find out where you can get this help should you ever need it. There will probably be posters up in the student union building or contact numbers in the information that you are given.

Insuring your possessions

Some universities suffer from more crime than others, but it is worth being aware that as a first-year student you may be slightly more vulnerable to theft than other people. Some estimates suggest that one in four students is a victim of crime. Taking out insurance for your possessions is one way of guarding against the misery and inconvenience that theft can cause.

Information point

Endsleigh Insurance specializes in student packages. For further information visit www.endsleigh.co.uk or telephone 0800 028 3571.

There are other companies that offer policies to students so do ask around for ideas.

Personal safety at university

Although campuses can be relatively safe places to be, you do need to make sure that you are aware of any potential risk situations that you are putting yourself in. You will almost certainly be given advice on your personal safety when you arrive at university. If you are not, find out for yourself what measures the university has taken to ensure your safety as you live and study there. Never walk alone after dark or in isolated places even with friends, and get into the habit of telling each other what you are doing each day and roughly when you will be back. If a friend is later than you expect, ring his or her mobile or just be aware of watching out for them. In short, look out for each other.

There are specialist books about going to university that will give you more detailed guidance on personal safety. Above all, never takes risks and trust your instincts. It may be a cliché, but it's better to be safe than sorry.

Information point

You can find out more about keeping safe from the Suzy Lamplugh Trust Website: www.suzylamplugh.org/home/index.shtml.

Moving away for work

If your new job requires you to be mobile, or it is simply too far away for you to continue living at home, you will have to move. This means finding suitable accommodation that is safe, comfortable and affordable. It is probably wise to do this only if there are no other alternatives. Staying at home with your parents for a while can help you to save some money and decide what you want to do – get your own place (if you can afford it), lodge in someone's house, share a house or flat with friends or stay put where you are.

If you will be moving away from home, here are the options open to you:

- Privately rented flats, houses and an array of other possibilities such as mobile homes and houseboats. These could be either furnished or unfurnished.
- Housing association properties.
- Lodging in a spare room in someone's house. Some meals may be provided too.
- Hostel or hotel/B&B accommodation.
- Buying your own home (although, unless you have a very good salary and pretty big deposit, or the assistance of a member of your family, for example, you are unlikely to be able to afford to do this in most parts of the country).

Living anywhere other than your parents' house is going to feel expensive. The first thing you need to do when deciding where to live is to work out what you can realistically afford to pay. Once you have done this, here are some other factors that you will need to take into consideration:

- How will you get to work? (Will you go by foot, use public transport, or go by car or bike?)
- How close you realistically need to live to your place of work. (You can save money by being within walking distance.)
- The additional bills you will have to pay on top of rent. (You can ask to see recent bills and be sure to find out what is included in the cost.)
- Any hidden costs there may be. Always ask for the full details of what you would be financially responsible for so that there are no hidden shocks!
- If the place is furnished, is there an inventory of what items of furniture, kitchen equipment, etc are there? There should be, and only when you have been through it to check that what should be there really is there should you sign it.

- How is rent to be paid? The usual arrangement is payment one month in advance with a month's rent as a deposit. You should get the deposit back unless you have caused any damage that needs to be repaired.
- How much notice of leaving would you have to give? Do not get locked into lengthy contracts in case you need to get out fairly quickly. A month's notice is common.
- You may be asked by the landlord or landlady for a reference. Don't forget, though, that the rental contract is a two-way thing. Are you happy with the landlord or landlady? Always trust your gut instincts and get advice from your family or friends if you are at all unsure.
- If you are lodging in someone's house, find out what they do and who else lives in the house. How much of the house do you have access to? Would your room be secure and private? Can you use the washing machine? Do you get a shelf in the fridge?
- Make sure that the place is clean and dry. Are there any telltale signs of damp? Does it smell musty? Are the windows secure?
- Consider the location of the property. Is it in a safe part of town? Is it near a busy main road? Is it somewhere you could envisage living?
- It may feel more like home if you can give it a fresh coat of paint and add your own personal touch to it. Do, however, check with the landlord or landlady before doing anything!

You may have to resort to living somewhere that does not match your ideal but the chances are that you will be able to make a go of it.

Information point

Always ask your boss to be if he or she knows of any accommodation that you could rent. There may be someone who works at the organization that you are about to join who has a spare room or flat to rent out, or you may be able to share a house with some of the other people starting at the same time as you. There is absolutely no harm in asking and your new place of work is likely to be a great source of contacts. Other places to look for accommodation are:

- *local lettings agencies;*
- *the* Yellow Pages*;*
- *the local paper and local radio stations;*
- *newsagents' and Post Office windows;*
- *the personnel department at the organization you are going to join.*

Lodging in a house ... View from Anna

When I first left home I lodged in a house owned by an elderly lady. She took lodgers so she didn't get lonely. I had to leave really early for work but she always got up even earlier than me to make my breakfast! When I got in from work she always wanted to know what sort of day I'd had and really took an interest in me.

Although I really appreciated all that she did for me, it did get a bit claustrophobic after a while. I wanted to move to be nearer some of the friends I'd made so I left and rented a room in a big family house. I'd really hoped that it would be a better situation but the family rowed all the time and sometimes the dad was in such a bad mood that everyone had to get out of his way. I'd have to wait until they were all out of the way before I could use the kitchen and when I was home I spent most of the time in my room regretting that I'd ever left my first place!

In the end I joined a house share with my mates, which was best of all. We had a real laugh and if I hadn't changed my job I'd still be there. I guess the lesson I learned is that you don't know what you like and don't like until you give it a go.

If you do leave home, make sure that you stay in touch with the friends and family that you leave behind. They will be a great source of support for you and will almost certainly appreciate your letters, telephone calls and e-mails home. If you do write regularly, ask the recipient to keep the correspondence (especially if it is to your parents) as this could become your diary or record of this time in your life.

Making friends

If you have just left school or college and started work for the first time it may seem a little strange having to start out making friends again. However, it is likely that there will be other people starting at the company at the same time and even if they are not exactly your type, you can support each other through the first few months as you all find your feet. And they may turn out to be good friends anyway!

You can also make friends by joining local clubs and societies or by doing some voluntary work in your spare time. Your local Citizens' Advice Bureau may have some contact details for you, as might the local Connexions office or local paper. Many towns have their own websites too, listing details of what's on. The local library will also be a great source of information.

Making friends at work ... View from Nikki

I found it really hard to make friends when I first started work. They were all older than me and it felt so different from when I was at college. I got quite down about it especially as I'd chosen not to go to university but a lot of my friends had gone and I was getting e-mails from them about what great times they were having.

I knew I had to do something about it and when I overheard a couple of the others talking about going to the local gym I actually asked if I could go too. They were fine about it! I felt really embarrassed about butting in like that but I just thought I'd got nothing to lose. We go out quite a lot now and I invited some of them round to my house and cooked a meal. It was a laugh and I think I'm quite accepted now.

I'd always found it really easy to make friends at school but starting out at work is completely different. You really have to make an effort and not expect everything to come to you. I've also joined my local Green Drinks group and that's been a great way to meet people. At least all my friends aren't from work!

●Information point

Nikki joined her local Green Drinks group. These are set up for people who are interested in the environment, sustainability and all things 'green'. To find out if there is one run in your town take a look at www.greendrinks.org.

Action

If you are finding it difficult to make friends, make a pact with yourself to do at least one thing a week that will help you to meet new people. Take a deep breath and go for it. Sometimes all it takes is a smile and you've broken the ice.

Summary

The key points from this chapter include:

- Going to university is an amazing experience for many students. It is exciting and challenging, new and yet daunting all at once.
- You should be given advice from your university on how to go about getting accommodation.
- When you start at university it is really important to make new friends.
- Taking out insurance for your possessions is one way of guarding against the misery and inconvenience that theft can cause.
- Living anywhere other than your parents' house is going to feel expensive.
- There are many sources of information about finding accommodation so it is important to look at as many of those as possible.
- Even if making friends and joining clubs and societies might seem daunting when you are in a new location, it is worth the effort and will help you to settle in.

17 Money

This chapter looks at:

- what money means to you;
- money management;
- opening a bank account;
- budgeting;
- 'cheap money';
- getting into debt;
- FE and money;
- HE and money;
- your first job and money.

Whether you are starting work or going to university, money is about to gain a whole new significance! Money means different things to different people, and this greatly affects the way they use it, so it is well worth taking a moment to think about what money means to you.

Action

What does money mean to you? Are you a spender or a saver? A risk taker or someone who always likes to play it safe? Can you stick to a budget or do you always overspend? Is money a means to take part in the world or a hindrance? Are you in control of your money or do you need people to bale you out? Do you see yourself as someone who wants enough money or who wants to be rich? Take some time to think about your answers to these questions. There is no real need to write your answers down, but do think hard about what your conclusions are.

Money management

It is essential that you manage your money, otherwise the consequences of debt and all the problems that brings could rule your life
for decades to come. That may sound gloomy, but the importance of
sound money management cannot be over-stressed.

Opening a bank account

The easiest way of getting in control of your finances is to have a
bank account. If you have not opened one already, these ideas may
help:

- Do you have any strong feelings over whether your money should
  be with a so-called ethical bank? If so, your choices are slightly
  more limited (see the Information point below).
- Forget the freebies, gimmicks and promotions. For each bank,
  look closely at the charges you would pay, what would happen if
  you went overdrawn (took more money out of your account than
  there was in it) or over your agreed overdraft limit, interest rates,
  and whether so-called interest-free loans or overdrafts really are
  that (ask what happens in the long term).
- Think about where you will be able to get cash out. Most banks
  have cash machines (check you will not be charged for using
  another bank's cash machine) and you can often get 'cash back' in
  many shops as well as the Post Office. Will there be opportunities
  near you? Does it matter if there are not? Does the bank offer telephone and internet banking?
- What banking services, exactly, would you have to pay for?
- Shop around and make sure you open an account with the bank
  that will serve your needs best. Always ask them direct questions
  about the level of support and understanding they would be
  prepared to give you in your circumstances.

Your bank will send you a statement of your account showing all
incoming money and all outgoing expenditure. They usually send
these out once a month although some banks are making statements
available to view anytime online. Make sure that you read these statements and check every item. It is a good idea to keep all your receipts

at least until the item appears on the statement. Do not throw these statements away when you have checked every item. Always file them away in case you need to refer to them at a later date. Ask your bank about anything you do not understand or that you want to question on your statement. Never leave statements unopened for weeks on end! Open them as soon as you receive them. Get into this habit and money problems are unlikely to get on top of you before you have a chance to realize what is happening.

It is extremely important to remember that the financial advice you get from a bank is not independent advice. It will be geared towards 'selling' you one of their products so always be hyper-vigilant.

Independent financial advice is quite hard to come by and you should be aware that some so-called financial advisers are simply promoting the financial products (such as accounts and pensions) of one particular company. If you need financial advice ask at your Connexions office to see what they suggest for your area.

Information point

Two banks that work to strict ethical codes are The Cooperative Bank and Triodos Bank. Neither has as many branches as some of the other banks but that is not a problem with telephone, internet and postal banking. If you would like to find out more visit www. co-operativebank.co.uk and www.triodos.co.uk.

Budgeting

All but the filthy rich have to budget! In fact, it is the only way to get on top of your money. This means planning for your known and expected expenditure (like rent, bills and food) and whatever is left over for your spending money.

The most essential thing to remember when budgeting is: do not spend, or plan to spend, money that you do not actually have. In order to draw up a budget, you first need to work out exactly how much money is available to you each week and exactly how much you spend. For example, it you are working and your take home pay (that is what is left after tax and National Insurance) is £200 a week, then that is the amount available to you.

Next, write a list of everything that you spend money on over a week. The following suggestions will help:

- rent or board and lodging (if you are at you parents' home you include any contribution to the housekeeping);
- food;
- utility bills such as gas and electricity;
- travel and transport costs (particularly if you own a car);
- laundry;
- insurance;
- mobile phone;
- hobbies;
- clothing;
- union or professional association fees;
- going out;
- presents and cards;
- books, magazines and newspapers;
- stationery, photocopying;
- equipment;
- other.

Next to each item write down as accurately as possible what you have to spend on it. Remember that essential items have to be paid for first (such as rent and food).

If there is any money left over you can put that towards some savings. OK, it is not always that simple, but you get the general gist!

When budgeting, do not forget these golden rules:

- Write yourself a budget sheet that shows your sources of income (for example job, student loan and so on), your expenditure (for example rent, bills and food), your budget for each item of expenditure and what you actually spend. Get in the habit of keeping an eye on what comes in and what goes out and you will almost certainly not get in a financial mess.
- Never go over your agreed overdraft limit. Always get in touch with the bank in good time to make sure that you can extend your overdraft; it is only polite! If you do not you may be hit with astronomical charges or a refusal for an extension (but remember,

they are allowed to do that). This could be right at the worst time – when your rent is due and you have no money left to buy food.

- Economize whenever you can. Before you buy *anything* always ask yourself: do I *really* need it? If you think you do, try going without for a week (not food, obviously!) and seeing if you still think you need the item then. The chances are that you won't and you will have saved yourself some money.

- Think about where you can cut back if you are consistently spending more than you have. For example, do you need to buy magazines or can you club together with a friend and share the cost? Can you buy anything in bulk with others and benefit from cheaper prices? Can you recycle anything that you might once have thrown away?

- If you are thinking of getting a job as a student to make ends meet (and about 75 per cent of students do) remember that your studies should come first so do not do anything that will take hours out of your study time or mean that you cannot have time off when you need it. Agency work might be best as you can usually choose your hours and decline work when you need to focus on your studies.

- Remember that every pound you overspend has to come from somewhere. Where is that? Blagging from your parents? Your overdraft? A student loan? Your credit card? Are you getting that money from the cheapest place possible?

Getting cheap money

The cheapest money you can get is an interest-free loan. If this is from a bank (in the form of a free overdraft) you will have to repay it, but if it is from your parents or a member of your family, there is a chance that you won't, or you will at least be able to arrange a way of paying it back that suits you all.

If you borrow money and have to pay interest on the loan it is essential to shop around so that you get the best deal. The things to look out for are the length of the loan and the annual percentage rate of charge (APR). The table below shows you how much you would have to pay back on a £1,000 loan over various lengths and at different APR rates. It is quite shocking when you see the figures in black and white!

Table 17.1

APR	1 year	3 years	5 years	10 years
5%	£1,027	£1,077	£1,129	£1,266
10%	£1,053	£1,154	£1,262	£1,557
15%	£1,078	£1,231	£1,398	£1,867
20%	£1,102	£1,308	£1,536	£2,191
25%	£1,126	£1,385	£1,675	£2,523
30%	£1,149	£1,461	£1,815	£2,860

If you need to borrow money, always ask your bank about what it can offer you. Don't be tempted to run up large credit card debts as the chances are you will be paying far more interest than you need to. Make sure that you fully understand the implications of borrowing money. If there is an interest rate attached to the loan you will pay back more than you borrow – considerably more in some cases. Personal debt is becoming an immense problem in the UK. The latest figures available show that consumer credit lending is growing at a rapid pace and now stands at £214 bn (June 2007). Total UK personal debt stood at £1,345 bn at the end of June 2007. Keeping debt under control is crucial.

Information point

BBC Radio 1's One Life Finance section is packed with useful infor-mation. It is well worth spending some time browsing www.bbc.co. uk/onelife/your_world/world/money/. You can find out more about debt from the Credit Action website: www.creditaction.org.uk.

Career Development Loans

If you are aged 18 or over and want to further your career by doing a vocational course, you may be eligible for a Career Development Loan. You can only apply for these if you do not have reasonable or adequate funds to pay for the course yourself. If eligible, you can borrow between £300 and £8,000 to help you to fund up to two years' learning (plus one year's practical work).

Information point

For further information about Career Development Loans visit www.lifelonglearning.co.uk/cdl/ or telephone 0800 585 505.

What if it all goes wrong?

The one thing to remember about getting into financial difficulties is that the sooner you seek help the less likely it is that you get into serious debt. Don't put your head in the sand about it. The problem will not go away and procrastination could land you in serious trouble. The sooner you get advice, the sooner you will be able to sort out a sensible budget and plan for the future. Do not borrow more money from potentially unscrupulous sources or simply increase your overdraft. Go straight to your bank or to your parents or another trusted relative or friend and be honest about the situation you are in. Gather all your bank statements and (if you have a credit card) credit card statements together and ask for help in getting straight for the future.

Don't feel that you are alone if you get into debt. Most people do at some stage of their lives and it is pretty hard to find a student that does not owe money! Just make sure that you face up to the reality of debt as soon as it happens and you will be able to keep it under control.

FE and money

You do not have to pay course fees for FE courses (post-16 education up to the age of 19). You may also be entitled to a little help with travelling expenses and living costs if you are suffering severe hardship. However, it is wise to get information on this as early as possible before starting the course as you will need to complete claim forms and some of these have to be in months before courses start. Your local Connexions office can help you to find out what you are entitled to, but do ask their advice as early as possible.

●
Information point

To find out more about funding for your FE courses contact your local authority (LA). Contact details will be in your telephone book, usually under the county or borough name, or listed in the front pages.

Education Maintenance Allowance (EMA)

Since September 2004 anyone who decided to stay on at school or go to college has been eligible for an EMA. This is a weekly payment of up to £30 which is intended to help you to cover the day-to-day costs of studying after the age of 16. For example, it could help towards the cost of books, equipment, travelling and so on.

The EMA is dependent on the amount of income your household receives so if this is below £30,810 a year, you will be eligible to apply. However, this is not money for nothing! Once you enrol on a course you must sign an EMA contract and attend all of your course sessions. There are also expectations of you in terms of course work and progress.

●
Information point

For more information about EMA you can ask at your local Connexions office or visit http://ema.direct.gov.uk/ema.html. You can also call the freephone helpline on 080 810 16 2 19. For details relating to Scotland visit www.emascotland.com, for information relating to Wales visit www.studentfinancewales.co.uk and for Northern Ireland go to www.delni.gov.uk

You may well be entitled to other forms of support to help you to stay on for FE so make sure that you ask your local Connexions or careers office all about what is available.

HE and money

If you are planning to go into HE you will almost certainly have given money some thought. HE is not just about having the qualifications to get on to the course you want, it is also about having a sensible idea about how you are going to fund your time at university.

Funding for students is often in the news and has been the subject of much debate and a few protests recently. It is important that you know exactly what you would be responsible for paying for as a student (fees and maintenance – in other words, living expenses) and what help you can legitimately claim. Most of this information will come either from your LA (the one where you live, not where you plan to study if it is different) or the university itself.

Action

Read the Information point below and visit the appropriate website for you. Make a list of what you think you are entitled to claim and the forms that you need to fill in. Now contact your LA to double check that you have all the relevant information. Remember to mention if you are a student with a child or with a disability.

Then, write out a timetable of what you need to do next. Pay special attention to the fact that most forms will need to be in by certain times. If you miss key deadlines, you will probably end up having to deal with disruptions to the start of your course or late payments of money you are entitled to.

•Information point

There is a lot of information on higher education student support on the Department for Children, Schools and Families (DCSF) website: www.dfes.gov.uk/studentsupport/.

See also: www.studentsupportdirect.co.uk.

If you are in Scotland visit www.student-support-saas.gov.uk.

For information about financial support in Wales visit www. studentfinancewales.co.uk and for Northern Ireland go to www.delni.gov.uk (Student Support branch).

Other sites to explore are:

http://moneytolearn.direct.gov.uk – Directgov;
www.nusonline.co.uk – the National Union of Students;
www.funderfinder.org.uk – if you are looking for charity support;
www.studentmoney.org – for funding sources.

Student loans

There are different types of student loan: tuition fees loans, and maintenance loans. On top of any contributions you will be making towards tuition fees, you will be paying for accommodation, books, travel, clothes, going out and so on. All of this can add up and unless you are lucky enough to have parents who can give you money to pay for it all, or large sums of money of your own saved from work that you have done during a gap year, you are likely to need to take out a student loan. Student loans are not unlimited. It is worth keeping in mind that the amount that you can borrow in student loans is almost certainly not going to be enough to live on. Think about how you can boost this through your own earnings, an agreed overdraft (make sure you know exactly what costs are involved in this) or borrowings from family members if possible.

Student loans, as the name implies, do have to be paid back, but only when you have left university. Even then, you only start to repay them when you start earning at a particular rate (at current rates you would start repaying when your income hits above £15,000). These loans are not interest free but the interest is based on the rate of inflation so is far lower than the rate charged for a bank loan (although higher than having an interest-free overdraft!).

Many student advisers feel that students should take out maximum student loans regardless of whether they think they will need them. If you find that you do have some money left over (this is not exactly likely but possible if your budgeting skills are on top form) put it into a savings account, quickly, and make sure that it is earning at an interest rate that is higher than inflation – that way you will make yourself some money; more than you need to pay back!

Don't delay in sending in your forms for a student loan; you need to make sure that you make all the deadlines otherwise you could face a delay in the money actually reaching your bank account.

Information point

All you need to know about student loans can be found on the Student Loans Company website: www.slc.co.uk.

A word about debt

It would be neglectful not to mention a word about student debt here. While there are definitely significant social and academic benefits of going to university and studying for a degree, it is a big financial commitment. Unless you are fortunate enough to receive substantial sums of money from your parents or family to see you through university, or you work like crazy every spare second to earn as much money as possible while studying (not advised!), it is likely that you will get into some degree of debt. You will see stories in the media about student debt levels and how they are rising. Some studies have also found that leaving university with debt that takes time to pay off prevents some students from even thinking about buying a home.

It would be a shame if fears of debt put you off studying for a degree. Do at least sit down and prepare a detailed budget, taking into account any money you have saved, any you can rely on from family members, any grants, loans and bursaries you have access to and any earnings you can expect from jobs you take while studying.

Be as realistic as possible and aim to think about any potential debt as an investment in your future. Yes, the prospect of debt needs to be taken seriously, but don't let it put you off studying without finding out all you can about the support available.

Sponsorship

It is possible for some students to be sponsored to complete a course. This is not as common as it used to be but there are still some sponsorships to be had, particularly if you want to enter the armed forces or have an NHS-funded place. The General Social Care Council also provides bursaries for degree or diploma courses in social work.

Some universities offer sponsorships and bursaries too, but these will have fairly strict criteria attached to them and will probably be snapped up early. Do your homework and get in touch with your university as early as possible to find out if there is anything you could apply for. It is best to do this before you get an offer of a place so that you have all the relevant information to apply for sponsorship as soon as you know you will be going to that university. Again, watch out for any deadlines as late applications probably will not be considered.

Don't ever depend on receiving sponsorship or bursaries. They are pretty few and far between and there may be a catch involved (read *all* the small print!).

•Information point

www.scholarship-search.org.uk/ is a comprehensive guide to all you need to know when planning and organizing your finances as a student. Check it out!

What funding is available for Scottish students studying in Scotland?

This section gives an overview of the funding available for **Scottish students** from August 2007. Whatever your age, abilities or family responsibilities you can apply to get help as there are many sources of funding available. One or more of them may well apply to you, whether you want to:

- stay on at school;
- go to college or university;
- study full-time or part-time.

What's on offer?

The financial support you get will depend on different factors such as:

- what course you want to study;
- your income and family circumstances;
- how old you are;
- where you want to study; and
- whether you want to study full, part-time or by distance learning.

Some funding comes as a grant, some as a loan and some in the form of free course fees. Most is income assessed and there is different support depending on the type of course you want to do.

Do I qualify?

To be eligible to apply for some funding you must meet certain residence conditions. These are complicated, and we advise you to contact your local college (for Further Education courses) or the Student Awards Agency for Scotland (SAAS) (for Higher Education courses) if you are in any doubt about your residence status.

See our Quick Guide presented in Table 17.2 (overleaf) for a breakdown of what's available.

Table 17.2

Type of Funding	Staying at School	Full-time Further Edutation	Full-time Higher Education	Part-time Further Education	Part-time Higher Education	Distance Learning FE	Distance Learning HE
Course Fees							
Tuition Fee		✔	✔	✔	✔	✔	✔
ILA Scotland		✔		✔	✔	✔	✔
Career Development Loan		✔	✔	✔	✔	✔	✔
Living Costs							
Education Maintenance Allowances	✔	✔					
Student Loans			✔		✔		✔
NHS Bursaries			✔				
HE Young Student Bursary			✔				
HE Young Student Outside Scotland Bursary			✔				
FE Maintenance Bursary		✔					
Travel Costs		✔	✔	✔		✔	
Study Costs		✔		✔		✔	
Help for Dependants							
Adult Dependant Grant		✔	✔				
Child Tax Credit		✔	✔	✔	✔	✔	✔
Lone Parents Grant			✔				
Lone Parents Childcare Grant			✔				
Childcare Funds		✔	✔	✔		✔	
Other Support							
Disabled Students Allowance			✔		✔		✔
Additional Support Needs for Learning Allowance		✔		✔			
Hardship Funds		✔	✔	✔	✔	✔	✔
Vacation Grant for Care Leavers			✔				
Charities		✔	✔	✔	✔		

NB: This is a general guide and only indicates the funding that you *may* receive.

Full-time
Staying at school

If you wish to stay on at school after your school leaving date you may receive an **Education Maintenance Allowance** (EMA)

- this gives you up to £30 a week during term time depending on your household income;
- plus two bonuses of £150 if you remain on your course and make good progress;
- find out more from www.emascotland.com

Further education students

Generally, full-time students do not pay fees. Check with your chosen college if you are in any doubt.

If you are a school leaver going to college you may also be eligible for an EMA (as above), or you could receive a non-repayable bursary of up to £84.69 per week, but this depends on age, family circumstances and income.

Some of the other financial help you may get is:

- **travel expenses** – if you are under 18 this allowance is not means tested;
- **Additional Support Needs for Learning Allowance** – this offers additional travel and study help to students with disabilities, on top of other disability grants and benefits, and is not means-tested;
- plus every college operates a **Hardship Fund** and students with particular financial difficulties or emergency needs can apply for assistance.

Contact your college bursary officer for advice on what support you may be eligible for.

Higher education students

The Student Awards Agency for Scotland (SAAS) pays the tuition fees for eligible students studying at publicly funded institutions in Scotland.

- the main source of help with living expenses is through an income-assessed **student loan**. The maximum loan is £4,400 for students living away from home and £3,485 for those living at home. An **additional loan** of £575 is available to young students from families with an income of up to £20,695;
- some young students may qualify for a **Young Student Bursary** (a means-tested non-repayable grant) of up to £2,510 a year instead of part of the loan, so it reduces the amount of loan you need to take out.

Talk to SAAS about the additional funding that is available, this includes:

- **travel costs**;
- **Disabled Students Allowance (DSA)** for those students who have additional expenditure whilst undertaking their course because of their disability;
- students who are experiencing particular financial difficulty can apply for assistance from their institution's **Hardship Fund**;
- there is also a **Vacation Grant for Care Leavers** of up to £100 a week to help students, who were previously in care, with accommodation costs.

Information point

Find out more from the Student Awards Agency for Scotland (SAAS) at www.saas.gov.uk or on 0845 111 1711.

Part-time
Further education
Most students studying part-time and on distance learning courses will have to pay tuition fees. However, if you are in receipt of certain benefits, on a low income or are disabled you may be eligible for free tuition.

- you may also be eligible for the **Individual Learning Account (ILA) Scotland** scheme (see below);

- you may also be eligible for support towards appropriate **study and travel expenses**, as well as the **Additional Support Needs for Learning Allowance**.

Higher education

Most students studying part-time and on distance learning courses will have to pay **tuition fees**. However, a **'fee waiver'** scheme can provide you with fee support if you are unemployed or on a low income.

- you may also be eligible for the **ILA Scotland scheme** (see below);
- students on a low income or benefits studying Higher Education part-time may be eligible for a £500 **student loan** provided you are studying at least 50 per cent of a full-time course;
- you may also be eligible for the **Disabled Students Allowance (DSA)** which is not income assessed.

Other sources of funding
ILA Scotland

ILA Scotland can help pay for a wide range of learning with a variety of approved learning providers. If you are aged over 18 and live in Scotland and earn £18,000 or less per year or are on benefit then you may qualify for up to £200 each year towards the cost of learning.

Information point

For information on ILA Scotland and to request an application pack call the free ILA Scotland helpline phone on 0808 100 1090 or visit the website at www.ilascotland.org.uk for advice about what learning is available.

Career Development Loans (CDLs)

CDLs are deferred repayment commercial bank loans available to cover a wide range of vocational training or education for adults. The Government supports these loans by paying the interest on the loan while the individual is undertaking their training. You can borrow between £300 and £8,000 to support any course of learning that will help you in your career.

● Information point

Further information about the CDL scheme can be obtained on free-phone 0800 585 505.

● Information point

Further Information

To find out more about the various financial help available contact:

Learndirect Scotland

If you want to get into learning but aren't sure where to start, contact Learndirect Scotland on their free helpline number 0808 100 9000. Alternatively browse around for ideas on their website at www.learndirectscotland.com.

Student Awards Agency for Scotland (SAAS)

For more information on higher education student finance contact SAAS at saas.geu@scotland.gov.uk or telephone 0845 111 1711 or visit the website at www.saas.gov.uk.

Your local college

For more information on further education student finance please contact your local college. Contact details for colleges can be found at the Association of Scottish Colleges: www.ascol.org.uk/contacts.

Careers Scotland

Careers Scotland gives guidance to anyone in Scotland about work or learning. The aim is to increase participation in learning, employment and provide guidance. Find out more on their website www.careers-scotland.org.uk.

Scottish Executive

You can visit their website www.scotland.gov.uk/fundingforlearners.

Your first job and money

Starting your first full-time job is incredibly exciting. It is probably your first taste of the adult world outside of education and your first experience of earning a wage.

Before you start work you should be told exactly what your conditions of employment are. This includes how many days of paid holiday a year you are entitled to and what benefits and bonuses you may be entitled to. You will also be given details of what is expected of you and what happens if you do not keep your side of the contract (usually called 'disciplinary procedures'). You will be asked to sign the contract. If none of this happens, it is important that you ask what the terms of your employment are. There may be a union or professional association that you can join and it is usually a good idea to do this. They can offer advice and protection as well as numerous other benefits. You usually have to pay a small amount each month to be a member.

Information point

There is a minimum wage which is the very least you should be paid. The rates since October 2007 are as follows:

- *16–17 year olds: £3.40 per hour;*
- *18–21 year olds (the development rate): £4.60 per hour;*
- *22 and over (the adult rate): £5.52 per hour.*

You can find out all you need to know about the National Minimum Wage either from your local Connexions office or from the Department for Business, Enterprise and Regulatory Reform website: www.dti.gov.uk/employment/pay/national-minimum-wage/index. html.

The chances are your earnings will be paid directly into your bank account on a monthly basis. Alternatives include being given a cheque to pay in to your account yourself or an envelope stuffed with money (although the latter is highly unusual now). The amount that you are paid will almost certainly be out of your control, although as you gain experience over the coming years you may be in a position to negotiate your salary upwards. As well as pay, you should also receive a pay slip.

Information point

If you think that you are being underpaid and want to make a complaint you can telephone 0845 6000 678 or visit www.direct. gov.uk/Employment/Employees/fs/en.

There is also 'A Short Guide for Young Workers' which can be down-loaded free of charge from www.berr.gov.uk/files/file34228.pdf.

When you get your pay slip you will notice that what you receive is less than your salary because tax and National Insurance will already have been deducted. If these contributions have not been deducted, it could be that you are not earning enough. Don't forget that you don't pay tax on the first £5,225 of your earnings. Above that, you get taxed at the rates below (figures are correct for 2007–08).

Table 17.3

Earnings (above first £5,225)	Income tax rate
£0–£2,230	10%
£2,231–£34,600	22%
£34,600 and above	40%

Information point

If you have any questions at all about tax and National Insurance your local tax office will be able to help you. Find the contact details in your local Yellow Pages. *You might also like to look at the HM Revenue and Customs website: www.hmrc.gov.uk.*

To find out about the National Minimum Wage and how it applies to you telephone 0845 600 0678. For information relating to Northern Ireland telephone 0845 6500 207.

Wages are usually paid at the end of the month for work done that month. This might mean that for the first month you have very little, if any, money. If this is a problem to you, you could ask your employer if your first month's wages could be paid weekly to help you to budget.

Summary

The key points from this chapter include:

- Part of understanding money is knowing what it means to you.
- It is important to open a bank account.
- Budgeting keeps you on top of your money. Do not spend, or plan to spend, money that you have not got.
- The cheapest form of money is an interest-free loan. Be very careful about any money that you borrow and check the rate of interest that you will be charged.
- If you start sinking into debt, ask for help. There are several places you can go.
- There is financial help available for FE and HE students.
- There is a minimum wage that school leavers wanting to find work should be aware of.
- Your earnings above a certain level will be subject to tax and National Insurance.

18 Advice: working with parents and advisers

This chapter looks at:

- careers advice – where can you get it?;
- working with advisers;
- the Connexions service;
- special needs and equal opportunities in FE;
- special needs and equal opportunities in HE;
- special needs and equal opportunities when starting work;
- discrimination.

There probably is not a person alive on the planet today who has not received advice at some stage of his or her life. We all need it to help us make potentially difficult decisions and you are fortunate in that there are many sources of help and advice out there for you as you make your decisions.

Careers advice

There are several sources of careers advice that luckily are usually free of charge for 16-year-olds (unless you choose to see an independent adviser who may make a charge). Just remember that the more involved you are in this whole process, the more likely it is that you will get something out of it. Don't be a passive recipient of advice! Be clear in your head exactly what it is you want to know and ask plenty of questions.

The Connexions service

There will be a Connexions office in your nearest town that is your point of contact for the Government's support service for all young people aged between 13 and 19 in England. Connexions offers a huge range of services and advice on just about everything you could ever want to make the transition between school and adult life as smooth as possible. It basically joins Government services together with private and voluntary organizations to ensure that young people have access to the best advice possible.

The support that Connexions offers is practical as well as informative. To get an idea of the full scope and range of what is on offer, do take a while to browse the Connexions website and remember to check this website every time you have an issue you need help with. The topics covered are not just about work and studying, but also health, housing, drugs and more. Most Connexions offices also have a careers library that you can browse as well as computers that you can use for careers-related work.

Information point

You will find your nearest Connexions office either through the website (www.connexions.gov.uk) or by looking in your Yellow Pages. *Connexions offices are staffed by qualified personnel, advisers and their support staff. You may well have already come across Connexions staff as they visit schools a lot.*

The careers teacher and library

Your school or college careers teacher and library are likely to be great sources of help and advice. The careers teacher can help you in many ways but in particular he or she is likely to:

- organize visits from local employers, careers advisers and colleges/universities;
- allow you to use computer guidance programs that can help you to identify careers paths and the qualifications that you need to follow them;

- help you to progress through the decision-making process – some careers teachers encourage students to keep careers logs or diaries documenting the process;
- run careers fairs;
- organize work-experience placements;
- keep the careers library well stocked with the latest information;
- tell you about useful websites to look at.

It is a good idea to talk to your careers teacher about any careers matter that you need help with or advice about. He or she is there to help you. If there is anything you particularly want to know about that has not been covered you could ask if an outside speaker could come in to talk to you about it. Or better still, ask if you can organize this yourself!

Independent consultants

Independent careers consultants charge for their services which are likely to be very good but it should be remembered that there is such a huge amount of excellent advice that is free of charge (in books, on the internet and via the Connexions service to name but a few) that it would be surprising if you needed to use the services of an independent careers adviser at this stage.

Information point

It goes without saying that if you want to use an independent consultant, try to get one on personal recommendation rather than picking one 'blind' from the telephone book. You need to know a little about the consultant, his or her business and specialist areas of knowledge.

Parents and carers

Your parents or other adults who act as parents are bound to be able to offer you practical advice and it is usually a good idea to enlist their help. You are facing a period of change in your life and this can make you and those who care for you feel apprehensive. Get them on board and involved and you will be able to gain from their experience and ideas at the same time as helping to reduce their anxiety!

However, don't forget that the decisions you make must ultimately be yours. You are the one who will need to follow them through and if you choose a course or job simply to please someone else you are likely to end up feeling resentful. That's no good for anyone! Use the help and advice of others, let them help you to research options and provide resources and perhaps some useful contacts but make sure that the decision you make is yours. This will ensure that you are as motivated as possible about the coming years. And the chances are, your parents will be in agreement with you.

Just remember that although you are in the middle of a really busy time, what with applications to write, coursework to complete and exams to revise for, showing your appreciation for all your family has done for you will go a long way in keeping them on your side, even if this is only a simple 'thank you'.

Special needs and equal opportunities

Everyone has needs. Often, these can be met within the usual framework of education and training available to all, but sometimes additional arrangements have to be made to ensure that we all have as equal an opportunity to succeed as possible.

If you have particular needs that are not 'mainstream', you will probably already be used to additional arrangements being made to ensure that you are being supported. Other people, such as your parents or your teachers at school, will have had the responsibility to arrange this support for you. However, now you will be responsible for it yourself, although of course you can expect to be helped through this process.

Information point

Laws which came into effect in October 2004 may have an impact on you if you are disabled. For further information visit the Disability Rights Commission website: www.drc-gb.org.

Special needs and equal opportunities in FE

If you find that you cannot pursue the FE courses that you want at your local college because of your particular needs, there are some possibilities:

- Some colleges of FE are able to offer courses for specific groups of people.
- Live-in facilities are available at some FE colleges to enable you to attend your courses either alone or with help.
- Some colleges of FE are fully residential and adapted specifically for the needs of their students.

●Information point

Your local Connexions service or LA should be able to help you to find out about FE colleges to suit your needs. The National Bureau for Students with Disabilities (SKILL) can give you up-to-date information too, in particular on funding issues. Find out more at www.skill. org.uk (and see also Part Six of this book).

If you are disabled, it is worth keeping in mind that you must not, by law, be treated any less favourably by your FE college than non-disabled students are. You should not be placed at a 'substantial disadvantage' so your college should make reasonable adjustments to avoid this.

Once you have chosen a college of FE to continue your studies in, it is a good idea to make an appointment to speak to the Student Welfare adviser or the equivalent to discuss exactly what support you might be entitled to and how you go about claiming it. It can be complicated to navigate your way through this as different funds come from different 'purses' (some will come from the college itself, some from the LA, and you may be entitled to claim some form of benefit too) probably meaning that you have to make several applications (more forms!). If you can get someone to take you through this process it will be very much easier than attempting it without advice and help.

Information point

After 16 – what's new?

www.after16.org.uk is a website for teenagers and young people who have an impairment or disability and need to know about what opportunities there are for them when they leave school.

Special needs and equal opportunities in HE

Depending on the nature of your particular needs, you should research suitable potential universities very carefully. The Connexions service may be able to help with this, as will SKILL and your current school or college. Contact your LA as soon as you know that you are applying for HE, and ask to be told about the full range of allowances and grants that might be available to you.

Information point

The Student Loans Company can tell you the latest details on how much you can borrow and how it will be calculated. You may be given longer to pay your loan off if you have extra costs because of your disability.

Starting work

Fortunately there is plenty of help out there for you if you have particular needs and plan to start work. Your local Connexions office will be up to date on what you need to know and your local Jobcentre Plus will have specialist advisers you can consult. They have a Disability and Financial Services team as well as Disability Employment Advisers. There may also be local groups and organizations who could offer you support. Ask at your local Citizens' Advice Bureau or look in your telephone book under Disability.

Information point

The Disability Rights Commission (DRC) is an independent body set up to stop discrimination and promote equality of opportunity for disabled people. It provides a crucial service for the (around) 10 million disabled people in Britain as well as their employers and others. Since October 2004 it has been unlawful for any employer to discriminate against a disabled person when choosing someone for a job or considering people for promotion, dismissal or redundancy. Check out the DRC website for further information: www.drc-gb.org.

Discrimination

Discrimination is illegal on many grounds and it is wise to be aware of exactly what your rights are when it comes to disability discrimination, sexual discrimination, racial discrimination and religious discrimination. There are laws to protect you, so if you suspect you are being discriminated against or treated unfairly in any way, do seek help and advice.

Information point

The Equal Opportunities Commission is an excellent source of help and advice for anyone who thinks he or she may be discriminated against. If you think this applies to you, take a good look through all the information on the Equal Opportunities Commission website: www.eoc.org.uk.

Information point

The Commission for Racial Equality (CRE) is an organization that works for a fair and just society. The CRE aims to help everyone to work, learn and live free from discrimination, racism and prejudice.

You can find out more by visiting the CRE website: www.cre.gov.uk.

If you think that you are suffering from discrimination you can either e-mail info@cre.gov.uk or look for the contact details of your nearest CRE office on the website.

Summary

The key points in this chapter include:

- Sometimes we all need advice to help us to make the right decisions.
- Careers advice can come from many sources.
- Connexions is the place to go to for information and advice about how to make the transition to adult life as smooth as possible.
- Your school or college careers teacher or library will be able to go through your career options with you.
- There are independent careers consultants but there is usually no need for teenagers to use their services.
- If you have particular needs that are not met within what is known as the 'mainstream' you will need to be responsible for making sure that you get the help that you need once you leave school.
- The student welfare adviser at your college or university will be able to help you to claim all the support that you are entitled to.
- Your local Jobcentre Plus office will be able to help you to look after your particular needs when you start work.
- Discrimination is illegal on several grounds but unfortunately it does still happen sometimes. If you think that you are being discriminated against there are organizations you can go to for specialist help.

19 Dealing with problems

This chapter looks at:

- feeling down or depressed;
- getting help;
- the meaning of stress;
- the symptoms of stress;
- dealing with stress.

Feeling down or depressed

It is a sad fact of life that there will be times when we feel that life is against us and it all seems too much. This can happen to everyone and if anyone tells you that it does not happen to them, the chances are that they are not being completely honest!

It is not always possible to detect our personal warning signs that things are getting on top of us until it feels too late. If you can be alert to changes in your mood, feelings and attitudes, you may be able to ask for help sooner rather than later.

Telltale signs that we may be struggling with our emotions are:

- general feelings of discontent;
- disturbed sleep;
- mood swings;
- inability to concentrate;
- feelings of isolation;
- getting frequent infections;
- not wanting to socialize with friends;
- feeling tired all the time;
- feeling tearful;

- feeling aggressive;
- being drawn to caffeine, alcohol, drugs, smoking.

If you find that you are experiencing any of these feelings it is really important that you talk to someone about it as soon as possible. Even if only one or two of these apply to you, don't struggle on alone. Take action sooner rather than later.

Action

Get a piece of paper and write at the top of the page the words: I feel...

Then write down everything that comes to mind. If it takes a while for your thoughts to flow don't worry.

Underneath that write the words: Things I would like to change are...

Then write down all the feelings and situations that you would like to change. If there is anything in your list that you know you need help with, underline it.

Choose the item on your list that is giving you the most grief right now and make a promise to yourself to get help to resolve the situation.

Getting help

There are many sources of help that you can go to if you feel in need. Even if you can objectively understand why you feel bad (for example, you have just failed your A levels and will have to resit them) you are still entitled to help to get through this time and start to feel better. The following ideas may help.

Friends and family

Our friends and family usually know us best of all and can detect even the smallest of changes in our mood. If you have a good relationship with your family they are likely to be a great source of support for getting through problems. That said, you may feel that you want to talk to someone who does not know you so well, in which case there are other places to turn to.

Your GP

Your GP will be able to point you in the right direction of appropriate support. You do not just have to have a physical problem to consult your GP – he or she can help with emotional issues too. You do not have to agree to what your GP suggests but you can at least find out what suggestions he or she has. While you are at the surgery for your appointment, have a good look at the notice board and leaflets that will be on display there. If you are not happy with the way in which your GP has dealt with you, ask to see a different GP.

Your school or college

There will be someone at your school or college who has responsibilities for student welfare. Not only will they be able to offer practical advice and guidance but they may also be able to make allowances for you if necessary.

Counselling

This is open to anyone and you can either go to a private practitioner (see your *Yellow Pages* for further details) or ask to be referred to a counsellor by your GP (this will be free of charge). There are different types of counselling so if you find that it does not work very well for you it could just mean that you need to try a different kind of counselling, or a different counsellor. Some counsellors use tools such as artwork and creative writing to help their clients to work through their problems. Finding a counsellor can be difficult if you do not know someone who could personally recommend one. If this is the case, visit the website of the British Association for Counselling and Psychotherapy (www.counselling.co.uk) for information on how to find an accredited counsellor in your area. Most reputable private counsellors will have a sliding scale of fees for students, young people and those on low incomes.

The Samaritans

This is a telephone listening service for those who need to talk. You do not need to be suicidal to call; the Samaritans are there to help all sorts of people with a huge range of problems. If they can direct you to a more appropriate service they will (for example, if you think you are pregnant and feel terrified they will give you the contact details of a local clinic to go to). You can telephone anonymously so that no one will know you have made the call.

Information point

You can telephone the Samaritans 24 hours a day, 7 days a week on 08457 909090.

For more information on what the Samaritans can do for you visit www.samaritans.org.uk.

Youth agencies

There will almost certainly be a drop-in centre in your town specifically for young people. It will also have loads of information on services for young people in the area and could be a good place to go if you need some confidential advice from someone you do not know. Check out your *Yellow Pages* or local library for more information.

Self-help organizations

There are hundreds of self-help organizations that may be able to help you with any problems or issues you have. Either contact your local Citizens' Advice Bureau or search the internet to see what you can come up with.

Solving problems ... View from Steve

I really didn't see my depression coming. I thought I was on top of things and didn't see any of my mates suffering so I didn't have anything to compare myself with. My family kept asking me if I was OK – they obviously thought something was wrong. I just felt worse and worse as the weeks went by. I'd taken my A levels and wasn't that worried about the results. I'd decided to take a year out but didn't yet know exactly what I was going to do with my time.

As I started looking around for ideas it just kind of hit me that I wasn't that interested in anything. I was really worried about how I was going to pay for my time at university as I don't like being in debt, but I just couldn't drum up any enthusiasm for anything. I started staying in and watching TV in my room rather than going out and days started to fly by. Some of my friends left for uni and I started wondering if I'd done the right thing. My parents kept trying to help but I pushed them away.

Then one day I was at the doctor's for a bad cough I couldn't shake off and he asked me if I felt depressed. Just as he said it I started to cry. I felt stupid but I knew that he'd hit on exactly how I'd been feeling for the last six months if I'm honest with myself.

I had a great GP. He encouraged me to talk to my family about how I felt and said he didn't want to prescribe any drugs until I'd tried some counselling. I was so nervous before my first appointment – I had no idea what would happen for a whole hour. But it's not that bad at all. In fact, I really enjoyed the sessions in the end and got so much better that I didn't ever need to take any prescribed drugs.

The one thing that still worries me about what happened to me is the nagging question: what would have happened if I hadn't gone to the doctor for that cough? How much worse would I have got without realizing? My counsellor told me that one in four British men suffer from depression. It's so common but how many could be helped if they only knew they needed to get advice?

In a funny way the whole experience has been great. I've learned a lot about myself and I'm sure I'd know the signs and symptoms in the future. It might sound crazy but I think I'm actually grateful for that! It's made me more aware of others' feelings too. You have to face up to it when life isn't going right, even if you don't know why, and then you have to deal with it and move on. I did tell a few of my friends and one had actually had counselling too and I didn't know! So, to anyone out there who feels even slightly that things aren't right, don't just get on with it by yourself. Get some help. You won't be the only one it's happening to and the sooner you deal with it the sooner you can get on with the rest of your life. Believe me, problems won't go away on their own.

Stress

We all hear people talking about stress all the time. People say that they are 'stressed out' or that something was 'really stressful'. Almost everywhere you look you will see references to stress: on the television, the radio, in books and newspapers, you name it, there will be something about stress and the impact it is having on us all.

Stress in the workplace is now at record levels, with enormous numbers of working days being lost to it. In fact, it is thought to be the number one reason for taking time off work – even more people have time off for stress-related problems than for other common reasons such as backache and colds.

Many people have theories about why we all seem to be more stressed than in the past, but regardless of the reasons for the apparent increase in stress it is really important to understand exactly what it is and how it can actually help us in certain circumstances.

Positive stress

Believe it or not there is such a thing as 'positive stress'. It is what motivates us and gives us the kick we need to push forward and get things done. We all need a certain level of drive and enthusiasm in our lives and positive stress can give this to us. When we are positively stressed, we feel that whatever it is that we have to do is achievable. Positive stress is still demanding and we may well feel exhausted after we've achieved a particular goal such as taking exams, but it helps us to respond to the challenges in our lives in a positive and creative way.

Negative stress

Negative stress is what makes us feel that we cannot achieve our tasks and goals. Everything seems too much and life seems like one big race against time. The motivating pressure of positive stress is now the crushing force of pure negative stress that can lead to a wide range of adverse physical and mental symptoms.

In fact, negative stress keeps us in a state of 'fight or flight' for longer than is healthy for us. We start to treat life as one big emergency and lose our perspective on what really matters.

Action

Take a moment to think about what stress means to you. The following questions may help to get you thinking:

- Do you see stress as a good thing or is it a bad thing in your life?
- When you think of stress do you also think of pressure, worry and fear?
- Does stress affect your sense of self-worth? For the better or worse?
- What do you think is the opposite of stress? Is that a good thing or a bad thing?
- How do you feel when you are stressed?
- How do you feel when you would describe yourself as 'not stressed'?

If you think it will help you in the future, jot your responses down. What conclusions can you reach about the thoughts you have had? Do you have a good understanding of what stress means to you?

Stress ... View from James

I hate it when I hear people saying stuff like 'I'm totally stressed out' or that life's so stressful. Mostly it isn't. There's bound to be stuff that winds us up and I think young people today do have to put up with a lot. Many of us haven't got a hope of ever buying our own house while prices are so high and we have to get into a lot of debt to go to university. There is stuff that could happen that would be really stressful so going on about all the small stuff isn't worth it.

I have been through a time when I felt totally stressed out. I was in the middle of doing my A levels and my mum was diagnosed with cancer. They didn't want to tell me about it but I knew what was going on and she went for treatment almost straight away so I had to know. It felt like everything was crushing in around me. Like real pressure. I came so close to walking out of a couple of my exams but managed to get it together enough to stay and finish them. Sometimes I felt really panicky and I told one of mum's nurses when she asked me how I was. She said that was normal under the circumstances but that I should try not to do too much for a while. As soon as my exams were finished I had some time off. I had planned to get a job for the summer before going to university but couldn't cope with anything new at that time.

Sometimes you just have to start cutting stuff out of your life for a while and just focus on one or two of the important things. As soon as you start to feel less stressed you can start to do more. I found that as long as I made changes to what I had to do I could cope better.

My mum had surgery but is much healthier now. It really taught me that sometimes you do just have to drop everything to deal with the big stuff and when you do, everything can seem more manageable than it did.

Symptoms of stress

There are some symptoms that you may experience if you are suffering from negative stress. You will not suffer from all of them – perhaps only one or two – but they are a signal that your body and mind may be suffering and that you should seek some support and advice (see the Information point on page 229).

Being self-aware (taking notice of your feelings, whether they are physical or mental) is crucial. Ignore the way that you are feeling and you are likely to be ignoring important messages from your body and mind that all is not well.

Here are just some of the changes that can take place in your body as a result of suffering from too much negative stress:

- the blood supply to the muscles increases;
- the adrenal glands produce more adrenaline;
- the pupils become dilated;
- the heart rate increases;
- blood pressure may rise;
- the sweat glands produce more sweat;
- breathing becomes more rapid or troubled;
- swallowing may become difficult;
- muscles may become tense;
- more headaches and migraines are experienced;
- the digestive system may become upset;
- the immune system becomes less effective, leading to frequent infections like coughs and colds;
- fatigue and exhaustion may develop;
- skin problems such as acne may develop.

Here are just some of the changes that can take place in your mind as a result of suffering from too much negative stress. You may:

- become more anxious and nervous;
- get depressed and moody;
- feel lonely and isolated;
- have emotional outbursts;
- find concentration and decision making difficult;
- get excessively self-critical;
- start to avoid certain situations;

- feel lethargic or 'lazier' than usual;
- feel over-dependent on stimulants like alcohol.

There are many more symptoms and feelings that could be added to this list but if you find yourself experiencing even just one or two of them do make sure that you seek help sooner rather than later.

Dealing with stress

The symptoms that your body gives you are not for you to ignore. If you think that stress is a problem for you the first thing you should do is talk to someone. There is a lot of advice out there for you (see the Information point below) and self-help techniques that you can learn, but it is essential to get the advice of someone who is not on the 'inside' of your stress so that you can get valuable perspectives and insights.

Never feel that a problem cannot be tackled or alleviated. Everything can be. Even if an issue cannot be removed entirely, you can certainly be helped to feel better about a particular situation or about your life in general. Don't suffer in silence!

Information point

If you suspect that negative stress is an issue for you, or you would like to talk to someone about the way that you are feeling, there are many sources of help for you.

In person
- *Your tutor at school or college may be able to help, especially if you get on well together.*
- *If you are at university there will be a student welfare office with staff who you can talk to.*
- *Your GP will be able to talk to you and may be able to arrange some counselling for you.*
- *Your family and friends may be a sound source of support.*
- *Your town may have a drop-in centre for young people to get advice on the way that they are feeling.*
- *Your local Connexions office will have staff who know where you can get good quality support.*

On the internet

Young Minds is a national charity that is committed to improving the mental health of young people. Take a look at www.youngminds. org.uk or e-mail info@youngminds.org.uk.

Connexions Direct has loads of advice for you on stress management too: www.connexions-direct.com.

On the telephone

The Samaritans are always there for you day and night. You can telephone confidentially and anonymously on 08457 909090 or e-mail jo@samaritans.org.

You can telephone Connexions on 080 800 13 2 19.

Summary

The key points in this chapter include:

- There are times in our lives when all of us can feel that life is against us and everything seems too much.
- You have to be self-aware to make sure that nasty symptoms do not creep up on you without you realizing.
- If you feel depressed or are struggling with your emotions it is essential to talk to someone about how you are feeling. There are many places that you can go for help.
- Stress can be divided into positive stress and negative stress.
- Positive stress can be inspiring and motivating.
- Negative stress can tip us into excessive anxiety and a whole host of physical and mental symptoms.
- It is essential to deal with negative stress sooner rather than later and there are many sources of help out there for you.

Part Seven

Spotlight on key professions

In looking at career options after school, there is a wealth of information available on all sectors of UK business. *A–Z of Careers & Jobs*, published by Kogan Page, provides detailed information for more than 300 different occupations and job types. We have taken five of those job sectors – construction, electrician, law, nursing and teaching – and included them here over the next five chapters as examples of the detailed material available. Each chapter discusses the various roles involved in that particular sector and includes useful contact details, helpful websites and realistic salary ranges. For further information on this and all other Kogan Page titles, look at our website: www.kogan-page.co.uk.

WANT A DEGREE, BUT DON'T WANT THE DEBT?

Rather than graduating after a degree owing thousands of pounds, there is now an exciting alternative. After your A-levels or Highers, you could join a prestigious company in full-time employment and study for a degree on a part-time basis.

The construction industry is the UK's biggest single industry, responsible for 10% of GDP and employing 1 in 9 of the working population.

By joining Balfour Beatty Construction you could work on a construction site in a management training scheme for four days a week and attend university the other day. It takes 5 years to get a degree – only one year longer than a full-time sandwich degree – and you would gain an enormous amount of work experience. Your tuition fees are paid and you receive a competitive and rising salary.

Trainees will develop their career during their training and will continue into management after qualifying as a Chartered Builder, Engineer or Surveyor. The final goal is Project Management – being responsible for turning an empty field into a new hospital, school or office!

The scheme gives young people the opportunity to both gain a degree and lots of work experience without having to suffer the financial hardships associated with full-time study today. The construction industry is booming and there are lots of long term opportunities to join a dynamic and interesting industry in which you can move up the management ladder quickly.

Balfour Beatty Construction manages the construction of building for both the public and private sectors throughout the UK. Annual turnover is over £600 million and we are part of the Balfour Beatty Group – a £7 billion turnover international construction, engineering and services company.

Opportunities are available across the North of England and Midlands.

20 Construction

The construction industry is the overarching sector for any occupation that is involved in the building and decorating of new and existing buildings. Building work involves the construction and maintenance of any structure. It is allied to civil and structural engineering, building and environmental engineering, municipal engineering, and highway and transportation engineering. There is a huge range of career options within the industry for graduates, technicians and at craft level.

Trades available include carpenters and joiners (see also Carpentry), formwork erectors, wood machinists, mastic asphalters, bricklayers, painters and decorators (see also Interior Decorator), crane drivers and mechanical equipment operators, electricians, refrigeration fitters, thermal insulators, plumbers and gas fitters, plasterers, glaziers, scaffolders, paviours, steel erectors, stonemasons, roofers, floor, ceiling and wall tilers, coiling fixers, heating and ventilation specialists. Each craftsperson is responsible for a specific part of the job but also works as part of a team whose collective responsibility is to produce high-quality work. The Construction Industry Training Board (CITB) predicted that the sector needed some 76,000 new recruits every year until 2006, to replace those leaving, and to fill new vacancies. Nearly 60 per cent of the new recruits needed are for trade occupations.

Building control surveyor

Building control is undertaken by local authorities and Approved Inspectors. The main activities involve the examination and assessment of plans, site visits to inspect work, and liaison with designers, builders and other professionals within the construction team, and the fire authorities to ensure that new building construction and alterations to existing buildings conform to building regulations. A broad knowledge of the many areas of building work and skills in dealing with people need to be developed.

Qualifications and training

There are two components to qualifying as a Chartered Building Control Surveyor: successful completion of a Royal Institution of Chartered Surveyors (RICS) approved degree or diploma, followed by enrolment onto the Assessment of Professional Competence (APC) which is two years' practical training while in employment, concluding with an RICS professional assessment interview. Postgraduate conversion courses are also available.

Personal qualities and skills

You have to be a good communicator, able to talk to property owners and builders, and you have to be firm and assertive when explaining, for example, why some work has to be redone. You have to have good technical knowledge and be able to convey this to other people. Maturity and common sense are vital.

Starting salary

Salaries begin at around £15,000 to £19,000, sometimes more for mature applicants with a lot of relevant industry experience.

Information point

Association of Building Engineers (ABE), Lutyens House, Billing Brook Road, Northampton NN3 8NW; 0845 177 3411; www. abe.org.uk/siteman/index.asp?orgid=791

Construction Industry Training Board, CITB – Construction Skills, Bircham Newton, Kings Lynn, Norfolk PE31 6RH; 01485 577577; www.citb.org.uk.

Royal Institution of Chartered Surveyors (RICS), RICS Contact Centre, Surveyor Court, Westwood Way, Coventry CV4 8JE; 0870 333 1600; www.rics.org.

Clerk of works

The clerk of works undertakes independent inspection of the works in progress to ensure that they conform to the specification so that the client obtains value for money.

Contract manager

The contract manager is the person responsible for the overall control of a building project. This means coordinating the subcontractors and specialist firms, the technical staff and the machine operatives and making sure that the whole project is completed within the specified time limit and to budget.

Construction trades

There are many different construction trades: carpenters, painters and decorators, electricians, plasterers, plumbers and roofers. While they each have their own specialist knowledge and technical skills, much of the training and qualification route is similar for all of these trades. Have a look at the Qualifications and Training section at the end of this chapter to see how to qualify and what kind of training to expect.

Carpenter

There are several different jobs covered by the general term carpenter – what they all have in common is that carpenters work with wood. They use wood to make doors, window frames, skirting boards, floorboards, cupboards and all the other woodwork you can think of in any domestic, public or commercial building. Some of the different roles include bench joiners, who prepare doors and window frames in a workshop ready for other workers to install them in properties; carpenters and joiners who work on site or inside or outside buildings, fitting cupboards, doors, window frames, etc; and wood machinists who prepare floorboards and skirting boards in the workshop ready for the carpenter and joiner to fix in place and finish.

Demolition work

Demolishing a building properly and safely is one of the most highly skilled areas in construction.

Demolition operative

Demolition operatives use heavy machinery to bring down walls, buildings and other structures. They have to be acutely aware of safety, calculating exactly how a building will collapse. They are also involved in clearance of the site once the building has been razed to the ground.

Scaffolder

Scaffolders build scaffolding that might be used in demolition, but more significantly in construction. They build scaffolding from steel tubes and wooden platforms, and it is essential they build scaffolding that is safe for other construction workers to stand on and work from.

Steeplejack

Steeplejacks work not just on steeples, but on any high structures, chimneys, clocks, etc. They have not only to work at a great height, using special safety equipment, but also have to have a good working knowledge of many different trades because they are likely to have to carry out repairs to and with many different materials: glass, wood, paint, plaster, mortar, etc.

Interior and finishing trades

Once a basic structure has been completed by bricklayers, carpenters, roofers, etc, there is still a great deal of work needed to make the building comfortable to live or work in and useful for the purpose for which it has been built. Ceiling fixers, floor layers, glaziers, painters and decorators, plasterers and plumbers are examples of some of the interior and finishing trades on offer.

Ceiling fixer

Ceiling fixers and dry liners install ceilings, especially in large modern buildings with large expanses of high ceiling. They build structures to fit large sheets of plasterboard to, and cover the whole thing with a very thin layer of plaster.

Electrician

See Chapter 21.

Glazier

Glaziers work with glass, installing glass windows, doors and glass partitions. They have to be skilled in cutting and fixing glass, from basic double-glazing to more ornate glass effects.

Painter and decorator

No building looks complete until the important finishing touches of painting, wood staining and papering have been applied. Interior decorators work inside and outside all kinds of buildings, from private houses to large warehouses, shops and offices.

Plasterer

This is a highly skilled occupation, as plasterers have to line walls or ceilings with a layer of even, smooth and attractive plaster to act as a basis for painting, wallpaper or other finishes. They have to work quickly, achieving the desired finish before the plaster dries out. Some plasterers go on to develop skills in ornamental and decorative plasterwork.

Plumber

Plumbers install and maintain all the necessary pipes, valves, tanks, boilers, etc that keep water and heating systems flowing through any building. They install and maintain drainage systems and repair flashing on roofs.

Roofer

Roofs come in many different shapes and sizes and are made from many different materials. It is the job of roofers to fix roofs onto buildings and to ensure that these roofs are safe and weatherproof. Within roofing there are several different specialist trades: felt roofing tiling and slating, lead roofing and many more. You may choose to work mainly with one of these materials, and become a specialist, or you may decide to work with all the different types of roofing material.

Trowel trades

If you work with brick or stone you will learn one of these trades. Of the many construction occupations available, these offer you the chance to be creative as well as using practical skills.

Bricklayer

Bricklayers build the external and internal walls of all kinds of buildings, from private houses to large hospitals, hotels and offices. They build garden walls and lay patios. They work mainly with ready-prepared bricks, building them up in layers, working to produce smooth and weatherproof results.

Stonemason

Stonemasons have employed their skills for hundreds of years, using natural stone as their basic building material. Today stonemasons work both restoring historic buildings and building modern structures. This is highly skilled work and a flair for design as well as practical ability is very important.

Supervisory roles

With so many different workers involved in building projects, both large and small, it is very important that there are people to take overall responsibility for employing workers, purchasing materials, health and safety, and day-to-day management.

Site technician

Site technicians get involved with the general running and safety of the site. Your role would include hiring and buying materials and machinery, and organising people and equipment. It would be your responsibility to ensure budgets and plans are followed, and that everything meets technical requirements.

To become a site technician, you will need to have a strong knowledge of building methods and materials, and health and safety requirements, which you will have to teach workers on your site. You will need good communication and organisational skills, have a high level of competence in computing, and work well as part of a team.

There are no specific academic entry requirements to train as a site technician, although it is helpful to have GCSE/Standard Grade passes in science, maths and technology for the measurements and planning.

Site manager

Many site technicians become site managers, taking on more responsibility for larger projects and being in charge of everything that happens on the site.

Construction project manager

Construction project managers have overall responsibility for the planning, management, coordination and financial control of a construction project. It is their responsibility to see that the clients' wishes are adhered to and that the project is completed on time within the agreed budget.

Qualifications and training

You do not need any formal qualifications to enter the building trades described above. For most trades it is a definite advantage to have GCSEs in maths, English and technology. There are several routes to entry and each route has its own specific entry requirements. Generally, training courses that do not require any formal educational qualifications lead to what are called craft level awards, and training that requires you to have four GCSEs leads to technician level awards. Many of the routes below offer both of these options. Most training takes between three and four years.

Foundation Certificates (FCs) are available at some schools and colleges in England and Wales and are really taster courses, to help you decide whether construction is for you. They are a good way of demonstrating your commitment if you are applying for further courses or traineeships in construction.

The Construction Apprenticeship Scheme (CAS) takes three to four years to complete, and you are based with an employer, earning a wage, but also receiving some structured training at your workplace and through college. At the end of your apprenticeship, if you are on a craft level scheme you will get a Construction Award (CA), and if you are on a technical level scheme you will get a National Certificate.

National Certificates (NCs) and National Diplomas (NDs) are technical qualifications available in many construction trades. You can study part-time or full-time for these awards. There are no formal entry requirements for these.

Higher National Certificates (HNCs) and Higher National Diplomas (HNDs) are one step up from NCs and NDs. You can either go from the basic level to the higher-level course or, if you have A levels, you can go straight onto a higher-level course.

National Vocational Qualifications (NVQs) are another way to combine practical on-site work and study at college, usually through day or block release. Most construction NVQs are based with employers, but there are some full-time college courses leading to this qualification. There are no formal exams with NVQs: your on-site and college work is assessed throughout the course. For most NVQ construction courses you need four GCSEs grades A to C, and these should include English, maths and technology.

Construction Awards are available at three levels: Foundation, Intermediate and Advanced, and are available in many construction occupations. They are college-based courses that you can study full time, or part time while working for an employer. All your assessments are based on what you do at college.

Construction project managers and site managers often have a degree in construction, civil engineering or quantity surveying.

There are increasing numbers of short, privately run training courses in some trades, particularly plumbing, painting and decorating and plastering, but others too. These are aimed at mature applicants wishing to change career. They can be extremely expensive and it is important that you check exactly what accreditation and qualifications they lead to.

If you are trying to sift through this rather bewildering set of options, start by considering whether you want to be mainly employed as you train or mainly based at college. It is also true that not every route is always available for every trade, and employment opportunities vary in different geographical areas. The CITB Construction Skills website is a very helpful and thorough starting point to help you compare trades and look at routes to qualification.

Personal qualities and skills

While a variety of trades have been described and each has its special requirements, there are many skills and qualities that are important for all these occupations. You need to have a special interest in and feel for the particular material you are working with – wood, metal, plaster, stone, etc. You must be good at measuring and calculating, working out how much material you will need, and measuring exactly to ensure that something fits.

For all jobs you must be physically fit, though some work, such as bricklaying, is especially demanding. You may have to climb up and down scaffolding, work outside in unpleasant weather, or work in cramped spaces such as somebody's loft.

You need to get on with people. You often work as part of a team, and if you progress to supervisory or management roles you have to be organised and be good at motivating other people. If you are working in private houses, you must be polite, pleasant and trustworthy, and good at coming up with solutions to problems. If you become self-employed you must develop good business and financial skills.

Starting salary

Salaries for apprentices throughout the construction industry are agreed annually. First-year apprentices earn around £7,500, second-year apprentices earn just under £10,000. Third-year apprentices earn around £12,000, more if they have achieved GNVQ level 3, and on completion of apprenticeships salaries rise to around £17,000. With experience, all trades can earn between £18,000 and £22,000. There is considerable regional variation in salaries. There may also be opportunities to earn overtime payments, or bonuses on very busy projects. Many people with experience in one of the construction trades choose to become self-employed.

Salaries for management posts range from £19,000 to £32,000.

Information point

CITB – Construction Skills, The Sector Skills Council for Construction, Bircham Newton, Kings Lynn, Norfolk PE31 6RH; 01485 577577; www.CITB-ConstructionSkills.org.uk.

Summit Skills, Vega House, Opal Drive, Fox Milne, Milton Keynes MK15 0DF; 01908 303960; www.summitskills.org.uk.

www.bconstructive.co.uk/.

Apprenticeships
www.apprenticeships.org.uk (England);
www.modernapprenticeships.com (Scotland);
www.elwa.org.uk (Wales).

Local Job Centre Plus and Connexions/Careers Centres.

21 *Electrician*

Electricians work in domestic houses, factories and commercial buildings and on road systems, railways and vehicles. They install, service and repair every kind of electrical system, from wiring to individual pieces of equipment.

Auto electrician

Auto electricians check, repair and replace the electrical/electronic circuiting and components in all types of motor vehicle.

Highway electrician

These electricians install, maintain and replace the electrical and electronic systems that operate street lighting and road traffic management systems. They work from high, mobile platforms.

Installation electrician

Installation electricians install, inspect and test wiring systems in every kind of building. They either strip out old wiring systems and replace them, or work with other members of the construction team on new buildings, installing new wiring systems.

Instrumentation electrician

Instrumentation electricians work mainly in the manufacturing industry, installing and maintaining the electrical and electronic systems that run the manufacturing process, whether this is a conveyor belt to fill bottles of drink, build cars, or pack frozen vegetables. They are involved in measuring how efficiently electrical and electronic operations are working.

Maintenance electrician

Maintenance electricians work mainly in manufacturing, maintaining and testing electrical and electronic equipment.

Panel building electrician

Panel building electricians work from diagrams putting together complex electrical and electronic control panels. An office building could have a central panel that controls heating and air conditioning, and this is an example of the kind of panel that these electricians build.

Repair and rewind electrician

When components in pumps, compressors or transformers go wrong, it is the repair and rewind electrician who analyses what the problem is and either repairs or replaces various components. They work both in industry and in domestic properties, repairing goods such as washing machines and fridges.

Service electrician

The dividing line between repair and servicing is not always distinct. Service engineers check equipment and make minor adjustments, to minimise the risk of things going wrong. These electricians also work in industry and private homes.

Theatre electrician

Away from the world of manufacturing or faulty TV sets, theatre electricians maintain and repair all the systems that operate lighting, sound and other specialist theatrical equipment. They need to be extremely good all-rounders.

Qualifications and training

To qualify as an electrician you must achieve an electrotechnical NVQ level 3. There are various routes to achieving this, but the most common, provided you are between the ages of 16 and 24, is to do a three to four year apprenticeship. These are mainly employer-based, but include some college work and practical and written assessments. Though it is not always essential, many employers require you to have GCSEs grades A to C in English, maths, technology and a science subject. If you are not eligible for an apprenticeship you can do college-based City & Guilds courses at GNVQ levels 2 and 3.

Electrotechnical NVQ level 3 offers several different pathways, including electrical installation, electrical maintenance, electrical instrumentation and associated equipment, installing highway electrical systems, electrical panel building and electrical machine rewind and repair. A great deal of training takes place on the job.

Recent changes to the Building Regulations have meant that many types of household electrical work must be approved either by a buildings inspector or by an electrician who has acquired an appropriate certificate. Electricians can take part in a short scheme to allow them to self-certify their work.

Personal qualities and skills

You must have good practical and technical skills and be able to follow technical drawings and diagrams. You should be reasonably fit, and for some jobs you need to be able to cope with heights or working in confined spaces. You should have good colour vision. You need to be able to work on your own, or as part of a team, and you must have good communication skills, and be able to talk to people without using a lot of technical jargon.

Starting salary

Apprentices earn from £11,000 to £15,000 and salaries for qualified electricians range from £16,000 to £19,000. There is a lot of scope for self-employment with this work.

Information point

Engineering Training Council,
10 Maltravers Street, London WC2R 3ER; 020 7240 7891;
www.engc.org.uk.

SEMTA, 14 Upton Road, Watford, Hertfordshire WD18 0JT; 01923
238441; www.semta.org.uk.

Summit Skills, Vega House, Opal Drive, Fox Milne, Milton Keynes
MK15 0DF; 01908 303969; www.summitskills.org.uk.

22 **Law**

The legal profession has many occupations within it, but all are based on upholding the laws of the land and dealing with those who contravene the laws. The word 'lawyer' is a blanket term that covers both solicitors and barristers. Solicitors advise clients and operate in the lower courts. Barristers are instructed by solicitors to act for clients, and work in the higher courts. Opportunities for lawyers can be found in the public and private sector as well as within the legal system. The legal profession also offers careers for those who have not trained as lawyers, such as legal clerks and executives.

Advocate/barrister

The services of a barrister are required by solicitors (see also Solicitor) who deal with the clients and then 'brief' the barrister. Barristers give specialised advice on the law and plead counsel in the higher court. They may also appear in the lower courts, where they usually begin their careers. Some are employed in the Army Legal Services, giving advice on all aspects of service and civil law that may affect the Army.

In Scotland, an advocate is the equivalent of a barrister. Advocates may not select their clients. Provided that a reasonable fee is tendered they may not, without good cause, refuse instructions to act in litigation. Advocates also work in the public sector, Crown Prosecution Service, the legal section of a government department or as Parliamentary drafters.

Barristers specialise in arguing a case in court and offer a legal opinion for solicitors when asked to consider a particular question of law. Barristers are instructed by solicitors on behalf of clients and never directly employed by clients.

The majority of barristers work independently through sets of 'chambers' (which are a collective organisation of barristers), and tend to be self-employed. Once established within chambers, barristers can advertise for work.

Qualifications and training

Full details of qualifications required for admission are available from the General Council of the Bar, but generally students are expected to hold a UK law degree with second-class honours or better, or a non-law degree at the same standard plus a pass in a special one-year course known as the Common Professional Examination/Postgraduate Diploma in Law.

Every intending barrister must join one of the four Inns of Court. Students intending to practise must also attend a one-year full-time vocational course. A list of institutions offering this is available from the Bar Council. This is followed by a one-year pupillage under the personal instruction and guidance of a barrister. Pupillage may involve researching relevant details of a case, setting them out in detail and drafting documents. During the first six months, pupils may attend court but may not accept briefs.

After completing pupillage a barrister has to find a 'seat' in an existing set of barristers' chambers. Some may choose to work as employed barristers and enter the civil service, local government or commerce and industry. About 15 years after being established at the Bar, a barrister may apply for a 'patent' as a Queen's Counsel. Although 'taking silk', as it is known, is usual (but not obligatory) if a barrister wishes to become a High Court Judge, it can have financial penalties and some barristers stay 'juniors' throughout their career at the Bar.

Full details of the qualifications and training required for advocacy in Scotland are available from the Clerk of Faculty. Generally speaking, applicants require a Scottish law degree with second-class honours or better, or a degree in Scottish law together with an Honours degree, second-class or better, from a university in the UK in another subject. In addition, they will have obtained a Diploma in Legal Practice from a Scottish university and served at least 12 months' traineeship in a solicitor's office in Scotland.

Personal qualities and skills

As it will be necessary to understand and interpret complex legal wording into clear basic English, barristers must have an excellent command of the English language and a meticulous understanding of the use of words. Barristers must understand and talk knowledgeably about technical matters in order to be able to cross-examine the most expert witness, for example, on complex aspects of technology. It is also useful if barristers present a highly confident and self-assured manner and can put on a 'good performance' in court. Since the work is confidential, a barrister needs to be trustworthy and discreet.

Starting salary

Barristers' earnings relate to the amount and type of their work, their reputation, and, if they share chambers, the apportionment and value of briefs. Barristers may find it a struggle to make a living at the beginning of their profession, but the rewards for those who succeed can be high.

Information point

General Council of the Bar, 2/3 Cursitor Street, London EC4A 1NE; 020 7440 4000; www.barcouncil.org.uk.

Details of education and training at the Bar: www.legaleducation. org.uk.

Faculty of Advocates, Advocates Library, Parliament House, 11 Parliament Square, Edinburgh EH1 1RF; 0131 226 5071; www.advo cates.org.uk.

Barrister's clerk/advocate's clerk

The barrister's clerk is the administrator or manager of the business chambers, deciding which briefs to accept, which of the barristers in the chamber to give them to, and negotiating the fees with the solicitor. The accounts, the barristers' appointment books and the efficient day-to-day running of the office are all part of the job of an experienced clerk.

Qualifications and training

The minimum qualification is four GCSE pass grades at A, B or C in academic subjects. Training is on the job and juniors can apply through the Institute of Barristers' Clerks to attend a two-year part-time Edexcel (BTEC) national certificate course studying organisation, finance, management, law, marketing and chambers administration. On obtaining the certificate, juniors may apply, after five years' service, for qualified Membership of the Institute of Barristers' Clerks. The Bar in Scotland is divided into 10 'stables', each of which is served by an advocate's clerk and a deputy clerk employed by Faculty Services Ltd. Training is provided in service. The job of advocate's clerk is very similar to that of barrister's clerk in England and Wales. Their rates of pay are linked to the civil service scale on a level that roughly relates to a comparable post within the courts' administration. The 10 advocate clerks have clerical and secretarial staff to provide them with administrative support.

Personal qualities and skills

In order to manage efficient chambers and the barristers who work from them, a barrister's clerk needs good organisational skills, the ability to lead a team as well as be part of a team, and to get on with the general public. A good command of written and spoken English and an appreciation of the necessity for absolute confidentiality at all times are vital to success in this career.

Starting salary

Starting salaries are in the region of £10,000. Junior clerks with two or three years' experience receive £13,500–£18,000, going up to £28,000 for very experienced juniors. Senior clerks may earn £60,000–£75,000 plus a performance-related bonus. Senior clerks were traditionally paid a fee which was a percentage of the barrister's own earnings. Some are still paid in this way, and the fee is usually around 5 per cent.

Information point

The Bar Council, 289–293 High Holborn, London WC1V 7HZ; 020 7242 0082; www.barcouncil.org.uk/

Institute of Barristers' Clerks (IBC), 289–293 High Holborn, London WC1 7HZ; 020 7831 7144; www.barristersclerks.com.

Court staff

Court administrative officer

Court administrative officers and court administrative assistants ensure the smooth day-to-day running of the courts. They book cases, allocate cases to courtrooms, prepare lists of the day's cases and send out correspondence. They may also be involved in the collection of fines and providing information to members of the public. More senior administrative officers lead teams of assistants, ensuring that all the tasks listed above are carried out efficiently.

Qualifications and training

To work as an administrative assistant you require two GCSEs grades A–C and to be an administrative officer you need five GCSEs grades A–C. If you have other useful administrative experience, you may be considered without these formal qualifications.

Personal qualities and skills

You must be able to deal calmly and politely with people. You should have good organisational skills and be able to stay calm in a busy environment. You should be able to pay attention to detail and work well as part of a team.

Court clerk

Court clerks are legal advisers who give advice to unpaid (non-stipendiary) magistrates who are trying cases in the magistrate's courts. They are qualified lawyers, but they do not take part in the decision making about judgments and sentencing. As magistrates do not have to be legally qualified, it is the court clerks who ensure that magistrates interpret and apply the law correctly.

Qualifications and training

Court clerks have to be either qualified solicitors or barristers, who themselves must have either a law degree or an approved postgraduate legal qualification. Court clerks follow a set training programme and also learn by working with more experienced clerks, finding out about the many different areas of work – road traffic, licensing, fines enforcement, sentencing, etc.

Personal qualities and skills

As well as a real interest in and broad knowledge of the law, court clerks must be logical thinkers, capable of undertaking fairly detailed research. They must be discreet, sensitive and calm, but also able to remain detached when dealing with stressful and upsetting situations.

Starting salary

Court administrative assistants earn between £12,000 and £15,000. Administrative officers earn between £14,000 and £16,000. Section managers and team leaders can earn up to £20,000. Court clerks start on £18,000 to £25,000. Senior court clerks earn up to £30,000.

Information point

Her Majesty's Court Service, 5th Floor, Clive House, Petty France, London SW1H 9HD; 0845 456 8770; www.hmcourts-service.gov.uk.

Scottish Court Service, Hayweight House, 23 Lauriston Street, Edinburgh, EH3 9DQ; 0131 229 9200; www.scotcourts.gov.uk.

Skills for Justice, 9 & 10 Riverside Court, Don Road, Sheffield S9 2TJ; 0114 261 1994; www.skillsforjustice.com.

Court reporter

Court reporters attend court sittings and take down a complete report of all the evidence, the summing-up or judgment and, on occasions, the speeches of counsel in the various cases. Formerly, the proceedings were taken down in shorthand; now a palantype or stenograph is used. This is a typewriter-like machine that enables the reporter to achieve 200 words per minute. In addition, computers may be used to prepare transcripts, with all the advantages of onscreen editing and speed of preparation. The work sometimes involves travelling to a number of different courts. The majority of verbatim reporters begin their careers in the courts but can also work for Hansard, producing reports of proceedings in the House of Commons and the House of Lords. Television subtitlers also use the skills of verbatim reporting.

Qualifications and training

No specific academic qualifications are demanded for court reporters, although GCSE and A level passes can be an advantage. Applicants need to have proven ability in shorthand or stenotyping (usually over 150 words per minute), good typing speeds, and a thorough knowledge of grammar and punctuation. Legal experience can also be an asset. Details of full-time, part-time and distance learning courses are available from the British Institute of Verbatim Reporters. In Scotland, there are no college courses but training is provided on the job by working alongside an experienced reporter.

Administrative officers need five GCSE passes (grade C or above), one of which must be English. The Scottish Court Service looks for applicants with Highers. Training lasts for two to three years, during which time trainees work and undertake courses run by the Court Service.

Personal qualities and skills

Anyone concerned with the courts must be discreet, honest and trust-worthy, as most of the work is confidential. Reporters must show a high degree of accuracy.

Starting salary

Qualified court reporters earn around £13,000. Freelancers can earn £140+ a day.

Information point

British Institute of Verbatim Reporters, Cliffords Inn, Fetter Lane, London EC4A 1LD; 020 8907 8249; www.bivr.org.uk.

Individual courts of law
Northern Ireland Court Service, Windsor House, Bedford Street, Belfast BT2 7LT; 028 9032 8594; www.nics.gov.uk/pubsec/courts/courts.htm.

Law Society of Scotland, 26 Drumsheugh Gardens, Edinburgh EH3 7YR; 0131 226 7411; fax: 0131 225 2934; www.lawscot.org.uk; e-mail: legaleduc@lawscot.org.uk.

Careers in the Law (Kogan Page)

Legal services commission research assistant

The statutory government advisory body on law reform, the Law Commission, is currently working on projects in a variety of fields including common law, company and commercial law, crime and property law, and on general revision of statute law. The work is carried out in small teams, each under the direction of a Commissioner, consisting of qualified lawyers and research assis-tants. Law graduates and graduates of other disciplines who have completed the Legal Practice Course or the Bar Vocational Course are recruited annually to work as research assistants. The work offers the opportunity to take part in the creation of new legislative measures, as well as the in-depth development of skills in a particular area of law. Extensive consultation and investigation takes place before proposals are formulated; a sizeable proportion result in legislation. Projects range from major investigations of controversial areas of law to the consideration of a specific problem.

Qualifications and training

The minimum academic standard required is a first or high upper second-class (or equivalent) degree achieved in legal studies (based on the law of England and Wales) of at least two years' duration.

Personal qualities and skills

You need a genuine interest in, as well as a thorough knowledge of the law and legal issues. You must have excellent research skills, including the use of databases. You must be able to think and write articulately, be good at solving problems and be able to communicate well.

Starting salary

Starting salaries range from £20,000 to £29,000. The highest salaries include London Weighting and are also paid to entrants with good postgraduate qualifications as well as a high class of degree.

Information point

Legal Services Commission, Legal Services Research Centre, 85 Gray's Inn Road, London WC1X 8TX; 020 7759 0000; www.legalservices.gov.uk.

Asset Skills, 2 The Courtyard, 48 New North Road, Exeter, Devon EX4 4EP; 01392 423399; www.assetskills.org.

Paralegal

Paralegals work for firms of solicitors, commercial companies and public sector bodies. They are not qualified solicitors or legal executives, but they develop considerable specialist knowledge. They normally specialise in a specific area of the law such as conveyancing, probate or family law. Their work involves researching information, drafting and managing documents, attending client meetings and some general clerical work. Paralegals also have to keep up to date with legal developments in their specialist field.

Qualifications and training

While there are no specific entry qualifications for paralegals, many hope to become solicitors, barristers or legal executives. This means that many applicants for these posts have law degrees. In any case, some firms ask for four or five GCSEs grades A–C or two A levels. Training is on the job and there are City & Guilds courses leading to a certificate level 2 and diploma level 3 available in paralegal studies. The Institute of Legal Executives (ILEX) also offers part-time and distance learning courses for paralegals.

Personal qualities and skills

You must be very well organised, able to manage your own workload and pay attention to detail. You should have good spoken and written English skills and be interested in legal matters.

Starting salary

Salaries for paralegals are between £14,000 and £22,000. For large city law firms, salaries can be much higher than this and some firms pay substantial annual bonuses.

Information point

Institute of Legal Executives, Kempston Manor, Kempston, Bedfordshire MK42 7AB; 01234 841000; www.ilexpp.co.uk.

National Association of Licensed Paralegals, 9 Unity Street, Bristol BS1 5HH; 0117 927 7077; www.nationalparalegals.com.

Legal executive

A legal executive is a professional lawyer employed in a solicitor's office or in the legal departments of commerce and central and local government. The training and academic requirements in a specified area of law are at the same level as those required of a solicitor. Consequently, with few exceptions, a legal executive is able to carry out tasks that are similar to those undertaken by solicitors. The main areas of specialisation are conveyancing, civil litigation, criminal law, family law and probate. In addition to providing a worthwhile career in its own right, the legal executive qualification provides access to those wishing to qualify as solicitors via the Institute route. In Scotland, the term 'legal executive' is not used, but solicitors engage assistants to do similar work.

Qualifications and training

The minimum entry requirement is four GCSEs to include English, but A level students and graduates are welcome. As an alternative, the Institute accepts a qualification in vocational legal studies, and has special arrangements for students who are over 21. In the main, training is on a part-time basis so that there is potential for trainees to 'learn while they earn'. For those already working in a legal environment, but with no formal legal qualifications, an NVQ (level 4) in legal practice is available, and the Institute of Legal Executives (ILEX) is the awarding body.

Personal qualities and skills

An ability to communicate, both verbally and in writing, with people at all levels, absolute discretion and trustworthiness, together with meticulous attention to detail, are essential.

Starting salary

Varies according to age and qualification, and the type of work undertaken. The average starting salary is around £12,000. Many established legal executives earn £60,000+.

●Information point

Institute of Legal Executives, Kempston Manor, Kempston, Bedfordshire MK42 7AB; 01234 841000; www.ilex.org.uk; e-mail: info@ilex.org.uk.

Notary public

A notary public is an international lawyer, whose main duty it is to prepare and verify legal documents for use abroad. These can be certified translations, powers of attorney and all manner of mercantile documents. There are two types of notaries: general notaries who are usually full-time solicitors with a part-time notarial practice, or scrivener notaries who are full-time notaries with linguistic skills. The latter are usually to be found in central London, the former anywhere in the UK. Although nearly all the work of scrivener notaries is of an international nature, they are competent to advise on certain domestic matters as well.

Qualifications and training

Qualification as a notary is open to solicitors, barristers and graduates, whose degree need not necessarily be in law. There is a unified system for the initial stage of qualification for both branches of the profession. This consists of a diploma course administered by Cambridge University. A general notary, having obtained this diploma, can then apply for a faculty to practise to the Faculty Office of the Archbishop of Canterbury. A scrivener notary, however, would need to take additional examinations such as those testing knowledge of two languages and the law of the country of one such language, with a requirement also to spend two years in a scrivener notary's office.

Personal qualities and skills

A notary public should be discreet, meticulous and knowledgeable.

Starting salary

A general notary will receive not only the remuneration earned as a notary but also any income earned as a solicitor. A scrivener notary, on the other hand, will only receive notarial income, and a starting salary upon qualification will be about £30,000.

Information point

Notaries Society, Administration Dept, PO Box 226, Melton Wood-bridge, Suffolk IP12 1WX; Fax: 01394 383772; www.thenotariessociety.org.uk; e-mail: NotariesSociety@compuserve.com.

Society of Scrivener Notaries; www.scrivener-notaries.org.uk.

Worshipful Company of Scriveners, HQS Wellington, Temple Stairs, Victoria Embankment, London WC2R 2PN; 020 7240 0529; fax: 020 7497 0645; www.scriveners.org.uk; e-mail: clerk@scriveners.org.uk.

Solicitor

The role of the solicitor is to provide clients with skilled legal representation and advice. The clients can be individual people or companies, or any type of organisation or group. A solicitor may work on all kinds of legal matters, from house purchases to defence of people accused of crimes; from selling a corporation to drafting a complicated will or trust. Solicitors may also represent clients in all courts, but will often brief a barrister (see Barrister) to represent the client, and then act as a liaison between them.

Scottish solicitors can appear in all courts and tribunals in Scotland up to and including the Sheriff Court. They can also gain rights of audience enabling them to appear in the higher courts by becoming

a solicitor-advocate, or may brief an advocate to represent their clients.

While some solicitors may deal with a variety of legal problems, others specialise in a particular area such as shipping, planning and construction, financial services or social security. Specialisation within the profession is increasing. The majority of solicitors work in private practice, with firms made up of several partners. Many others work as employed solicitors in commerce, industry, local and central government and other organisations.

Solicitors are instructed directly by clients and have a lot of contact with them. They have rights of audience in the magistrates' court and the county court. Unlike barristers, solicitors do not wear wigs but do wear gowns if they appear in county court. Solicitors are governed by a professional body called the Law Society.

Qualifications and training

England and Wales: the Law Society governs the training of solicitors in England and Wales, which takes place in two stages – the academic and the professional. Most, but not all, entrants to the profession are graduates. Fellows of the Institute of Legal Executives over the age of 25 with five years' qualifying experience do not need to complete the academic stage. Non-law graduates take the Common Professional Examination (CPE) or a Postgraduate Diploma in Law; those with the qualifying law degrees are exempt from this. The next stage, the vocational stage, is taken via the legal practice course, available at a number of colleges or universities. It is a one-year full-time or two-year part-time course. The trainee solicitor then has to undertake a two-year training contract with an authorised firm or organisation. During the course of this, a 20-day professional skills course is undertaken, usually on a modular basis.

Scotland: the Law Society of Scotland governs the training of solicitors in Scotland. It is possible to study for a Bachelor of Laws degree at five Scottish universities: Aberdeen, Dundee, Edinburgh, Glasgow and Strathclyde. Alternatively, it is possible to take the Law Society's own examinations by finding employment as a pre-diploma trainee. After completion of the LLB degree or professional examinations, all graduates who would like to become solicitors must take the diploma in legal practice – a 26-week postgraduate course, which also offers training in office and business skills. After successful completion of the degree and the diploma, those who wish to become solicitors then serve a two-year training contract with a Scottish solicitor. Trainees must undertake a further two-week course of study, keep training records, which will be examined and monitored by the Society, and take a test of professional competence. The trainees can then apply to the Law Society of Scotland for a practising certificate. All Scottish solicitors must hold a Law Society of Scotland practising certificate.

Personal qualities and skills

A high level of academic achievement, integrity, good communication skills, patience, discretion, a good command of language and problem-solving skills are all required.

Starting salary

The range of starting salaries is very wide in this profession. The Law Society suggests that trainees should be paid around £15,000 in the regions and £17,000 in London. In practice, large city firms pay far more than this, somewhere in the region of £25,000 to £35,000. Another factor affecting earning is the field of law in which you practise: commercial law tends to offer higher earnings than family or employment law, for example.

Information point

Law Society, 113 Chancery Lane, London WC2A 1PL; 020 7242 1222; fax: 020 7831 0344; Legal Education Line: 0870 606 2555; ww.lawsociety.org.uk; e-mail: legaled@lawsociety.org.uk.

Law Society of Scotland, 26 Drumsheugh Gardens, Edinburgh EH3 7YR; 0131 226 7411; fax: 0131 225 2934; www.lawscot.org.uk; e-mail: legaleduc@lawscot.org.uk.

So… you want to be a lawyer? (Kogan Page)
Careers in the Law (Kogan Page)

23 Nursing, health visiting and midwifery

Nurses are employed in a wide variety of settings in hospitals, institutions (such as prisons and colleges), the armed forces, schools, industry and private organisations. There are four specialisms or 'branches' within nursing: adult nursing, children's nursing, mental health nursing and learning disability nursing. Midwifery and health visiting are regarded as separate professions although still part of the nursing family. Healthcare assistants now work with nurses and other healthcare professionals.

Applicants must decide which branch of nursing they want to qualify in before training. Specialist training within community nursing or other areas of nursing can be pursued once registration as a general nurse has been achieved. Specialist qualifications in district nursing, health visiting, community psychiatric nursing, learning disability nursing (community practice), occupational health nursing, school nursing and practice nursing can be taken at degree or diploma level.

Nurses working in the 'adult nursing' branch spend time not only working on hospital wards but also in outpatient departments, operating theatres, intensive care and with elderly patients. They also work in the community under the supervision of district nurses, health visitors and community midwives. A qualification in adult nursing could lead to specialising in areas such as accident and emergency, practice nursing or health visiting.

Children's nursing, usually referred to as 'paediatric nursing', covers community care, surgical nursing, medical nursing and caring for children with physical and learning disabilities. Children's nurses need to be able to deal with the fears and anxieties of sick children and provide support for their family. Communication skills are very important in this branch of nursing. A children's nurse will care for newborn babies and teenagers, support the child's family and help them care for the child, work with the family to plan care, and work within the paediatric team. Specialisms following on from qualification in children's nursing might be in intensive care, child protection or cancer care.

The mental health nurse will care for people who are mentally ill. Mentally ill people are increasingly being cared for at home or in homes within the community setting. Mental health nurses care for patients suffering from a wide range of illnesses. Some patients simply require help, counselling and support from the nurse. Others with more serious mental health illnesses will require monitoring and help with medication. The mental health nurse assesses individual needs and works with the patient to develop a plan of care; monitors the effectiveness of planned care; administers and monitors the dosage of prescribed medicine; and explains the effects of medication to the individual. He or she works as part of a team of professionals and acts as 'key worker' coordinating the care of an individual. The mental health nurse will require skill, tact and patience in caring for people.

A nurse working within the learning disability branch of nursing assesses each individual and works with the person to develop a plan of care. Some people need to be taught basic skills such as bathing, and the nurse breaks each skill into a series of small tasks and works with the individuals. People with learning disabilities often have physical handicaps, and nurses work with other professionals such as physiotherapists, occupational therapists and doctors in providing care and promoting independence. More people with learning disabilities are cared for at home and in the community than ever before, and increasing numbers of nurses are undergoing specialist training to offer care in the community.

Qualifications and training

To qualify as a nurse you need to complete a degree or diploma course that is approved by the Nursing and Midwifery Council (NMC). At the point when you apply for a course, you must choose the type of nursing in which you wish to specialise – care of adults, children, patients with mental health needs, or patients with learning disabilities. Institutions offering nurse training can set their own academic entry requirements, but there are broad general guidelines. For nursing diploma courses you need five GCSEs grades A–C, including English, maths and a biological science. For degree courses the same GCSE requirements apply, but you also need two A levels. Applicants must be aged 17.5 in England and Wales, 17 in Scotland and 18 in Northern Ireland. In England you must apply through the Nursing and Midwifery Admissions Service (NMAS) – the contacts for Scotland, Wales and Ireland are listed in the info panel. Applicants who do not meet these entry requirements may be successful if they can demonstrate literacy and numeracy skills and provide some evidence that they have recently undertaken successful study of some kind.

There are other routes to qualification. If you are between 16 and 19 you can train through a cadet scheme and healthcare assistants and other healthcare support workers may be able to achieve GNVQ level 3 qualifications which are normally accepted for entry onto nursing diploma and degree courses. All applicants to nursing will have to undergo a Criminal Records Bureau (CRB) check, to ensure that they can work with children and/or vulnerable adults.

Personal qualities and skills

Nurses have to have very good interpersonal skills, and be able to be sympathetic and calm when working with patients. They have to be practical and physically and emotionally resilient. Nurses have to work as part of a team and often have to work in highly pressured and stressful situations.

Starting salary

(These figures are based on working for the NHS.) Newly qualified nurses earn between £19,000 and £25,000. With experience, specialist knowledge and management responsibilities, this rises to between £25,000 and £32,000. A few nurses in consulting roles will earn higher salaries than these.

Healthcare assistant

Healthcare assistants work alongside nurses and provide basic care for patients. They help with treatments, keep wards tidy and complete basic paperwork. They work on general hospital wards, in clinics and outpatient departments, psychiatric hospitals, hospices and care homes. There are also opportunities for community-based work, providing physical care to individuals who might otherwise have needed to go into hospital or residential care homes.

Qualifications and training

No prior qualifications are needed to start work as a healthcare assistant, but hospitals, care homes and other organisations do provide training and there is currently a drive to ensure that everyone doing this work will achieve at least NVQ level 2.

Personal qualities and skills

Like qualified nurses, healthcare assistants must have patience, tact, tolerance and an ability to communicate with the patients in their charge. Physical fitness is essential as the job sometimes involves heavy work (such as lifting and turning patients).

Starting salary

Health care assistants in the NHS aged 18 or over start on a salary of between £11,100 and £13,300. More experienced staff with a relevant NVQ level 2 or 3 can earn up to £17,000. There are also allowances for antisocial hours, and some overtime payments are possible.

Information point

Nursing and Midwifery Council (NMC), 23 Portland Place, London W1B 1PZ; 020 7637 7181; registration contacts: overseas 020 7333 6600; general 020 7333 9333; www.nmc-uk.org.

Nursing and Midwifery Admissions Service, Rosehill, New Barn Lane, Cheltenham, Gloucestershire GL52 3LZ; 0870 112 2206 for general enquiries; 0870 112 2200 for application packs; www.nmas.ac.uk.

NHS Careers, PO Box 376, Bristol BS99 3EY; 0845 606 0655; www.nhscareers.nhs.uk
NHS Education for Scotland, Careers Information Service, 66 Rose Street, Edinburgh EH2 2NN; 0131 225 4365; www.nes.scot.nhs.uk.

National Leadership and Innovation Agency for Healthcare (Wales), Innovation House, Bridgend Road, Llanharan CF72 9RP; 01443 233333; www.wales.nhs.uk/sites3/home.cfm?OrgID-484.

Northern Ireland Practice & Education Council for Nursing & Midwifery, Centre House, 79 Chichester Street, Belfast BT1 4JE; 028 9023 8152; www.n-i.nhs.uk/nipec/index.htm.

Nursing Careers Centre (NCC), 31/32 Fitzwilliam Square, Dublin 2; 01 639 8500; www.nursingcareers.ie.

Health visitors

Health visitors promote health and contribute to the prevention of mental, physical and social ill health in the community. This involves educating people in ways of healthy living and making positive changes in the environment. Education may be achieved by teaching individuals or families in their own homes, in health centres, clinics, in informal groups, or through campaigns for the promotion of good health practices through local or national mass media.

The health visitor may work with people who are registered with a GP or who live within a defined geographical area. The work includes collaboration with a wide range of voluntary and statutory organisations.

Qualifications and training

Applicants must hold a first-level nurse or midwifery qualification with post-registration experience. One-year health visitor courses are provided at institutions of higher education.

All approved programmes now lead to the award of Specialist Practitioner (Public Health Visiting/Health Visiting). These programmes are at a minimum of first degree level.

Personal qualities and skills

Health visitors must be excellent communicators, able to convey information to all types of people without being patronising. They must have self-confidence, tact and a lot of common sense. They must be able to work alone, yet know when to seek advice. They should be confident, articulate public speakers.

Starting salary

Approximately £18,000, rising to £25,000.

Information point

NHS Careers; Careers Helpline: 0845 606 0655; www.nhscareers. nhs.uk.

Community Practitioners and Health Visitors Association, 40 Bermondsey Street, London SE1 3UD; 020 7939 7000; fax: 020 7403 2976; www.msfcphva.org; e-mail: infocphva@amicustheunion.org.

Midwifery

Midwives (who may be female or male) provide care and advice to mothers and fathers before, during and after birth; they are either employed by the NHS in hospital and/or community settings, including home births, by private hospitals, or work independently. The midwife provides care during normal pregnancy and birth, and up to 28 days following the birth. The midwife will also care for women who have complications. The midwife is an integral part of the multidisciplinary team responsible for delivering care, working closely with obstetricians and other health professionals in ensuring the wellbeing of mothers and babies.

Qualifications and training

To qualify as a midwife you need to complete a degree or diploma course in midwifery that is approved by the Nursing and Midwifery Council (NMC). Institutions running courses can set their own academic entry requirements, but there are broad general guidelines. For nursing diploma courses you need five GCSEs grades A–C, including English, maths and a biological science. For degree courses the same GCSE requirements apply, but you also need two A levels. Applicants must be aged 17.5 in England and Wales, 17 in Scotland and 18 in Northern Ireland. In England you must apply through the Nursing and Midwifery Admissions Service (NMAS) – the contacts for Scotland, Wales and Ireland are listed in the info panel. Applicants who do not meet these entry requirements may be successful if they can demonstrate literacy and numeracy skills and provide some evidence that they have recently undertaken successful study of some kind. If you have a nursing degree or diploma (adult branch) you can do a 12 to 18 month midwifery diploma.

Personal qualities and skills

Midwives must have extremely good interpersonal skills, be caring, practical, friendly and encouraging. They must be able to work as part of a team, but also to take responsible decisions on their own.

Starting salary

Newly qualified midwives earn between £19,000 and £25,000. With experience, specialist knowledge and management responsibilities, this rises to between £25,000 and £32,000.

●
Information point

Nursing and Midwifery Council (NMC), 23 Portland Place, London W1B 1PZ; 020 7637 7181; registration contacts: overseas 020 7333 6600, general 020 7333 9333; www.nmc-uk.org.

Nursing and Midwifery Admissions System, Rosehill, New Barn Lane, Cheltenham, Gloucestershire GL52 3LZ; 0870 112 2206 for general enquiries, 0870 112 2200 for application packs; www.nmas.ac.uk.

NHS Careers, PO Box 376, Bristol BS99 3EY; 0845 606 0655; www.nhscareers.nhs.uk.

NHS Education for Scotland, Careers Information Service, 66 Rose Street, Edinburgh EH2 2NN; 0131 225 4365; www.nes.scot.nhs.uk.

National Leadership and Innovation Agency for Healthcare (Wales), Innovation House, Bridgend Road, Llanharan CF72 9RP; 01443 233333; www.wales.nhs.uk/sites3/home.cfm?OrgID-484.

Northern Ireland Practice & Education Council for Nursing & Midwifery, Centre House, 79 Chichester Street, Belfast BT1 4JE; 028 9023 8152; www.n-i.nhs.uk/nipec/index.htm.

Nursing Careers Centre (NCC), 31/32 Fitzwilliam Square, Dublin 2; 01 639 8500; www.nursingcareers.ie.

24 *Teaching*

Most formal teaching is done in schools, while lecturing is carried out in universities and other further and higher education establishments.

Lecturer

Further education

Lecturers in this field may teach anyone over the age of 16. The range of subjects taught in further education is diverse and growing rapidly. Most lecturers have a particular expertise but are increasingly expected to teach outside their specialist area. They may work on vocational and/or academic courses. In order to meet the demands of their clients, further education colleges offer courses on a full- or part-time basis. These include evening courses and short courses.

Higher education

Lecturers in universities and other higher education institutions (HEIs) teach mainly undergraduates. As well as teaching, many carry out research, write articles and books, give outside lectures and broadcasts. Competition is fierce and it is unlikely that a new graduate will be able to enter higher education as a first job.

Qualifications and training

Lecturers in HEIs must have first- or upper-second class degrees; many have postgraduate qualifications, and some have further degrees. In the new universities, lecturers may be drawn from industry or commerce.

Qualifications for lecturers in further education vary, depending on the subject taught. A degree, a professional qualification and a teaching qualification are all acceptable and desirable. There are one-year full-time and two-year part-time courses available for those intending to teach in further education.

Personal qualities and skills

All teachers/lecturers must have a high level of knowledge of, and enthusiasm for, their subject, combined with a desire to communicate this to others. They must have the ability to organise and deliver their material in a way that is understandable to their students.

Starting salary

In further education, salaries range from £16,000 to £21,000. These are based on rates recommended by the National Association of Teachers in Further and Higher Education, but not all colleges pay at these rates. In higher education, salaries range from £24,500 to £30,000. Senior lecturers earn around £37,000.

Information point

Lifelong Learning UK (LLUK), 4th Floor, 32 Farringdon Street, London EC4A 4HJ; 020 7332 9535; www.lifelonglearninguk.org.

The Higher Education Academy, Innovation Way, York Science Park, Heslington, York YO10 5BR; 01904 717500; www.heacademy.ac.uk.

Association of University Teachers (AUT), Egmont House, 25–31 Tavistock Place, London WC1H 9UT; 020 7670 9700; www.aut. org.uk.

Teacher

Teaching offers a wide variety of openings working with children and young people of all ages and backgrounds.

The work of a teacher varies according to the age group being taught. Nursery and Foundation Stage teachers take the under-fives, Key Stage 1 primary teachers take five- to seven-year-olds and Key Stage 2 teachers take 7–11-year-olds. Secondary education (Key Stages 3 and 4) starts at 11 and continues (in some cases) to 18 or 19. In addition, teachers are needed in sixth-form colleges and the numerous further and higher education establishments. Teachers at primary level (up to age 11) generally teach a variety of basic subjects, and specialist subject teachers are not introduced until secondary level, although specialist music or sports teachers may be brought in at an earlier age.

The majority of pupils attend state schools, although there are also openings in private education. There are also opportunities for teachers in special schools: for the handicapped (either boarding or day establishments), for disturbed children (in community homes or approved schools), for those with special educational needs and in children's hospitals, where long-term patients are expected to take lessons.

Qualifications and training

To teach in state schools, you must attain Qualified Teacher Status (QTS) by undertaking a course of Initial Teacher Training (ITT). This is not essential to work in the independent sector, but many schools prefer it. There are several types of ITT, but there are certain criteria which you must meet for all of them. You must have GCSEs grade A–C in English and maths. If you are teaching beyond Key Stages 2/3 your GCSEs must also include a science at grades A–C. You must pass QTS skills tests in English, maths and information and communications technology (ICT). These tests are computerised and run at more than 40 centres throughout England. In Wales, you do not have to take these. You must have a satisfactory Criminal Records Bureau (CRB) check, and some experience of working with children and young people is a great advantage.

There are a number of different routes to QTS, such as a degree in the subject you want to teach at secondary level or in a subject related to the core curriculum at primary level, followed by a Post-graduate Certificate in Education (PGCE). A PGCE can be one year full time college-based, two years part time college-based, or one year full time school-based. If you already have some relevant teaching experience there is an option to do a flexible tailor-made PGCE programme by distance learning. The Graduate Teacher Training Registry (GTTR) provides details of courses and an online applications system.

Alternatively, you can do a three- or four-year BEd (Bachelor of Education) or a BA or BSc which awards QTS. Most of these degree courses are for primary teachers, but a few are available at secondary level.

A third method is to undertake a School Centred Initial Teacher Training (SCITT) – this is considered to be at PGCE level. Schools run Graduate Teacher Programmes (GTPs) where graduates work as unqualified teachers while undergoing training. You can find details of course providers on the Training and Development Agency for Schools website. On this website you can also find details of other employer-based schemes for people with HNDs, two years of degree level study, or overseas qualifications.

Teach First is a special scheme operating in London and Manchester for graduates with a 2.1 in a curriculum subject who are prepared to work in challenging schools and take part in special leadership training courses.

Personal qualities and skills

Teachers must enjoy working with the age group they teach. They must be excellent communicators, able to motivate and encourage their students. They have to have great self-confidence, be able to handle difficult situations and discuss issues with parents as well as students. They must be able to work under considerable pressure, be well organised administrators and come up with imaginative solutions to problems.

Starting salary

New entrants are paid on a scale ranging from £19,000 to £29,000. Incremental points are awarded for taking on particular responsibilities or for working in challenging schools. Senior teachers are paid on a scale of £30,000 to £49,000.

Information point

Fast Track Teaching Recruitment Team, National College of School Leadership; 0845 058 1066; www.ncsl.org.uk/programmes/fasttrack.

Graduate Teacher Training Registry (GTTR), Rosehill, New Barn Lane, Cheltenham, Gloucestershire GL52 3LZ; 0870 112 2205; www.gttr.ac.uk.

Teachernet; www.teachernet.gov.uk.

Department of Education Northern Ireland, Rathael House, Balloo Road, Bangor BT19 7PR; 028 9127 9279; www.deni.gov.uk.

Training and Development Agency for Schools, 151 Buckingham Palace Road, London SW1W 9SZ; 0845 6000 991; www.tda.gov.uk.

Teaching assistant

Teaching assistants or classroom assistants provide help and support for qualified teachers in the classroom. They can work in any school, but there are more employed at primary school level helping younger children with reading, writing and mathematics. They often provide particular support to children with special needs or whose first language is not English. They also help prepare lesson materials.

If a job ad describes the post as 'Learning Support Assistant' rather than a classroom or teaching assistant, the work involves supporting an individual child who has particular special needs, such as a sensory impairment, or a physical or psychological disability.

Qualifications and training

At present, this varies from LEA (local education authority) to LEA, though the government does plan to introduce a standard training model. Many LEAs do not ask for any formal qualifications, but some ask for GCSEs in English and mathematics.

Personal qualities and skills

Teaching assistants must be able to build good relationships with children and have a lot of common sense. They should be able to work well as part of a team, and being imaginative and creative is also useful.

Starting salary

Teaching assistants are often paid on an hourly rate and this is sometimes close to the minimum wage, though it can be £6.50 to £8.00 an hour. A lot of the work is part time and available only during term time.

Appendices

Appendix 1:
Useful information

If you think there is a useful book, website or anything else that should be included in this directory of useful information, you can e-mail the author at eh@elizabethholmes.info and it will be considered for inclusion in the next edition of this book.

Glossary

A level – Advanced level of the General Certificate of Education; a qualification in FE

Academic – as opposed to vocational: a subject or course that is not aimed at a particular profession or career

Accreditation of prior learning – a way of having your skills and knowledge recognized when you have no recognized qualifications for them. You can also get accreditation for prior learning when you have completed some units of a course but have not actually finished it

Admissions tutor – the person at colleges and universities responsible for selecting candidates for courses

Apprenticeships – training schemes that combine working and studying

AS level – Advanced Supplementary qualification (taken in the first year of sixth form)

AVCE – Advanced Vocational Certificate of Education

Awarding body – an organization that sets and monitors the standards for qualifications

BA – Bachelor of Arts

BEd – Bachelor of Education

BDS – Bachelor of Dental Surgery

BMus – Bachelor of Music

BNurs – Bachelor of Nursing

BPharm – Bachelor of Pharmacy

BSocSci – Bachelor of Social Science

BSc – Bachelor of Science

BVetMed – Bachelor of Veterinary Medicine

C&G (City and Guilds of London Institute) – an awarding body committed to vocational qualifications

Commune – a group of people living together and sharing responsibilities and/or possessions

Connexions – the Government's service to help young people aged between 13 and 19

Day release – time off work to attend educational courses

DCSF – Department for Children, Schools and Families

DEAs – Disability Employment Advisers

Degree – a qualification gained at university after three or more years of study

DipHE – Diploma of Higher Education

DIUS – the Government's Department for Innovation, Universities and Skills

European Employment Service EURES – the European Job Mobility portal on the Europa website. EURES is a network to help workers move around Europe

ECCTIS – Educational Counselling and Credit Transfer Information Service which is a database for university and college courses

EDEXCEL – one of the largest awarding bodies in the UK

FE – further education (study usually between the ages of 16 to 18 or 19)

FD – Foundation degree

FDA – Foundation degree (Arts)

FDSc – Foundation degree (Science)

Freelance – a person working for different companies at different times or at the same time: not employed by one company

Gap year – a year off, usually taken after FE or HE but sometimes later in life

GCSE – General Certificate of Education (these are usually taken at school at the age of 16)

HE – higher education

Highers – exams taken in Scotland instead of A levels

HNC – Higher National Certificate

HND – Higher National Diploma

Induction – an introduction to a new job or course

Jobcentre Plus – local drop-in agencies run by the Jobcentre Plus Network to get people who are 18+ into work

Kibbutz – a communal settlement in Israel, usually a farm

Learning and Skills Council – the organization responsible for all post-16 education and training in England

LEAs – local education authorities (which are part of the county or borough council) responsible for state maintained primary and secondary education in the area. They also administer awards for HE, among other things

LLB – Bachelor of Law

MB/BS – Bachelor of Medicine and Bachelor of Surgery

Modular – a course that can be built from separate units and modules

Moshav – a cooperative Israeli village or settlement

NVQ – National Vocation Qualification (SVQ in Scotland)

OCR – one of the three largest awarding bodies

Outsourcing – contracting goods and services from outside a company rather than from employees

Profession – usually described as an occupation that involves prolonged training

Progress File – an interactive tool for career and study planning designed to be used from the age of 13 onwards

Prospectus – a printed or online 'booklet' which advertises a university or college

QCA – Qualifications and Curriculum Authority

Recruiter – someone who selects applicants for interview and then decides who gets the job

Referee – someone who testifies verbally or in writing about someone's skills and character

S grade – Standard Grade in Scotland, the equivalent of the GCSE

SQA – Scottish Qualifications Authority

SVQ – Scottish Vocational Qualification (National Vocational Qualification, or NVQ, elsewhere in the UK)

TEFL – teaching English as a foreign language

UCAS – Universities and Colleges Admissions Service (handles admissions to most undergraduate courses in the UK)

Vocational education or training – education or training targeted at a particular occupation or career.

Further reading

There is a huge amount of reading material out there for young people – everything from writing CVs to cookery books for students on a budget is available. It is well worth spending time browsing your local library or good quality book shop to see if there is anything that looks interesting to you. Don't feel restricted by what is suggested below – this is just the tip of the iceberg!

The internet

It is probably fair to say that just about all you need to know for your post-16 decisions can be found on the internet. The trouble is that it is not all in one place on the world wide web, which is why this book has gathered together URLs for all the websites you are likely to find of value and included them in the relevant place in each chapter. If you want to write to any of the organizations you visit online, you will find contact post and e-mail addresses on the relevant websites.

The websites listed below are useful starting points for further information. This is not a definitive list by any means but it is worth bookmarking these sites and dropping in to see what is new as often as possible. All of these sites have lots of suggested links for you to follow. Have fun!

www.aimhigher.ac.uk – information on the road to HE

www.aimhigher.ac.uk/uni4me/home – for information about going to university

www.basic-skills.co.uk – information on improving skills, such as reading and numeracy

www.bbc.co.uk/learning/ – study, work, money and travel advice for 16–24 year-olds

www.careers-portal.co.uk – careers and HE advice

www.connexions.gov.uk – packed with all kinds of advice for 13- to 19-year-olds

www.dfes.gov.uk/hegateway/ – information on a wide range of topics to help students make effective decisions

www.eurochoice.org.uk – a guide for opportunities in Europe including travel, careers and study

www.hero.ac.uk – the official gateway to universities, colleges and research organizations in the UK www.learndirect-advice.co.uk – for advice on learning and working

www.parentscentre.gov.uk – advice for parents and carers

www.springboard.hobsons.co.uk – a guide to careers, study and gap year opportunities

www.support4learning.org.uk – good starting point for UK and foreign courses

www.thebigchoice.com – for careers ideas and choices

www.thesite.org.uk – packed with information including lots on careers and education

www.universityoptions.co.uk – for impartial advice on HE

Books

This is just a starting point from which to launch your search for useful books. Don't forget that many good books have further reading sections at the back so you will get more ideas by going through those too.

General careers information and advice

The A–Z of Careers and Jobs (2007) 14th edn, Hodgson, S, Kogan Page, London
British Qualifications: A complete guide to educational, technical, professional and academic qualifications in Britain, 38th edn, Kogan Page, London
Careers In... series, Kogan Page, London
Choosing Your Career: Work out what you really want to do with your life (2004) 2nd edn, Longson, S, Kogan Page, London
Net that Job! Using the World Wide Web to develop your career and find work (2000) 2nd edn, Krechowiecka, I, Kogan Page, London
Odd Jobs (2002) Kent, S, Kogan Page, London

The Sustainable Careers Handbook, (2000) Shepherd, A and Rowe, F,
    Centre for Alternative Technology
What Can I Do With ... series, Trotman Publishing, Richmond
Your First Job (1997) 3rd edn, Grose, R and Donald, V, Kogan Page,
    London

Going abroad

Browse through the online catalogue of books at the Vacation Work
Publications website: www.vacationwork.co.uk as there will be a lot
there to tempt you!

In particular:
The Directory of Jobs and Careers Abroad, Boothby, D, Vacation
    Work Publications, Oxford
Live and Work In... series, Vacation Work Publications, Oxford

Also browse through the Kogan Page online catalogue at www.
kogan-page.co.uk as there is plenty to be found on this topic, in
particular:

Working Abroad (2007) 28th edn, Reuvid, J, Kogan Page, London

Living and Working in France: Chez Vous en France (2004) 3rd edn,
    Brame, G, Kogan Page, London

Applications and interviews

Great Answers to Tough Interview Questions, (2005) 6th edn, Yate, M
    J, Kogan Page, London
Your Job Search Made Easy, (2002) 3rd edn, Parkinson, M, Kogan
    Page, London
*Preparing the Perfect CV: How to improve your chances of getting
    the job you want* (2007) 4th edn, Corfield, R, Kogan Page,
    London
Preparing the Perfect Job Application (2007), Corfield, R, Kogan Page,
    London

Taking a gap year

Before You Go: The ultimate guide to planning your gap year (2002) Griffiths, T, Aspect Guides
Directory of Work and Study in Developing Countries, Milner, T, Vacation Work Publications, Oxford
The Gap Year Guidebook, annual, Withers, A, John Catt
Making the Most of Your Gap Year (2002) Flynn, M, Trotman, Richmond
Summer Jobs Abroad, Woodworth, D and Pybus, V, annual, Vacation Work Publications, Oxford
Summer Jobs in Britain, Woodworth, D and Hobbs, G, annual, Vacation Work Publications, Oxford

www.yearoutgroup.org
www.gapyear.com
www.teaching-abroad.co.uk
www.statravel.co.uk
www.whatsonwhen.com
www.vacationwork.co.uk

FE and HE

There are hundreds of books and guides that could be included here, but as that would not be as useful as it might sound, here is a selection for you to browse! You local library and Connexions office are likely to have a copy of many of these.

The Art and Design Directory 2005 (2004) Widmer, J, ISCO Publications
Choosing Your Degree Course and University (2004) Heap, B, Trotman, Richmond
Degree Course Guides annual, Trotman, Richmond
Degree Course Offers 2005 Entry (2004) Trotman, Richmond
Disabled Students' Guide to University 2006 (2005) Trotman, Richmond
Making the Most of Being a Student, Kogan Page, London
Net That Course! Using the internet to research, select and apply for degree courses (1999) Krechowiecka, I, Kogan Page, London

The Student Book 2006 (2005) Boehm, K and Lees-Spadling, J, Trotman, Richmond

University and College Entrance: Official Guide 2006 Entry (2005) UCAS

The Virgin 2005 Alternative Guide to British Universities (2004) Dudgeon, P, Virgin Books, London

You Want to Study WHAT?! (2003) Houston, K, Trotman, Richmond

Magazines and newspapers

You will find copies of local and national newspapers in your local reference library but it is also worth talking to the librarian about any other newspapers or magazines that he or she buys that you may not have thought of looking at. The national broadsheet newspapers (just to confuse matters, some are now published in a compact size as well) cover different themes (such as media, secretarial, technology, education and so on) on different days, so find out what days you should not miss reading them. It is a good idea to browse the education and HE supplements of these newspapers too.

Local papers nearly always carry job advertisements. Some will be published weekly and some daily so make sure that you know when yours comes out. There may well be a local glossy monthly magazine too, so check that out as well.

Another good source of information on magazines and newspapers is your local large newsagent. Staff there will know exactly what is available and will be able to tell you if there is a specialist publication that you might like to order (make sure that these are not in your local library before paying for your own copies).

Your careers library at school may have some free magazines so it is worth checking and picking copies up when you see them.

Money

Balancing Your Books: The CRAC Guide To Student Finance (2004) Warrior, J, Trotman, Richmond

Directory of Grant Making Trusts (Charities Aid Foundation)2005/06

Students' Money Matters 2005 (2005) Thomas, G, Trotman, Richmond

University Scholarships and Awards (2004) Heap, B, Trotman, Richmond

Self-employment

Getting into Self-employment (1999) Grigg, J, Trotman, Richmond
Start Up and Run Your Own Business (2007) 6th edn, Reuvid, J, Kogan Page, London

Software

There are several software packages that you may be able to use either at school/college or at your local Connexions office. Look out for the following:

Higher Ideas Careersoft (database of HE courses);
Kudos CASCAiD (to help you find job ideas);
Odyssey VT Career Progressions (database for information on occupations);
Pathfinder HE VT Career Progressions (careers guidance as well as suggestions for possible HE courses);
SkillCheck VT Career Progressions (helps you to identify key skills as well as work-related skills);
StudyLink Undergraduate Entry (CD ROM – database of courses available through UCAS).

Tests

How to Succeed at an Assessment Centre (2005) 2nd edn, Tolley, H and Wood, R, Kogan Page, London
Test Your IQ (2006) 2nd edn, Russell, K and Carter, P, Kogan Page
Test Your Own Aptitude (2003) 3rd edn, Williams, G and Barrett, J, Kogan Page, London

Appendix 2: Recruitment tests

Recruitment tests are an increasingly popular part of the job interview within all industry sectors. Psychometric, aptitude and IQ tests are common, as are personality questionnaires. The testing is designed to highlight potential skills and to identify an individual's attributes.

There are a number of ways in which an applicant can prepare for recruitment tests. Online practice tests are now readily available as are a number of books that offer practice tests (see details in Appendix 1). The more the job applicant can practise the better as there are set patterns and rules in psychometric testing which can be learned.

The following tests are from Carter, P (2004) *IQ and Psychometric Tests*, Kogan Page, London, and offer examples of numerical and verbal reasoning tests which are similar to ones that a job applicant might be asked to do.

Verbal reasoning

Test 1: Synonym test

A synonym is a word that has the same meaning as, or a very similar meaning to, another word. Examples of synonyms are: calm and placid, error and mistake, select and choose. This test is a series of 20 questions designed to test your knowledge of language and your ability to identify quickly words that have the same or very similar meanings.

You have 30 minutes to complete the 20 questions. You should work as quickly as possible as some questions will take more time to solve than others.

Questions 1 to 5

In the following five questions select the word in brackets that means the same or has the closest meaning to the word in capitals.

1. BRUSQUE (crude, curt, unkind, elastic, wieldy)

2. DISTIL (reduce, liquefy, soften, purify, rarefy)

3. SINGULAR (remarkable, free, routine, natural, upright)

4. FASTIDIOUS (chic, loyal, protective, choosy, viable)

5. WAX (souse, fade, shrink, strengthen, dilate)

Questions 6 to 10

In the following five questions, from the six words given identify the two words that you believe to be closest in meaning.

6. flawless, ulterior, unwelcome, secret, overt, literate

7. circle, row, pedal, track, flaw, line

8. relative, common, exoteric, indolent, careless, apposite

9. ascribe, profess, aspire, judge, hanker, daze

10. vote, composite, blend, proposition, element, total

Questions 11 to 20

The following are a miscellaneous selection of question types where, in each case, you have to identify two words with similar meanings. Read the instructions to each question carefully.

11. Complete the two words, one in each circle and both reading clockwise, which are similar in meaning. You have to find the starting point and provide the missing letters.

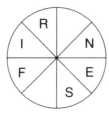 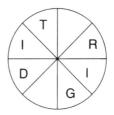

12. Complete the two words, one in each circle and both reading clockwise, which are similar in meaning. You have to find the starting point and provide the missing letters.

13. Complete the two words, one in each circle, one reading clockwise and the other anti-clockwise, that are similar in meaning. You have to find the starting point and provide the missing letters, and work out which word is clockwise and which is anti-clockwise.

14. Which two words below are most similar to the phrase 'get the wrong idea'?

    misconceive, miscalculate, misconstrue, misinform, misapply, misconduct

15. Which two words below are most similar to the phrase 'put in a good word for'?

    concilate, recommend, pacify, advise, endorse, enliven

16. Which two words below are most similar to the phrase 'down-to earth'?

    subservient, dismayed, practical, earthward, explicit, realistic

17. ROPE OF CREW is an anagram of which two words (5, 5 letters) that are similar in meaning?

18. VINCIBLE OIL is an anagram of which two words (4, 7 letters) that are similar in meaning?

19. Each square contains the letters of a nine-letter word. Find the two words, one in each square, that are similar in meaning:

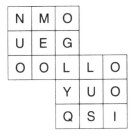

20. The circles contain the letters of two eight-letter words which can be found reading clockwise. Find the two words which are similar in meaning. Each word starts in a different circle, and all letters appear in the correct order and are used once only.

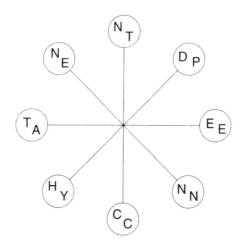

Answers to Test 1

1. curt
2. purify
3. remarkable
4. choosy
5. dilate
6. ulterior, secret
7. row, line
8. relative, apposite
9. aspire, hanker
10. composite, blend
11. firmness, rigidity
12. accredit, sanction
13. sediment, residuum
14. misconceive, misconstrue
15. recommend, endorse
16. practical, realistic
17. power, force
18. bill, invoice
19. monologue, soliloquy
20. tendency, penchant

Assessment

Each correct answer scores one point

8–10   Average
11–13   Good
14–16   Very good
17–20   Exceptional

Numerical reasoning

As well as diagrammatic tests, numerical tests are regarded as being culture-fair to a great extent, as numbers are international. In addition to testing your powers of calculation, many of the tests in this chapter also test your powers of logic, and your ability to deal with problems in a structured and analytical way.

We all require some numerical skills in our lives, whether it is to calculate our weekly shopping bill or to budget how to use our monthly income. Anyone who has ever taken an IQ test will be familiar with the types of numerical tests encountered, and the flexibility of thought and often lateral thinking processes needed to solve them. The more one practises on these types of little puzzles, the more proficient one becomes at solving them.

Test 1: Calculation and logic A

This test is a battery of 15 number puzzles designed to test your numerical ability. You have 60 minutes in which to solve the 15 puzzles. The use of a calculator is permitted in this test.

1. What number should replace the question mark to continue the sequence?

    1, 5, 13, 29, ?

2. How many minutes is it before 12 noon if 40 minutes ago it was four times as many minutes past 10 am?

3. What number should replace the question mark?

4. What number should replace the question mark to continue the sequence?

   100, 96.5, 92, 86.5, ?

5. What value of weight should be placed on the scales to balance?

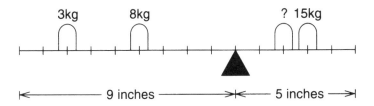

6. Tony and Cherie share a certain amount of money in the ratio 2 : 5. If Cherie has £195.00, how much money is shared?

7. Insert the numbers 1, 2, 3, 4, 5 into the circles, one per circle, so that:

   the sum of the numbers 2 and 1, and all the numbers in between total 7

   the sum of the numbers 2 and 3, and all the numbers in between total 10

   the sum of the numbers 5 and 3, and all the number in between total 15

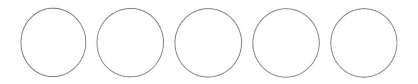

8. What is the difference between the sum (added together) of the largest two odd numbers in grid A and the product (multiplied together) of the smallest two even numbers in grid B?

A	17	14	9	5
	11	24	19	18
	12	13	10	7
	23	28	15	16

					B
5	20	7	18	
22	32	24	4	
26	14	23	36	
9	21	16	15	

9. What two numbers should replace the questions marks to continue the sequence?

1, 10, 2.75, 8.25, 4.5, 6.5, 6.25, ?, ?

10. If Peter's age + Paul's age = 39
and Peter's age + Mary's age = 44
and Paul's age + Mary's age = 47
how old are Peter, Paul and Mary?

11. What numbers should replace the question marks?

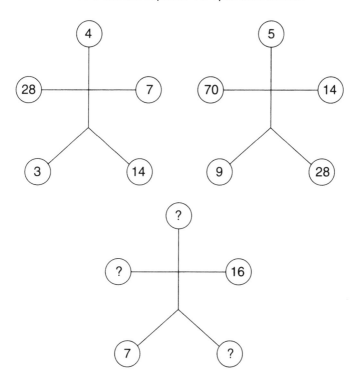

12. What is 3/11 divided by 18/44 to the smallest fraction?

2	7	10	15
5	10	13	18
10	15	?	23
13	18	21	26

13. What number should replace the question mark?
14. What number should replace the question mark to continue the sequence?

17, 34, 51, 68, ?, 102

15. What number should replace the question mark?

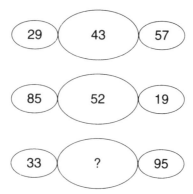

Answers to Test 1

1. 61: add 4, 8, 16, 32.
2. 16 minutes: 12 noon less 16 minutes = 11.44. 11.44 less 40 minutes = 11.04. 11.04 less 64 minutes (4 × 16) = 10 am.
3. 14: 8 × 7 = 56; 56/4 = 14. Similarly 7 × 9 = 63; 63/3 = 21.
4. 80: less 3.5, 4.5, 5.5, 6.5.
5. 4 kg

4 × 8 = 32	3 × 15 = 45
7 × 3 = <u>21</u>	2 × 4 = <u> 8</u>
53	53

6. £273.00. Each share is 273/7 (2 + 5) = £39.00. Therefore Cherie's share is 5 × 39 = 195 and Tony's share is 2 × 39 = 78.
7. 5 2 4 1 3 or 3 1 4 2 5
8. 14: A = 19 + 23 = 42 and b = 4 × 14 = 56.
9. 4.75, 8. There are two alternate sequences, one starting at 1 and adding 1.75, and the other starting at 10 and deducting 1.75.
10. Peter 18, Paul 21, Mary 26.
11. A + C = E, A × E = B, A + E + C = D.

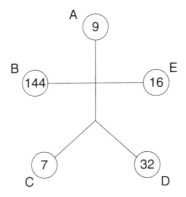

12. 2/3

    3(1)/11(1) × 44(4)/18(6) = 2/3
13. 18. Looking across each line add 5 and 3 alternately. Looking down each column add 3 and 5 alternately.
14. 85: add 17 each time.
15. 64: (33 + 95)/2. Similarly (29 + 57)/2.

Assessment

Each correct answer scores one point.

6–7   Average
8–9   Good
10–13 Very good
14–15 Exceptional.

Index

Index of advertisers